"Tracy Marks has written a fascinating study of the 12th house in a manner that is highly readable and very understandable. It is the most complete study of the subject I have ever seen. This book has taken much of the mystery out of the 12th house."

—Mercury Hour Magazine

"Few of us have the talent necessary to share our insights as well as Tracy Marks, the author of a new inspiring, and delightfully well written treatment of this most elusive of houses. . . . Tracy Marks reveals her intelligence and psychological acumen in her imaginative and witty examples of possible expressions or manifestations of planets in the 12th house."

—Biblioscope

Books by the Author

The Astrology of Self-Discovery

Planetary Aspects: From Conflict to Cooperation
(New edition of *How to Handle Your T-Square*)

The Art of Chart Interpretation

*Your Secret Self: Illuminating the Mysteries
of the Twelfth House*

For information on the above titles,
write CRCS Publications at the address
given on the title page.

Your Secret Self

Illuminating the Mysteries of the Twelfth House

Tracy Marks

CRCS PUBLICATIONS
Post Office Box 1460
Sebastopol, California 95473

Library of Congress Cataloging-in-Publication Data

Marks, Tracy, 1950–
    Your secret self : illuminating the mysteries of the 12th house /
by Tracy Marks.
        p.   cm.
    Bibliography: p.
    ISBN 0-916360-43-1
    1. Astrology.   2. Dreams.   I. Title.   II. Title: Title: 12th
house.
BF1711.M44   1989
133.5--dc19   88-27091
                                                                  CIP

INTERNATIONAL STANDARD BOOK NUMBER: 0-916360-43-1

Published simultaneously in the United States and Canada by:
CRCS Publications
Distributed in the United States and internationally by
CRCS Publications
(Write for current list of worldwide distributors.)
Cover Design by Rebecca Wilson

A small amount of material in this book (specifically "The Lunar Nodes in the
Twelfth House," some paragraphs of "The Twelfth House: Its Hidden Wisdom,"
and the poem, "And Then the Chart Spoke") are reprinted from *The Twelfth
House,* by Tracy Marks, Sagittarius Rising, Arlington, Mass. 1978. The vast ma-
jority is entirely new material, including most of the twelfth house interpretive
material.

Many of the quotations are from secondary sources (quotation anthologies)
and personal journals. Apart from the author, documentation is not possible.

Acknowledgments

I wish to thank the following people for their contributions to this book: Jill Goldman, Jane Graham, Michael Jaro, Helen Landerman, Martha Marks, Patricia Mokry, Christian Palocz, Ilana Rhodes, Tom Watkins, Stuart Weinberg, and Ellen Wilson.

Dedication

This book is dedicated to Ellen Wilson,
who helped me to regain my secret self,
and to discover my dreams.

Contents

Whatever we fight about in the outside world
is also a battle in our inner selves.
                    —Carl Jung

He who lives in harmony with his own self, his demon,
lives in harmony with the universe.
                    —Marcus Aurelius

Not in the clamor of the crowded street,
Not on the shouts and plaudits of the throng,
But in ourselves, are triumph and defeat.
                    —Henry W. Longfellow

To the possession of the self the way is inward.
                    —Plotinus

I broider the world upon a loom,
I broider with dreams my tapestry;
Here in a little lonely room
I am master of earth and sea,
And the planets come to me.
                    —Arthur Symons

Introduction

The purpose of *Your Secret Self* is to help you to understand and make contact with unconscious facets of yourself which subvert your aims, and which could, if consciously integrated into your life, contribute to your well-being. These latent and repressed parts of yourself are likely to be indicated by the planets and signs in and ruling the twelfth house of your astrology chart.*

Although this book is written for astrology students who know their natal charts and have learned the rudiments of the planets, signs, and houses, you need not study astrology in order to benefit from most of the theory, interpretations, and guidance presented here. You need only be willing to look within yourself, and to pay attention to the material in the book which resonates for you. Those of you who are students of astrology are advised also to follow your inner signals in regard to the meaningfulness of this material to your lives, apart from the specific planets and signs you have in your twelfth house. The value of astrology is in helping you to attune to your own wisdom, not in learning to block your intuitive promptings in order to embrace concepts which do not feel relevant to you.

Your Secret Self is divided into four sections, each with a particular aim. In "The Twelfth House: Your Hidden Wisdom," you will be introduced to most of the meanings of the twelfth house, with specific examples relating different twelfth house functions to various planet and sign placements. In the second and largest section, "Twelfth House Planets and Signs," you will have the opportunity to study

---

*It would be best for beginners to have a competent astrological practitioner calculate the birth chart and show the reader how to understand the basic symbols and placements in his or her chart. If that is not possible, the reader can obtain an accurate complete birth chart by sending name, address, birth date, place, *and exact time*, along with $4, to Astro-Computing Services; P. O. Box 16430; San Diego, CA 92116-9987.

the meanings of twelfth house planets which are important to you—planets positioned in your twelfth house, or which rule your twelfth house signs. Inspiring images and quotations will help you to access your intuitive right brain, which is more essential than your left brain in the process of attuning to twelfth house energies.

The third section of this book was written for those of you who wish to progress beyond mere intellectual understanding, and to begin a deeper psychological exploration of the conflicts which may occur when twelfth house energies are manifesting in self-defeating ways. Conducting psychotherapy with many astrology students who wish not only to diagnose and understand their patterns, but also to create greater fulfillment in their lives, I find that many of my clients benefit from gaining deeper theoretical understanding of their psycho-dynamics and of the process of psychological change. The two chapters included here are therefore written for those of you who are committed to your own personal growth and involved in psychotherapy or self-therapeutic pursuits. In "The Psychodynamics of Twelfth House Conflicts," you will consider some of the disturbances associated with twelfth house conflicts, particularly in regard to shame, fear, guilt, and dissociation. In "The Process of Integration," you will discover how psychological change occurs and become more adept at facilitating your own growth process.

Because my specialty during the past few years has been working with dreams, and because dreamwork is one of the most effective gateways into the hidden meanings of the twelfth house, the last section of *Your Secret Self* is about recalling, interpreting, understanding, and constructively utilizing your dreams. In "Self-Transformation through Dreamwork," you will learn about the value of working with your dreams, the process of recalling dreams, dream symbology, and hints for interpretation. In "The Dream Experience: Twelfth House Case Studies," you will be introduced to the charts, dreams, and lives of six people with twelfth house planets who have attended my dream groups during recent years. Finally, in "A Twelfth House Dream Journey," I reveal several years of my own growth through dreamwork, as it reflects my twelfth house planets and signs both natally and by transit.

Your journey into your twelfth house, through astrological and psychological understanding, through dreamwork, and through direct emotional experience, is likely to be both a painful and joyful process. Through confronting, contacting, and transforming your twelfth house energies you may have to face the darkest, most distorted, destructive, or wounded facets of yourself. But you are also likely to discover hidden talents and sources of fulfillment which lie buried within those shadow selves, as well as new dimensions of your own wisdom, love, and spirituality which you have previously been unable to acknowledge or access.

If you wish to liberate yourself from past patterns which interfere with your goals and keep you feeling empty or powerless, and if you wish to discover, recover, and develop facets of yourself which can empower you and contribute to greater wholeness, satisfaction, and life purpose, then you are ready to open the door to your twelfth house and to explore the rich and varied rooms of your secret self.

Twelfth House Inspirations

When from our better selves we have too long
Been parted by the hurrying world, and droop,
Sick of its business, of its pleasures tired,
How gracious, how benign, is Solitude.
                           —William Wordsworth

The man who has no inner life is the slave of his surroundings.
                           —Henri Frederic Amiel

A man who is unconscious of himself . . . sees everything that he is not conscious of in himself coming to meet him from outside as projections upon
his neighbor.
                           —Carl Jung

They say, best men are molded out of faults,
And, for the most, become much more the better
For being a little bad.
                           —Shakespeare, Measure for Measure

Good does not become better by being exaggerated, but worse, and a small
evil becomes a big one through being disregarded and repressed.
                           —Carl Jung

So every bondman in his own hand bears
The power to cancel his captivity.
                           —Shakespeare, Julius Caesar

PART I

The Twelfth House: Your Hidden Wisdom

Have you noticed when the Sun ascends each day, that the first house of the horoscope through which it travels is the twelfth house? As it crosses the horizon, beginning its cycle through space and time toward the midheaven and around the wheel, it calls upon you to move first downward and backward into the past. The twelfth house is the reservoir of the past, of all that lies beneath the surface of consciousness—feelings, thoughts, images from early childhood, and further back still, from past lives. It is what we hide from ourselves and others, and what emerges within us, threatening and enriching us, in solitude.

The twelfth house is the storehouse within us in which both our inner demons and angels reside. In order to move upward and contact the angels—the sources of our creative inspiration, spirituality, and the highest expressions of love and service to humanity, we must first move downward. We must face the ghosts of the past, the failures, the humiliations, and the painful experiences which haunt us. We must encounter our unresolved problems, and all that we dislike within ourselves—our anger, greed, cruelty, extravagance, vanity, as well as all the qualities in ourselves which we like and value but nevertheless hesitate to acknowledge.

Later, we will explore together the process of confronting twelfth house energies, a very difficult but ultimately freeing process, full of dangers and joys. But first, we need to understand the numerous and related meanings of the twelfth house itself. Whether you are a beginning astrology student, still learning basic definitions of planets, signs, and houses, or an advanced student, deepening your understanding of the chart, you will most benefit from this book if you relate the material in it to the planets and the signs in your twelfth house.

Take a few moments now and recall your twelfth house. What sign appears on your twelfth house cusp? . . . . Is it the same or a different sign than the sign of your eleventh house or your ascendant and first house? . . . . What, if any, other signs are in your twelfth house? . . . . What planets rule your twelfth house signs, and where are these planets located in your chart? . . . . If you have no twelfth house planets, then you may not need to focus on your inner world as much as people with twelfth house planets do. But the planets which rule your twelfth house sign or signs will have a special significance in your life, because they will indicate how and where you channel your subtle and often unconscious twelfth house energy.

Look again at your twelfth house. What planets reside there? . . . . In what sign or signs? . . . . What other houses do they rule in your chart? The twelfth house meanings of each of these planets will influence the houses that these planets rule. If you have several twelfth house planets, your twelfth house energies may extend into many realms of your life.

If you have three or more planets in your twelfth house, (or two, if one of them is the Sun, Moon, or Neptune), then a large part of your consciousness is already in the twelfth house, digging through its garbage and its gold mines. If you have one or perhaps two planets there, you particularly need to come to terms with twelfth house energies. These planets may hinder or support the drives indicated by other planets in your chart.

Consider now all the aspects which your twelfth house planets or rulers make to other planets, signs, and houses. . . . How many planets, signs, and houses are involved with your twelfth house energies? . . . . These aspects to other houses are pathways of energy through which your twelfth house planets manifest themselves, seeking compensation and escape from conflict, as well as outward expression for their inner gifts.

Do conjunctions predominate? If your twelfth house planets conjunct each other, but make few aspects to other dimensions of your chart, then you may need to retreat deeply within yourself, you may feel disconnected from your twelfth house energy, and you may experience a split between your inner and outer selves. . . . Do squares predominate? Then you will be drawing from but battling with your deeper energies; you may be forced repeatedly to confront and change your behavior. . . . Do oppositions predominate? Then you are likely to gain understanding of yourself through projecting your deep-seated patterns onto others, and through viewing yourself through the mirrors of your personal relationships. . . . Do trines and sextiles predominate? These will aid you in discovering constructive outlets for your twelfth house energies. But your primary problem may be lack of motivation; you may not feel challenged enough to develop your psychological resources. Peace with yourself may be too easy.

In addition to the planets in your natal chart, consider also the planets by transit and progression which are passing through your twelfth house now. . . . Transiting outer planets and progressed planets may have been influencing your twelfth house for many years and operating within the recesses of your psyche like natal twelfth house planets. These planets too rule houses in your chart, and make aspects to other planets.

As you reflect upon planets in your twelfth house natally, planets ruling it, and planets temporarily passing through it, consider both their positive and negative manifestations. Saturn, for example, can indicate repression and oppression, limitation and restriction, fear, withdrawal, and deprivation. But Saturn in the twelfth house, operating in an inward manner, can help you fully commit yourself to inner development or to a path of service; it can mobilize the self-discipline required for solitary work. You have the potential to express both positive and negative meanings of your twelfth house planets, but you are not likely to be able to find their most constructive expressions until you have at least begun to confront, own, and work through the negative, destructive tendencies within you.

Your Twelfth House Profile*

SIGNS IN YOUR 12th HOUSE

Sign on the cusp _____

Second sign _____

Third sign (if interception) _____

The planetary ruler of the cusp, _____ , is in the

   sign _____ in the _____ house, and

   makes these aspects:

      aspect _____ to planet _____ orb _____

      aspect _____ to planet _____ orb _____

      aspect _____ to planet _____ orb _____

      aspect _____ to planet _____ orb _____

Does a sign rule the 11th & 12th, or 12th & 1st? _____ .

PLANETS IN YOUR 12th HOUSE

Which planets? _____ , _____ , _____ , _____ .

Planet #1 _____ is in the sign _____ and rules the

   _____ (and _____) houses of my chart. It makes

   the following aspects:

      aspect _____ to planet _____ orb _____

      aspect _____ to planet _____ orb _____

      aspect _____ to planet _____ orb _____

      aspect _____ to planet _____ orb _____

   Is this planet in mutual reception, in its own sign,

      or in its own house?

   Is it the focal planet of a pattern or aspect configuration? _____ .

Planet #2 _____ is in the sign_____ and rules the

   _____ (and _____) houses of my chart. It makes

   the following aspects:

      aspect _____ to planet _____ orb _____

      aspect _____ to planet _____ orb _____

---

*See page 44 for information on completing and interpreting your twelfth house profile.

Your Twelfth House Profile

aspect _____ to planet _____ orb _____
aspect _____ to planet _____ orb _____

Is this planet in mutual reception, in its own sign,
   or in its own house?

Is it the focal planet of a pattern or aspect configuration? _____ .

Planet #3 _____ is in the sign _____ and rules the
_____ (and _____) houses of my chart. It makes the
following aspects:

    aspect _____ to planet _____ orb _____
    aspect _____ to planet _____ orb _____
    aspect _____ to planet _____ orb _____
    aspect _____ to planet _____ orb _____

Is this planet in mutual reception, in its own sign,
   or in its own house?

Is it the focal planet of a pattern or aspect configuration? _____ .

**Diagram the planets in-
volved in your 12th house.
Include planets in and ruling the 12th house, and the
planets that they aspect.**

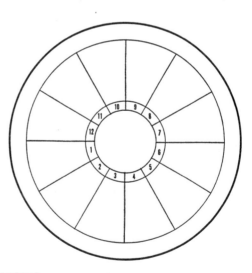

TRANSITS AND PROGRESSIONS

What outer planet transits or progressions are passing through your
12th house? What is their position in your natal chart (house position, house rulership, etc)? _____

_____   _____ .

The Inner Life

What then are the debilitating and life-enhancing meanings of the twelfth house? What does the twelfth house represent? First of all, it is the house of solitude. If you have several planets there, (especially the Sun, Moon, Venus, Jupiter, or Neptune), you probably crave times alone and enjoy remote environments where you can commune with your inner world. What emerges within you when you are alone? The Sun here indicates an inner warmth, vitality, a confidence in your inner resources; the Moon, emotional needs and sensitivities which demand your attention; Mercury, a frenzy of thoughts and worries, nervous mental energy which may motivate you to read or write; Venus, feelings of peace and love, and an appreciation of beauty which you may channel into artistic pursuits; Mars, sexual desire, previously unacknowledged resentments, and a restlessness which goads you to keep busy; Jupiter, rich and expansive faith, and a questing for the wisdom gained through exploring and expanding your inner horizons.

Saturn in the twelfth house indicates deep-seated loneliness, fear or guilt, despair or negativity which may be difficult to confront. But it also shows the ability to apply yourself with determination or concentration to some solitary task—perhaps to your work, which helps you to bring order to the internal chaos. Uranus inclines you to express yourself in inventive, often unconventional ways when alone, seeking activities which allow for constant change and mental stimulation. Neptune suggests creative inspiration, transcendent experience, or fantasies and dreams which captivate you. Finally, Pluto in the twelfth house indicates so much intensity lurking beneath your calm surface that you feel driven with your total being to explore the depths of your psyche; or in contrast, you may feel driven to move outward, away from the threats of volcanic eruption, to focus single-mindedly on some activity which requires you to use all of your energies.

The twelfth house is the house of confinement as well as solitude, and may indicate either voluntary or involuntary confinement at some point in the life cycle. Many people with strong twelfth houses have chosen to live in ashrams or alone in some remote location. Others have been confined in prisons, hospitals, or mental institutions, often because they have misused their energies, or because they have become so out of touch with their minds, bodies and emotions that they were drawn into seclusion so that they might regain contact with themselves. Many people with twelfth house planets, wishing to serve humanity, feel called to work with the institutionalized and to vicariously experience their conflicts. Such confinement may be a choice which a soul makes in order to confront and integrate otherwise inaccessible facets of itself.

Apart from solitude and confinement, your twelfth house planets may suggest that you are oversensitive to public attention, and that you desire to operate behind the scenes, quietly expressing yourself and sustaining yourself without public acknowledgement. If you have Mars or Saturn here, you may in particular be threatened by competition and prefer to work on your own, or in an environment free from external pressures.

Often, the twelfth house desire to remain in the background results in indirect or evasive action. Mercury in the twelfth house may incline you to ramble in speech rather than directly express your thoughts; Mars, to assert yourself or express your anger in subtle, circuitous ways, such as by making wisecracks or by edging your way to the front of a line rather than overtly asserting yourself; Pluto may unconsciously motivate you to gain power in your relationships by using your penetrating psychological insight as a means to manipulate others.

Whatever planetary energies are located in or ruling your twelfth house, you are generally quite protective of them. Many planets here suggest that you are a private person; one or two indicate that you keep to yourself certain vulnerable facets of your experience (as indicated by the nature of these particular planets). Although you may talk about your personal life, you only directly reveal these twelfth house energies with the few people you most deeply trust. Because they indicate your Achilles heel, your points of maximum vulnerability, you are easily wounded by other people's unempathic reactions to these parts of yourself.

If your Moon is in your twelfth house, you are unwilling to disclose when you are hurt or need comfort or sympathy, or to let people directly see your feelings, perhaps because you fear being regarded as weak or childish. With Mercury or Jupiter here, you may feel threatened by the mental abilities, beliefs, or methods of communication of other people, and may hesitate to share what you are really thinking. Venus in the twelfth house may indicate that you are affectionate in private but unwilling to display affection openly; Mars, that you keep your anger to yourself, so as not to hurt other people or drive them away; Uranus, that you hide your idiosyncrasies or unconventional habits, interests or activities from the public eyes so as not to be considered abnormal or odd; Pluto, that you keep your deepest desires and passions to yourself, and are reticent about facing and expressing your real issues in regard to money, sex, or death.

Thus, planets in the twelfth house, like retrograde planets, indicate energies turned inward rather than outward. With the Moon here, you nurture or baby yourself rather than function outwardly in a nurturing role. If you have a twelfth house Mercury, you talk to yourself or write, rather than communicate or interact with many people. Jupiter inclines you to turn inward for understanding rather than reach out openly, and Saturn, to control yourself and to maintain internal stability rather than pursue external expressions of power, control or security.

Your tendency to direct the energies of your twelfth house inward rather than outward is both advantageous and detrimental. On the one hand, you may cultivate your inner resources; on the other hand, you may use these energies against yourself or become narcissistic and self-absorbed. If you have a twelfth house Venus, and you are unable to develop an intimate relationship which satisfies your unrealistic images of love, you may turn away from human contact and invest more energy into self-love than love of others. If you have a twelfth house Mars, and you have not learned to effectively express your anger, you may direct your aggression against yourself and experience painful bouts of self-hatred and depression. Your twelfth house planets and rulers are both hidden helpers and internal saboteurs which may prevent you from developing your capacities to cope effectively with the outer world.

Karmic Experience

Another way of understanding your twelfth house planets is to view them from a karmic perspective, as expressions of unresolved issues and tasks you carry with you from past lives. According to esoteric astrology, not only does the Moon's South Node reflect what you're manifesting from a past life, but the sign on the cusp of your twelfth house indicates your ascendant in your last life, and the planets contained within or ruling your twelfth house express your primary focus within that lifetime. Aspects to these planets denote how you used these energies and show the conflicts you may have experienced. Squares or oppositions to the twelfth house (or difficult conjunctions, such as a Saturn/Pluto conjunction) suggest karma which must be paid—hurts you inflicted upon others for which you must now make amends. An abundance of trines and sextiles to the twelfth house, or the placement of benefic planets and conjunctions there (such as Venus/Jupiter) suggest a previous life characterized by love, generosity, or inner development. During this incarnation you may be rewarded for all that you have given in the past.

If you have the same sign on the cusps of the twelfth and first houses, you are most likely dealing with the same issues that you dealt with in a previous lifetime. Perhaps you failed to learn your life lesson, or you need to learn more about the expression of this particular sign before you can move forward to another life lesson or task. Because the energies of the twelfth house are pulled outward at the ascendant, there is no escape for you this time. You are compelled to use these energies. You are your best friend and your worst enemy; you take in at the twelfth house the same energies which you give out at the ascendant. Although you tend to be unconscious of the image which you project to others (because of the twelfth house dynamics underlying your ascendant), you will face the consequences of your behaviors and grow in consciousness.

If the same sign is on your eleventh and twelfth house cusps, then you are likely to confront your past life karma through friendship, group activities, and social causes, as well as through the pursuit of your goals. If a sign is intercepted within your twelfth house, you have a double task in this lifetime. First, you must face the issues related to the sign on the cusp and the planets in that sign; then you plunge downward still deeper to encounter the energies of the intercepted sign. These latter issues may be very old ones, unresolved problems from many past lifetimes.

Many people who view the astrology chart from a karmic perspective focus on the personal karma which we carry from incarnation to incarnation. But that personal karma is often a part of larger karmic dramas—those of our families, of our society, of our planet as a whole. Famous Greek myths, such as the stories of the House of Atreus, express how children frequently repeat the crimes of their forefathers, or are driven to atone for them. Family dramas may not be clearly revealed in the natal chart, yet comparing the charts of family members may reveal significant karmic ties.

Consider a family in which not only do both parents have planets on their daughter's South Node, but both have Plutonian temperaments. The mother is a Scorpio, and the father has a t-square to Pluto. Not only does the daughter (and coincidentally, her only brother) have a twelfth house Pluto, but her Pluto is the same degree as her mother's

Moon and her father's Jupiter. Such twelfth house connections suggest deep psychological ties between family members which may have past life origins. Indeed, this woman, in a past life regression, experienced herself as a political leader in ancient Rome, who sentenced both her parents to death. In this lifetime, in reaction to her parents' powerful expressions of energy, she has inhibited both her power and aggression, and struggled with a life-threatening illness which she views as a form of punishment for her destructive impulses.

Most likely, the twelfth house suggests not only personal and family karma, but also societal or collective karma. Those of you who have Uranus, Neptune or Pluto in your twelfth houses may be bearing some of the burdens of the larger collective; your own inner struggles with these energies may feel insurmountable at times because you are confronting the disowned shadow of humanity—the anarchistic, chaotic and violent energies which often seem to rule this planet. Perhaps your own experiences in facing and learning to harness or transmute these energies may have an impact upon planetary evolution; perhaps your own pain will be easier to bear if you believe that your own internal battles may have a meaning which extends beyond yourself.

Childhood and Parental Influences

Apart from issues connected with past lives, energies related to your twelfth house were likely to have been a significant focus in childhood. As indicators of emotionally charged residue which you carry from the past, they may point to deep-seated stress early in life which still subliminally influences you today.

According to Howard Sasportas,[1] twelfth house planets and signs not only reflect the issues of early childhood, but they also reflect life in the womb. The nature of your twelfth house energy indicates those dimensions of your mother's experience which you absorbed prenatally and which colored your earliest perceptions of life on earth. If, for example, you have a twelfth house Saturn, you may have felt particularly constrained and confined within the womb, in part because you were sensitive to your mother's experiences of fear, restriction, and depression during her pregnancy. While your twelfth house indicates your fetal experience, your ascendant (and planets conjunct your ascendant) suggest your experience of birth—how you entered and reacted to the outer world.

At least as significant as past lives and prenatal influences is your experience of early childhood—particularly if you have fourth house/

twelfth house connections in your chart (e.g., your twelfth house planet rules your fourth house, your twelfth house ruler is in your fourth house, or you have fourth house/twelfth house aspects). During your earliest years, the structure of your personality developed; never again in your life will you be as malleable as you were then. Your perceptions of the world, new and fluid from the start, eventually hardened over time and became filters through which you still perceive yourself and the world around you. The Moon, its South Node, and the planets and signs influencing your twelfth house were the primary filters through which you encountered life outside yourself. No matter what thoughts, feelings, and behaviors were directed toward you, you were nevertheless likely to process them according to the web of expectations indicated by these astrological variables.

Perhaps one of your parents strongly manifested the energy of your twelfth house planet or sign, without allowing space for anyone else in the family (especially you) to outwardly express it; as a result, you were overstimulated in regard to this energy, while simultaneously learning to inhibit it. Perhaps your parents directly or indirectly communicated to you that the expression of this energy was unacceptable and would be punished.

If you ask yourself what "don'ts" prevailed during your childhood, prohibitions which were either overtly or latently enforced, you may discover that many of them are related to your twelfth house energies. "Don't cry," a mother repeatedly tells a child with a twelfth house Moon. "Don't be a baby." Parents of a daughter with a twelfth house Mars assertively let her know that her own assertion, aggression, sexuality, and spontaneous expressions of physical energy are unfeminine and unwelcome. "Smile," they say, and "Don't be angry!" Because you as a child were powerless and dependent upon your parents for your emotional and physical survival, their "don't" had life-or-death impact upon you. Without their care, help, and support, you faced an unfathomable terror of loss and annihilation. Now, when you question their prohibitions, you may experience that same terror.

The Sun in the twelfth house suggests that your parents were not supportive of your ego development and did not help you to develop self-confidence; the Moon, that they did not respond to your emotional needs or nurture you. Frequently, a twelfth house Moon also suggests the loss of a mother at an early age, and profound psychic ties which were never openly acknowledged. A twelfth house Mercury may indicate that you never felt free to communicate with your family, or that they treated you as mentally inferior; Venus here suggests a prohibition in regard to expressing affection and love, or pursuing cultural interests.

If you have Mars in the twelfth house, you may have not been allowed to express your anger or to be physically active; because Mars is the sense of "I am," your identity as separate from your parents may have been unacknowledged. Jupiter in the twelfth house indicates that your parents discouraged your attempts to grow and expand beyond their narrow world through your own philosophical quest for meaning, or in regard to travel and the exploration of new outer horizons. Saturn suggests the psychological or physical absence of a father (or authority figure) who worked, or who provided a model for you in terms of discipline, organization, and coping with the realities of everyday living; you were not encouraged to develop your ambition or your competitive spirit, or to believe in your potential for success.

A twelfth house Uranus suggests that your individuality and originality were stifled, and that you felt forced to conform to parental expectations; Neptune, that your creative and spiritual development were neglected or ignored, and that as a result you turned inward to fantasy. Finally, a twelfth house Pluto suggests a parental ban upon facing and expressing the primal dimension of life—the turbulent energies of passion and sexuality, as well as indicating emotionally charged issues surrounding money, death, occult experience, and the use of power.

Because you were not able to openly express twelfth house energies in childhood, you are likely to be uncomfortable with them and to deny them. But pushing them beneath the surface of your consciousness does not get rid of them; rather, it causes them to fester, to grow in distorted, excessive ways within the darkness of the unconscious. Beyond your awareness, the ghosts of the past, the memory images of emotionally charged experiences and the reservoir of denied, unexpressed thoughts and feelings become lenses through which you perceive reality. Adult experiences which in any way inwardly resonate with significant past experiences trigger your earliest learned responses and behaviors—often preverbal responses which you cannot remember or even conceptualize.

Displacement Patterns: Aspects

As a result of being pushed into the unconscious, your twelfth house energies operate subliminally; often, the primitive anxiety they evoke fuels automatic and compulsive activities, usually indicated by squares to twelfth house planets (or in the case of projection onto others, through oppositions). Often, you repeat the same pattern again and again until you are able to consciously examine it, discover and re-experience its origins, and grow beyond needing it.

An examination of the squares to your twelfth house planets can reveal useful information in regard to how your twelfth house issues are manifesting themselves. You may not even be aware of problems in regard to your twelfth house planets because the planets which square them are bearing their energy and seeking compensation. If you have a square from the twelfth house to the second house, you may be compulsive about spending money, accumulating possessions, earning money, or proving your value and self-worth. From an early age, your sensitivities and conflicts in regard to your twelfth house planet may have been channelled into second house issues. Likewise, such channelling and compensation behavior occurs with other twelfth house squares.

A twelfth house/third house square suggests subconsciously moti-vated energy directed toward writing, communication, daily interac-tion, and relationships with sisters and brothers. A square from the twelfth to the fourth house directs your subliminal and often com-pensatory energy into a focus on the home and family. An eighth house/twelfth house square may be the most helpful of the squares because your twelfth house planet may seek an outlet which is directly psychological or spiritual; your focus upon psychology, psychotherapy, life/death issues, the occult, and sexuality is likely to be motivated by the energy of your twelfth house planet. You may, however, use sex as a means of escaping from twelfth house conflicts.

What about a square from a twelfth house planet to the ninth house? Such a square can fuel a quest for consciousness and understanding which illumines twelfth house issues; but it can also motivate you to avoid the direct experience of your twelfth house wounds and con-flicts by retreating into mental realms, by reading, attending courses, and pursuing degrees in order to avoid painful inner experience. Likewise, a tenth house/twelfth house square can motivate you to use your twelfth house planet successfully in your career, or can drive you to avoid facing the issues inherent in it by becoming a compulsive workaholic or status-seeker.

If you have no twelfth house planets, but have one or more squares to the planetary ruler of your twelfth house, the nature of this planet, sign, and house may likewise indicate your means of channelling your twelfth house energy, or seeking compensation for its unresolved issues.

Sextiles and trines to twelfth house planets also direct the energy of the planets into other houses, where they can be constructively expressed or where they can find a means of escape from their conflicts. Sextiles and trines are easier to handle than squares because energy flows freely into an outlet which provides some satisfaction; however, such satisfaction is not necessarily beneficial—a sextile from a twelfth house Pluto to a second house Neptune may incline you to buy and consume alcohol as a means of avoiding the self-condemnation and inner turmoil of a twelfth house Pluto. Your sextiles and trines may provide easy escapes from twelfth house issues, whereas your squares will continually force you to deal with your psychological conflicts, even if displaced and directed into other areas of your chart

All-or-Nothing Patterns

Because the energies of your twelfth house are emotionally loaded and often repressed, they tend to manifest indirectly. Yet frequently they will burst into your consciousness and into your behavioral expressions in a forthright and urgent manner; to the extent which you have disowned them, you may feel a lack of control when they assert themselves. One day, you feel small and disconnected from yourself, Lilliputian; the next day (often in response to a twelfth house transit), you are inflated with your own energy, as if you have entered the Brobdingnagian world of Gulliver, or swallowed Alice in Wonderland's potion which spurs sudden growth. Soon, however, you may feel carried away with needs, desires, feelings, fantasies, thoughts, or impulses which seem overwhelming.

This all-or-nothing twelfth house pattern can be quite disruptive to your life if you do not make choices which take into account your twelfth house energies; whenever these parts of yourself are excluded for any length of time, they tend to reappear quite dramatically. Like the fairy who was not invited to Sleeping Beauty's wedding, they may indeed appear to curse you when they do appear; any energy that has been denied will first burst into consciousness in distorted and troublesome form.

Consider Spiro Agnew, whose twelfth house Mercury inclined him to faulty slips of the tongue, or Anita Bryant, whose twelfth house Pluto vehemently burst onto the scene in opposition to homosexuality. The less an energy is acknowledged and integrated, the more powerful it will express itself, and the more inappropriate it may appear to be.

Because twelfth house energies often exist in primal, archaic form, since they were deprived of the early socialization experiences which would have made them more civilized and adaptable, they usually respond to inner promptings rather than the cues of the social environment. If you have a twelfth house Mars and a friend unintentionally slights you, you may unconsciously perceive him as the father who abused you when you were a child; you may lash out at him with a rage which is clearly overreactive. When your "anger button" is pushed, you respond not only with the anger you feel in your current circumstance, but with the entire bag of anger you have been carrying around with you since childhood. To everyone else, your response seems inappropriate; but to you, perceiving your situation through the lens of Mars, it feels perfectly justifiable. You may not even be aware that you unconsciously brushed aside your irritated reactions toward your friend for many months, because they seemed trivial or because you didn't want to disturb the apparent harmony existing between you. But now you remember every intended or unintended slight, as if your friend has never been your friend at all, but only an antagonist born to persecute you. You may not be aware of the degree to which you are repressing your thoughts or feelings until your brakes wear out from overuse, and the unacknowledged thoughts and feelings flood into consciousness.

Thus, your twelfth house energies become your hidden weaknesses, ways in which you delude or defeat yourself, facets of yourself which you fear or dislike, and psychological problems which are painful to acknowledge. Without your awareness or acceptance, these traits seem like alien forces threatening to overwhelm you; they become distorted in their expression, and operate in negative, self-destructive ways.

Hidden Weaknesses

How can you know what energies you repress and what your hidden weaknesses are? If the twelfth house is indeed your blind spot, then how can you cast light into that darkness and begin to see the shadows which reside there? Again, begin with a mental assessment. Look to the planets in or ruling your twelfth house. Ask yourself how you experience these energies in your daily life, and how the negative dimensions of these energies emerge within you. Doing so may make you uneasy; you can confront your twelfth house energies only when you are ready to confront them, when you feel secure enough in yourself to allow them to surface. Without an attitude of compassion toward yourself, the capacity for self-forgiveness, and the acceptance of human limitation, the integration and transmutation of twelfth house energies cannot happen. The willingness to learn humility, and the desire to love yourself as you are, rather than to focus solely on your grandiose ideals, are prerequisites to the integration of twelfth house energies.

Whether or not you have yet developed these qualities, you may want to take a moment now to at least briefly examine the hidden weaknesses which might be indicated by your twelfth house planets and signs.

With the Sun or Leo in the twelfth house, you may outwardly appear self-effacing, but you may carry within yourself considerable egotism, narcissism, and arrogance. For you, the bottom line may be the protection of your ego from outer forces which threaten your pride and self-esteem. If you have Virgo rising, you may cover up this pride with a humble, self-serving persona.

With the Moon or Cancer in the twelfth house, you may be oversensitive and passive; you may deny your childish hungers, your need to be taken care of, your desire for mothering. As a result, you may be ill at ease around children, or (if you are female) deny your maternal instincts. Your hidden weakness is your unwillingness to deal directly with emotional needs.

Mercury here can incline you to suffer from nervous tension, incessant mental chatter, self-criticism, and worry. Gemini indicates excessive thinking and ruminating, as well as a tendency to lose yourself in monologues and soliloquies. Virgo in the twelfth house is self-critical, obsessive about details and order, and prone to negative thinking.

Having a twelfth house Venus suggests that you deny your desire for an intimate partner, or relate primarily to fantasy, rather than the person in front of you. Your hidden weaknesses are likely to be excessive self-love, vanity, self-indulgence, or materialism. If Taurus is in your twelfth house, you disavow your materialistic tendencies, dogmatism, laziness, or sensuality. If you have Libra here, you avoid facing the compulsions and illusions which interfere with your personal relationships; your peace-at-any-price attitude, applied to yourself, may prevent you from honestly looking inward.

With Mars or Aries, you avoid dealing openly with your physical and sexual needs, or with your anger, which you are likely to turn against yourself or experience as paranoia. You may feel uncomfortable acknowledging the extent to which you are motivated by self-interest. You need to learn how to openly go after what you want, and to stand up for yourself.

With Jupiter or Sagittarius in the twelfth house, you avoid confronting your extravagance and self-righteousness. By holding onto beliefs or assumptions about yourself which no longer serve you, you limit your expansion in the outer world. Yet you also are inclined to overextend yourself and to become emotionally overinvested in your experiences.

With Saturn or Capricorn here, you hesitate to openly express and come to terms with your negative feelings, particularly fear, guilt, loneliness, and mistrust. Because you haven't dealt with the fear and self-doubt which inhibit you, you may deny your desire for professional accomplishment. This Saturnian influence can manifest as psychological rigidity and withholding, due to inability to let go of past patterns. You, above all, need to come to terms with your repressions.

If Uranus or Aquarius is in your twelfth house, you suppress your need for independence, change, freedom, or individualistic self-expression. But on an inner level, you may be willful, a law to yourself, irresponsible, or undisciplined. You may experience constant inner turmoil.

Neptune or Pisces in its own house suggest that your hidden weakness may be hypersensitivity, addiction, escapism or fantasy, self-deception, or a willingness to drift through life without determining your direction. You may avoid openly developing and expressing your creative or spiritual capacities.

Finally, if you have Pluto or Scorpio in your twelfth house you may deny and fear your inner power, and your potential for cruelty and violence, as well as for totally regenerating sexual experience. Your hidden weaknesses may be your harsh judgment of yourself, your tendency to drive yourself mercilessly, and your volatile explosiveness which results from repressing rather than constructively channelling your intense primal energy.

Relationships

Whatever planets or signs influence your twelfth house, you are likely to be unaware of their outer manifestations; however, you are unlikely to hide them from other people. Frequently, you subliminally broadcast these signs and planets, communicating mixed messages which may be confusing or indecipherable.

These energies which you unconsciously communicate also have a magnetic effect; they seek overt expression in your life, through the people with whom you come into contact and the circumstances with which you grapple. To the extent that you are not consciously attuned to your twelfth house energies, you attract people who express them for you, particularly if you have oppositions to the twelfth house or its ruler. The more out of touch you are with these energies, the more negatively they will manifest—as compulsive attractions or seemingly unwanted intrusions from people who are larger-than-life expressions of your twelfth house. Your hidden enemy is not only yourself, but also the people in your life who express the negative dimensions of your twelfth house planets.

This phenomenon, of attracting people who express your twelfth house energies, is a form of projection—of noticing in other people and overreacting to the qualities which you don't accept in yourself. Your twelfth house planets and signs incline you not only to attract people into your life who manifest these qualities, but also to see those qualities enlarged in people who are only minimally expressing them; you may then either resent or idealize these people, depending upon whether you have disowned these qualities in yourself because you are more uncomfortable with your strengths or with your weaknesses. If you have oppositions to your twelfth house or twelfth house ruler, you are particularly likely to get rid of your uncomfortable twelfth house experiences by projecting these qualities onto others.

If your Moon is in your twelfth house, you may be conscious of, and actively dislike, childish, needy people; if Mars, you may be quick to label someone aggressive and to reject him because of it. You will stop being unduly disturbed by your negative qualities as perceived in other people when you have fully acknowledged and accepted them in yourself.

Not only the twelfth house, but also the seventh house, can be considered to be the projection houses of the horoscope. Each day after the Sun rises, it casts the longest shadows after dawn, when it passes through the twelfth house, and before sunset, when it crosses the seventh house. The "shadow" in Jungian psychology is the dark side of ourselves, the facets of ourselves which are most hidden from our consciousness. Your seventh house does not indicate your subliminal energies to the degree that your twelfth house does, but it does indicate those portions of yourself which you most elicit and seek in others. If the seventh and twelfth houses are linked in your chart—because the ruler of one resides in the other, because aspects occur between these houses or their rulers, or because the same planet rules both houses—then you are especially prone to act out unconscious psychological and karmic patterns in your relationships.

Having your seventh house ruler in your twelfth house indicates that you are drawn to a partner who triggers your unconscious complexes, or who expresses your twelfth house energies for you, and with whom you experience a deep-seated psychic or spiritual bond. Rather than valuing the external dimensions of your relationship, you seek internal values—perhaps the capacity that both of you have together to share the secret realms of yourself or to commune on nonverbal levels. You are also likely to be quite emotionally sensitive to your relationship experiences, and may even deny your desire for a partner because of the vulnerabilities which intimate relationships awaken within you. Having your twelfth house ruler in your seventh house is similar, except that you are even more likely to project your internal experience onto your partner and to view other people in your life through the filter of the past.

Not only are you likely to reject in others and project onto others your own twelfth house energies; you may also act in a manner which elicits responses that are related to your twelfth house planets and signs. Your twelfth house Saturn provokes rejection; your twelfth house Venus invites affection, as well as indulgent behavior; your twelfth house Sun requests that the other party take center stage so that you may revolve around him, and experience a center that you otherwise lack.

In addition to attracting people into your life, your twelfth house planets and signs may magnetically catalyze events; when your twelfth house is aspected, you may experience the manifestations of these energies happening around you, but not directly affecting you. If you have a twelfth house Moon or Neptune, you witness a flood; if your Mars is in the twelfth house, you are on the scene frequently during an accident or a fire. Consider, for example, Marilyn Monroe, Judy Garland, George Wallace, Patty Hearst, and Anita Bryant—all of whom had to deal with issues related to violence, death, or sexuality. All of these people have Pluto in their natal twelfth houses.

Sensitivity, Service & Imagination

Facing the dark side of your twelfth house energies may involve considerable suffering. But whether or not you confront these facets of yourself, your twelfth house planets (especially Moon and Neptune) are likely to indicate suffering, vulnerability, and sensitivity which you may hide from others. Experiences which might not be disturbing to other people may be emotionally overwhelming to you.

This sensitivity has positive and negative ramifications. On the negative side, it can lead to a weak-willed personality with psychological problems involving excessive emotional insecurity, phobias, timidity, self-pity, addiction, or escapism. If you have several planets in the twelfth house, you may feel persecuted; you may become a victim or martyr, or may allow yourself to be exploited by other people.

On the physical level, the twelfth house can suggest chronic illness, particularly if the sixth house is involved in opposition aspects, or if twelfth house planets (or rulers) square or oppose Mercury, Neptune, the sixth house ruler, or Pisces or Virgo planets. Aspects to the ascendant or first house ruler can also indicate physical weakness, as can the placement of the ascendant ruler within the twelfth house. The nature of the illness may be indicated by the most afflicted planets associated with the twelfth house. The Sun, for example, might suggest heart trouble, or Venus, hormonal imbalance or even diabetes. Many people with polio, or suffering from partial paralysis, have one or more twelfth house oppositions, sometimes involving Neptune in Virgo opposing Mercury in Pisces. Physical problems related to twelfth house planets usually have psychological origins and suggest emotional conflicts which need to be experienced and worked through in a safe environment.

The psychological roots of such a problem as paralysis may be evident to you if you have several planets in your twelfth house, or the Moon, Mercury, or Neptune there. Most likely, then, you often feel psychologically paralyzed, overwhelmed because you are taking in more than you can assimilate. Naturally psychic and impressionable, you pick up every emotional vibration around you, every nuance of expression. Unless Saturn is strong in your chart, you may lack a filtering mechanism for shutting out the influx of energies. You may feel other people's feelings, needs, problems, and experiences as if they were your own. If you can control this openness, you have the potential to be an outstanding counselor or psychologist. If Mercury or Pluto are in your twelfth house, you possess remarkable psychological insight; if the Moon or Neptune are here, you experience considerable empathy and compassion.

These qualities of empathy and compassion are two of the most constructive expressions of the twelfth house. Planets here influence your concern for and responsiveness to people in need. A twelfth house Venus or Neptune in particular give you the natural ability to expand beyond personal love to a spiritual love for humanity—to devote yourself to the mission of helping other people. You may therefore feel drawn to a social service profession, perhaps involving working in an institution with the sick, disturbed, or imprisoned; you may do volunteer work or contribute money to a charitable organization.

When I was doing volunteer work in a prison, giving astrological consultations to the inmates, I noticed similar patterns in their charts. First of all, many had t-squares to Uranus; these men had been involved in riots or socially disruptive activities. Many had t-squares to Neptune; these prisoners were incarcerated for drug-dealing activities. Another high percentage of the inmates possessed t-squares to Pluto; many of these men were imprisoned for crimes of violence. Not only these charts, but others I studied as well, were characterized by affliction, natally or by transit, to the twelfth house, to Neptune, and frequently to Pisces planets.

During this brief period of volunteer work, I was fortunate enough also to do consultations for half a dozen members of the prison staff. In these charts, I found similar characteristics to the charts of the inmates. What was the primary difference between the staff and the prisoners? Not their charts, but rather the opportunities open to them, and how they had chosen to express their twelfth house energies.

Your twelfth house planets can indicate that you possess such hypersensitivity that you are unable to adapt to life's demands; on the other hand, that sensitivity can enable you to become a helper, a healer, or an artist. The nature of your twelfth house planets and signs indicate the energies to which you are psychically sensitive, and through which you easily attune to the needs of others. Since twelfth house planets indicate a desire to serve humanity, you may experience a sense of mission in regard to expressing your twelfth house energies by responding to the needs of the people around you.

This desire to serve is likely to be motivated by many factors. First of all, the suffering which you have experienced in regard to your twelfth house energies legitimately fuels your compassion toward people experiencing similar suffering. Second, the spiritual sensitivity of the twelfth house inclines you to feel that your life is not your own, and that its fullest expression is in service to a cause which transcends yourself. Third, you may doubt your worthiness as a human being and your right to follow your own self-interest, and you may build your esteem through dedicating yourself to others. Fourth, you may be burdened, consciously or unconsciously, with guilt and shame for which you need to atone.

Your need for atonement may be influenced primarily by karmic factors, or by real or imaginary "crimes" in this lifetime which consciously or unconsciously burden you. The guilt and shame which you carry may have its roots in early childhood, when the infantile ego perceives the destructive fantasies it has toward its parents to influence reality. Guilt in regard to fantasied or overtly expressed aggression, or in regard to your sense of "badness" in not living up to the internalized standards of your family, may fuel your desire to make reparation and seek atonement through service.

In many ways, the twelfth house is the house of inner images and ideals, not external reality. Here, you seek escape from the bad or unpleasant images which haunt you; you also seek fulfillment through images of experiencing the ideal—whether through service, beauty, love, or transcendent experience.

Because of the image-oriented nature of the twelfth house, your twelfth house planets (particularly Moon, Mercury, Jupiter, or Neptune) can indicate a vivid imagination and active dream life. Of course, these may have negative ramifications—you may feel perpetually pulled into a fantasy world where you eventually lose the ability to differentiate reality from illusion. For example, a planet such as Venus in the twelfth house may incline you to require an ideal love relationship and be unable to accept an imperfect one. But the positive ramifications of twelfth house sensitivity are enriching. With a twelfth house Jupiter, you may be able to grow considerably from the wisdom you gain from dreams and meditations; with Pluto here, you may tap deeply into the powerful archetypes common to humanity.

Planets in the twelfth house are fuel for the imagination and an aid in doing visualization work such as is practiced by various schools of meditation, by Silva Mind Control, or by spiritual schools of psychotherapy such as psychosynthesis. By fantasizing vividly what you want to be, you can generate a thought form powerful enough to manifest desired changes in your life. Mercury, Mars, or Saturn here can also help you to make practical use of your imagination.

This power of imagination indicated by twelfth house influences is related to creative inspiration. Many writers (such as Ernest Hemingway, Pearl Buck, Germaine Greer, Gertrude Stein, John Ruskin, and Anatole France) have had Mercury in the twelfth house; many singers (such as Barbra Streisand, Janis Joplin, and Judy Garland) and musicians (such as Jimi Hendrix, Richard Strauss, and Claude Debussy) have had twelfth house Venuses. The placement of Moon in the twelfth house is common for both poets (William Blake, Percy Bysshe Shelley, Arthur Rimbaud, and W. B. Yeats) and musicians (Jose Feliciano, Liberace, Eric Satie, and Paul Simon). Your twelfth house planets may help you to become a channel for creative energies, and may increase your openness and your capacity to surrender yourself to inspiration.

Spirituality and Transcendence

Twelfth house inspiration is often a source of transcendence, faith, and spirituality. In an emotional, experiential sense, the twelfth house is a deeply religious house. Unlike the ninth house, and the influence of Jupiter and Sagittarius, it is not concerned with philosophical and religious beliefs; rather, its realm is the inner realm through which the divine energies of God (Goddess) are directly experienced. If you have several planets in the twelfth house, particularly Moon, Jupiter, or Neptune, you may possess the ability to reach high planes of consciousness, to lose your separateness in the awesome experience of cosmic unity, to attune yourself to the divine light within you. This openness to cosmic energies can lead to a sustaining faith and to the security that you are protected by forces greater than the human and worldly; it can actually allow those radiant, healing, and guiding energies to penetrate every facet of your life, every house of your chart, as the Sun each day carries those energies around the circle of houses.

Your twelfth house is where you receive an influx of cosmic energies. The planets in and ruling your twelfth house may be keys to the ways in which you can most easily open yourself to these energies—Venus, through love or the arts; Jupiter, through study or travel; Saturn, through work, particularly work which is service-oriented; Neptune, through service, poetry, music, or meditation.

Because the twelfth house is the dimension of yourself where you tap into both superconscious (transpersonal) and collective or archetypal energies, the planets and signs which influence your twelfth house have meanings which extend beyond the personal. They seek universal expression; they are not satisfied with operating within a limited subjective sphere. Therefore, your twelfth house Venus is attuned to spiritual love, which touches the souls of many, rather than focusing exclusively on a one-to-one relationship; your twelfth house Mercury wishes to write and communicate about large, universal issues; your twelfth house Saturn works not for profit and self-interest but as a service to humanity.

You can lose yourself in your twelfth house and drift rudderless through life, lost in your private world, afraid to move out of yourself, submissive to other people's will, or dependent upon drugs or alcohol. Or, you can learn to open to transforming experiences of love, faith, or transcendence, and become motivated to express your experience outwardly through your relationships, creative projects, and work.

Although the difficulties of your twelfth house may be many, its gifts are likely to be legion as well. Your twelfth house indicates not only your hidden weaknesses, but also your hidden strengths.

Hidden Strengths

What can your individual planetary placements or rulerships tell you about your hidden strengths? Just as you looked to your twelfth house planets to discover your hidden weaknesses, look now to their most positive expressions to discover your hidden strengths. These strengths are hidden because you may not be aware of them until, in a stress situation, you are forced to draw upon your deepest inner resources. What then are you likely to discover in yourself?

If your Sun influences your twelfth house, your hidden strengths are your confidence in your inner wealth, your ability to revitalize yourself, your centeredness, your potential for leadership. The Moon in your twelfth shows your emotional self-sufficiency, your ability to care for yourself and nurture yourself, your emotional responsiveness to people who need you.

Your twelfth house Mercury suggests that you have an uncanny ability to communicate clearly with yourself, to involve yourself in mentally stimulating activities, and to use writing as a tool for your inner development. Venus indicates love for yourself, kindness, enjoyment of your own company, devotion to your ideals, and inner peace.

If your Mars influences your twelfth house, you have the capacity to repeatedly begin anew, to motivate yourself, and to initiate activities. You demonstrate courage and determination as you explore your psyche, and as you battle for yourself or the causes in which you believe. Jupiter here indicates a deep-seated sense of faith in yourself and in the future, the supportive strength of your philosophical or religious beliefs, positive attitudes, your ability to grow from every experience, and the richness of your inner life.

Saturn provides inner strength and self-discipline, a capacity to cope with loneliness and handle responsibility, and a willingness to work on your own with determination and perseverance. The hidden gifts of your twelfth house Uranus are psychological independence and freedom, open-mindedness, deep-seated intuition and originality, and an ability to both change yourself and to handle disruptive, unexpected life circumstances.

Neptune here suggests abiding faith, compassion, attunement to high levels of inspiration, dedication to your ideals, and your willingness to give of yourself to those who need you. Finally, your twelfth house Pluto suggests deep psychological insight, an indomitable will, and a remarkable degree of power available to you for withstanding stress and regenerating yourself.

All of these meanings of your twelfth house planets and rulers are, of course, modified by their sign placements, their aspects, and the other houses which they rule in your chart. You must consider the whole picture, and the whole picture of your twelfth house involves more than your twelfth house alone.

Becoming Whole

In order to become open to all the positive, healing twelfth house energies which you have shut out of your awareness, you may first need to confront the past fears, hatreds, sufferings, losses, humiliations etc. which inhibit you, and which prevent you from awakening to your true self. Why should you deal with these twelfth house energies? Is it really worthwhile to allow your negativity to surface? If you consciously choose to open the doors to your hidden self, might you fall apart, or break down, and function less adequately than you do now? Why not leave the experience of your subconscious alone and content yourself with safe intellectual exploration?

Certainly, if you primarily have trines or sextiles to your twelfth house planets, you may not need to confront your hidden energies. They may be already flowing smoothly into your consciousness. But you may not be using these energies to their fullest extent, or even expressing their constructive potential; you may be neglecting your responsibility to yourself to develop yourself still further.

If you have three or more planets in your twelfth house, you may not need to turn inward more than you are doing now. Much, however, depends upon whether in your inner journeys you are really coming to terms with these energies emotionally, or whether you are wallowing in them or escaping from them. You may need to balance your twelfth house emphasis by consciously and realistically examining your fantasies, by learning to shut off the influx of incoming energies, by moving out of yourself, by facing and accepting the outer world, and by practically applying your vision and inspiration in the world.

What if you have unresolved squares or oppositions to your twelfth house planets or twelfth house? Why should you confront your twelfth house energies? What might happen if you don't?

First of all, experiences associated with twelfth house planets are emotionally charged. You have a lot of psychological energy invested in them. When you repress these experiences, and the thoughts, feelings, and impulses associated with them, you push a considerable amount of energy beneath the surface of your consciousness. The more energy you repress, the less is available for daily living. You become physically and emotionally depleted.

Second, the more you restrict your awareness of your experience, the more your ego and self-image develop apart from your whole self.

Your consciousness of yourself becomes narrow; you function like a small circular fortress with walls erected against the larger circle of your total being. You must defend yourself repeatedly against the alien forces apparently outside yourself which threaten your self-image. At the same time, you make choices which appear to satisfy your conscious self, but which may be counter to the needs of your unconscious self.

You cannot, however, shut off the rest of yourself so easily. Not only do these denied energies operate compulsively, indirectly, or through people and experiences which you attract to yourself, but when you are stressed, exhausted, or overburdened, they tend to burst through and gain control over your feelings and behaviors. The more you have denied them, the more you experience them as alien forces possessing you, threatening your ego, your self-worth, your sense of control. You may then act in ways which you can't understand, and which acutely embarrass you. If you have Moon in the twelfth house, you unexpectedly burst into tears; if Mars, you lash out at a friend for no apparent reason; if Jupiter, you indulge in a spending spree; or if Saturn, you reject someone you love. An extreme result of denied energies bursting through and possessing you is psychosis.

Most likely, if these denied energies gain control over you too frequently, you will stop and question yourself about them. But you may hesitate to plunge too deeply into experiencing them, because you are afraid of the forces which lurk within you and what they will do to your self-esteem and your relationships if they emerge any further. You may be afraid that they will completely take you over.

People with afflicted twelfth house planets often make the following statements:

SUN—"If I take center stage, I'll never let go of it."

MOON—"If I start crying now, I'll never stop."

MERCURY—"If I start to tell you my experience, I'll never stop talking."

VENUS—"If I allow myself to fall in love, I won't be able to do anything but live and breathe love."

MARS—"If I really let out my anger, I'll drive everyone away."

JUPITER—"If I go for abundance in my life, I'll be insatiable in my greed."

SATURN—"If I feel how sad and lonely I really am, I'll become so depressed that I'll hide in my room and never come out."

URANUS—"If I let people see how unconventional and weird I
    really am, they'll lock me up."

NEPTUNE—"If I feel and show how vulnerable I really am, I
    won't be able to bear the pain."

PLUTO—"If I express the destructive feelings inside of me, I'd
    explode like a volcano. I might kill someone."

These fears may have some justification. There are considerable
dangers in confronting twelfth house energies. First of all, you may
experience the Neptunian effect of the dissolution of your self-image,
emotional chaos, helplessness, resignation, or psychological paralysis.
If you judge yourself too severely for these qualities which are emerging within you, you can drain yourself with self-hatred, and plunge
into despair and suicidal fantasies. On the other hand, if you have
Jupiter or the Sun in or ruling your twelfth house, you may have the
reverse experience—a manic reaction of overconfidence, megalomania,
overestimation of your powerfulness or godliness.

According to Carl Jung, the "shadow" is the dark side of ourselves
which we hesitate to acknowledge and integrate into our awareness
of ourselves. Jung wrote:

> The shadow is a moral problem that challenges the whole ego-
> personality, for no one can be conscious of the shadow without con-
> siderable moral effort. To become conscious of it involves recognizing
> the dark aspects of the personality as present and real. This act is the
> essential condition for any kind of self-knowledge, and it therefore, as
> a rule, meets with considerable resistance. Indeed, self-knowledge as
> a psychotherapeutic measure frequently requires much painstaking
> work extending over a long period of time.[2]

For most people, the confrontation with repressed material must
be a slow process, occurring within the context of safe, therapeutic
human relationships. Usually, you must acknowledge the presence
of these energies, emotionally experience them (often while gaining
insight in regard to their origin), and begin to accept them before they
can begin to transform themselves. This kind of process may require
the empathic, caring presence of a psychotherapist, friend, or partner who is unafraid of archaic, often infantile experience. As they
are made conscious and accepted, your twelfth house planets and
signs will begin to reveal your hidden gifts, and to integrate themselves
with the rest of your life. You are then likely to experience vitality
and joy, and a sense of personal substance, wholeness, and integrity
which you may never have imagined could exist for you. Your real

self will inevitably provide a greater sense of self-worth and well-being than your fantasied ideal self could ever provide.

My first experience of directly encountering my twelfth house energies was not a slow one. In the early seventies, during the height of the personal growth movement, I plunged into week-long primal therapy and gestalt therapy workshops. Transiting Neptune had just completed its conjunction to my twelfth house Mars, and transiting Pluto was sextiling my Mars and conjuncting my natal Sun. For a while I became an "intensity addict," enraptured with the sense of aliveness I felt while contacting and ventilating emotion. Because at the time I believed that the amount of catharting I did would be directly proportionate to the amount of change I would experience, I had little respect for my own ego defenses, and little awareness of the time required to integrate the material flooding my consciousness. Psychologically, I began to feel as if I were dying; experiencing the darkness and nothingness at the center of myself reduced me to a state of near powerlessness. My ego felt shattered; I needed several years to rebuild myself—three years in which the intense experiences I had undergone began to manifest themselves positively in my life.

At the same time as I was confronting these primal levels in myself, I was weekly experiencing a form of deep massage, akin to rolfing, which released such powerful energy in me that I literally shook for hours after each session. This was an ecstatic experience more than a painful one, but it was too much too fast. Often, within a few days after a session, my body began to reconstellate the tension patterns it had relinquished. The experience of this often-poisonous energy pouring back into my system against my will was very disturbing; I felt as if I were aging years in a few hours, re-experiencing all the psychological pollution of a lifetime.

I do not advocate this intense approach to purging yourself of your repressions, unless your Pluto, Scorpio planets, or eighth house planets demand it. What I do recommend is practicing some form of meditation several times a day, keeping a journal of your inner experience, working with your dreams, and possibly committing yourself to psychotherapy with a practitioner who is skilled in facilitating the process of recovering, reowning, and integrating disowned facets of the self. You must choose the method appropriate to you, whether it means working totally on your own, with a friend or group, or with the support of a professional whom you trust.

Whatever method you choose, uncomfortable feelings will emerge within you. You need not fight them; you will benefit from breathing with them and letting them happen. In most forms of psychotherapy, you will normally talk them out slowly, week after week, giving them time to work their way into your consciousness and begin to alter your self-image, attitudes, and behavior patterns. In gestalt therapy, you will identify with them, express them and frequently dialogue between the different parts of yourself (as you may also choose to dialogue between the planetary personalities which aspect each other in your chart). In meditation, you will sit, close your eyes, and let your feelings and thoughts flow past you. Rather than identifying with them and discharging them, you will simply observe them; in some forms of meditation, your focus will be not on your thoughts and feelings, but upon your breathing, or upon a mantra which you inwardly chant.

Whatever approach you use, you need to learn to suspend your self-judgment of the feelings and thoughts which you are newly encountering as parts of yourself. Over time, you are likely to develop faith and confidence in your capacity to move through and beyond your negative feelings to the positive feelings which lie beneath them. But as your center of consciousness grows, you will become less identified with both the "negative" and "positive," and more aware of a self which transcends your feelings, thoughts, and behaviors. As this self grows and solidifies, your self-image will change, and become less important to you than your direct experience of self. Now you will be more invested in being fully who you are, rather than in maintaining the image of who you think you are, or who you want to be.

Because of my own experience with too much intensity, I wish to encourage you *not* to push yourself to become aware of more than you can assimilate in a short period of time. The more you have repressed, the longer you may need to digest this new material, to move from the pain of acknowledging it to acceptance, and then to the love, joy, and free-flowing energy which is locked behind it.

This process of confronting twelfth house energies does not always have to be done apart from daily activities, in blocks of time set aside for this purpose. It can also be done in moments throughout the day—recalling a dream when waking, observing what irritates you in other people and how those same qualities operate in yourself, catching thoughts which you normally push out of your mind (like a movement at the edge of your line of vision), or writing in a small notebook which you carry with you a few words about a theme, a memory, or a feeling which repeatedly haunts you.

Remember that the twelfth house does not exist apart from the other houses. The boundaries between houses are not solid barriers. The Sun moves through the twelfth house first every day after dawn. Its energies can then infiltrate all the areas of your life, all the houses of your chart—revitalizing them, renovating them, opening their windows to take in the radiant, warming energy which the Sun releases.

Many years ago, living in Greece and traveling through its islands, I became aware that most of my experiences there were vivid and enriching. So much of what I observed and experienced then I can still clearly recall, while many other events in my life are foggy and forgotten. At first, I thought that this vividness was the result of travelling, of continually seeing new lands and people, but then I began to realize that the landscapes and people were not always changing, and that the vividness of my experiences was partially a result of what I was bringing to each moment—a receptivity, an expectancy, a total openness to the world within me and around me.

At home, I attempted to retain this way of looking at the world, so that I might carry this vividness and aliveness of experience into my daily life. I also moved out of the city, lived alone, worked at home, and narrowed my social horizons. Gradually, the four walls of my apartment began to close in on me, and in solitude, many of the feelings, thoughts, and behaviors indicated by my own twelfth house influences began to surface. But rather than push them away, or seek teachers, therapists, spiritual leaders, or astrologers to help me (to give me answers or generate cathartic experiences for me), I began to face myself in ways I had been unable to do before. I listened to those hidden messages, learned from them, and began to channel my insights into writing.

Gradually, my life began to fill again with people who were important to me. I no longer had large blocks of time available to listen to myself. But did I lose this openness, this inspiration? At times, yes. The demands of reality, often accompanied by Saturn transits, could be overwhelming. But at other times, I experienced further unfolding, further opening, further awakening to both the demons and the angels of my twelfth house energies—an awakening that began to have positive ramifications in regard to the depth of my work and my personal relationships.

Another result of striving to bring twelfth house energies more fully into my daily living was that I began to find that many of the little, mundane details of everyday life—details normally appreciated only for a moment or ignored, became replete with meaning. A cup of coffee, a few words to a stranger in line at the bank, a letter in the mail, one autumn leaf distinct from the rest on a tree—all of these little details became full of magic. I firmly believe that this openness to the beauty and richness of daily living is accessible to all of us, and is a direct result of making peace with our twelfth house energies.

Twelfth House Keywords

solitude
introspection
what emerges in us when alone
our sense of privacy
secret relationships or actions
indirect activity
how we operate
    behind the scenes
automatic or compulsive
    responses
all-or-nothing behavior
inappropriate expressions
unconscious habits and
    motivations
confinement, service, retreat
    in: prisons, ashrams,
    hospitals,
    secluded places
inner suffering
sensitivity
vulnerability
our Achilles heel
the burdens we carry
psychic ability
resourcefulness
our mixed messages
what we project
what we attract in others
what we absorb/introject from
    others
events we attract in our lives
victim/martyr tendencies
self-exploitative behavior
escapism into the past
karmic obligations
family and collective karma

psychic/occult experiences
empathy and compassion
responsiveness to people in
    need
the desire to serve others
how we serve others
volunteer work
sacrifices we make
our sense of mission
the nature of our illnesses
psychosomatic illnesses
invalidism
self-defeating behavior
what we repress
what we disown
psychological complexes
self-delusion
hidden weaknesses
shame and guilt
deep-seated fears
hidden enemies
how we relate to ourselves
psychological insight
intuition
archaic/infantile energy
secret fantasies
imagination
internal images
dream life
how we sleep
openness to creative
    inspiration
openness to our feelings
receptivity to higher states of
    consciousness
faith in the cosmos or God

Twelfth House Keywords continued

the nature of past lives
our self-undoing in a past life
gifts/talents from past lives
prenatal experiences
childhood prohibitions
early traumas
past experiences which haunt us
the family shadow
unfinished business
developmental fixations

spiritual interests
spiritual devotion
meditation
selfless love
the inner power we draw upon in
  crisis
our hidden resources and
  strengths

Your Twelfth House Profile

SIGNS IN YOUR 12th HOUSE

Sign on the cusp _____

Second sign _____

Third sign (if interception) _____

The planetary ruler of the cusp, _____ , is in the

    sign _____ in the _____ house, and

    makes these aspects:

        aspect _____ to planet _____ orb _____

        aspect _____ to planet _____ orb _____

        aspect _____ to planet _____ orb _____

        aspect _____ to planet _____ orb _____

Does a sign rule the 11th & 12th, or 12th & 1st? _____ .

PLANETS IN YOUR 12th HOUSE

Which planets? _____ , _____ , _____ , _____ .

Planet #1 _____ is in the sign _____ and rules the

    _____ (and _____) houses of my chart. It makes

    the following aspects:

        aspect _____ to planet _____ orb _____

        aspect _____ to planet _____ orb _____

        aspect _____ to planet _____ orb _____

        aspect _____ to planet _____ orb _____

    Is this planet in mutual reception, in its own sign,

        or in its own house?

    Is it the focal planet of a pattern or aspect configuration? _____ .

Planet #2 _____ is in the sign_____ and rules the

    _____ (and _____) houses of my chart. It makes

    the following aspects:

        aspect _____ to planet _____ orb _____

        aspect _____ to planet _____ orb _____

Your Twelfth House Profile

aspect _____ to planet _____ orb _____

aspect _____ to planet _____ orb _____

Is this planet in mutual reception, in its own sign,
or in its own house?

Is it the focal planet of a pattern or aspect configuration? _____ .

Planet #3 _____ is in the sign _____ and rules the
_____ (and _____) houses of my chart. It makes the
following aspects:

aspect _____ to planet _____ orb _____

aspect _____ to planet _____ orb _____

aspect _____ to planet _____ orb _____

aspect _____ to planet _____ orb _____

Is this planet in mutual reception, in its own sign,
or in its own house?

Is it the focal planet of a pattern or aspect configuration? _____ .

Diagram the planets involved in your 12th house. Include planets in and ruling the 12th house, and the planets that they aspect.

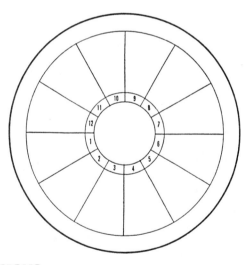

TRANSITS AND PROGRESSIONS

What outer planet transits or progressions are passing through your
12th house? What is their position in your natal chart (house position, house rulership, etc)? _____

_____   _____ .

Notes on Your Twelfth House Profile

Planets in the Twelfth House

The nature of each of your twelfth house planets indicates which energies in you operate subliminally, in solitude, and according to your ideals and inspiration. The sign of each planet describes the way in which its energy operates. The house or houses each planet rules indicates the areas of life in which this planet can function in a conscious, overt manner. Planets ruling but not positioned within your twelfth house operate in the house in which they are positioned, but carry the emotional charge of twelfth house issues, as described in this chapter.

The aspects each planet makes reveal how it operates in relation to other characteristics of your personality and other areas of your life. The tighter the orb, the more important its functioning will be to your overall personality. Conjunctions blend this planet's functioning with that of another twelfth house planet. Conjunctions to the ascendant influence the first house as well as the twelfth, and are more overtly expressed. Squares indicate areas of personal conflict and friction, but provide the energy and motivation necessary to use the planet advantageously. Often the issues of the twelfth house planet are transferred to, and subliminally influence, the squaring planet.

Oppositions to the twelfth house are often expressed through work issues and work relationships, as well as health. Oppositions usually result in more awareness of twelfth house energies than do squares, but one or both planets of the opposition may be projected onto someone else.

Trines and sextiles provide constructive outlets for twelfth house energies, which are channelled into the expression of the aspecting planets. However, such aspecting planets may also be negatively influenced by your twelfth house planet. You may be influenced by unconscious motivations here, compulsive in your behavior, or inclined to take the "path of least resistance." The house placements of the aspecting planets indicate areas of life which affect and are affected by your twelfth house planet.

Signs in the Twelfth House

The sign on your twelfth house cusp denotes the energy which you most frequently repress, or which you reveal only in private. Its ruler indicates a function of your personality which you overtly express (according to the ruler's sign and house), which may operate in a semiconscious manner, and which you may express in solitude or behind the scenes. The aspects of the ruler will indicate how it operates in relation to other characteristics of your personality and other areas of your life. For example, a twelfth house Aries woman who has Mars in Gemini in the second house square Saturn in Virgo in the fifth house may have a secret compulsion in regard to buying and accumulating books. After a bookstore spending spree, she then experiences Saturnian guilt and anxiety because she has indulged in a pleasurable but costly activity.

The above information is true for an intercepted twelfth house sign and its ruler, as well as for the sign and ruler of planets in the twelfth house which are in the sign of the ascendant, but not the sign of the twelfth house cusp. However, the former may be buried too deep beneath your consciousness for you to discern, while the latter expresses itself outwardly, since it influences your persona, or outer self.

Twelfth House Progressions and Transits

The meaning of a progressed or transiting planet passing through your twelfth house is similar to the natal twelfth house placement of that planet, except that the influence is temporary, and the progressed or transiting planet carries with it the influences of its natal placement. The energies denoted by its natal position in your chart are now operating in a subliminal, introspective, and private manner. The aspects it makes as it passes through your twelfth house indicate how it functions in relation to other planets, signs, and houses in your chart.

A progressed or transiting planet aspecting one of your twelfth house planets provides an outlet for that twelfth house energy. The nature of this outlet is suggested by the sign of the progression/transit and the house through which it is passing in your natal chart. The meaning of its natal position is now being expressed through its current position. This progression/transit is influencing and being influenced by the twelfth house planet, according to the nature of the aspect, and how you direct its energies.

And Then the Chart Spoke
by Tracy Marks

The astrologer sat
stationary
turning retrograde.
"I have reached the nadir of my life,"
she said. "For years,
I have been descending. It is time
to rectify the path I've charted,
to decrease my orb of influence,
to seek my own part of fortune.

"I have lived
in opposition to life,
transited
from house to house,
eclipsed by larger bodies
occupying space
I thought was mine.
I have spoken a garbled language
of signs,
unaspected,
noting aspects linking
other people's planets,
calculating logarithms
of other people's pains and joys,
orbiting a sun which was not my own,
observing from afar
each fixed star performing its cosmic drama,
witnessing the declination of my hopes.

"It is time," she said,
"to give myself latitude,
to determine my primary direction."

Each day then she swam
in the symbols of her chart,
immersed herself in their secret meanings,

noting each cusp of her life,
each progression and converse
progression, seeking an alchemical answer
to her questions.

But the chart spoke
with babbling tongue, vague phrases,
a delirious Delphic oracle.

In vain she delineated
obscure aspects, plotted asteroids,
eclipses, fixed stars,
tried cosmobiology, harmonics,
to no avail.
Each path
only confirmed the diagnosis,
gave no hint of cure,
failed to expose the blessing
buried beneath each affliction,
to transmute each square into a trine.

In frenzy then
she threw aside her books and tables,
turned to the man she loved for comfort,
sought out family, friends,
wrote poems
through the long night, dispensing
with her dreams
until the early morning rays
illumined her dark corner.

The morning dawned on her.
She rose then, opened the windows
of her twelfth house. The solar rays
flooded her with warmth and wonder.
Her eyes drank in the dimming stars,
the fading fullness of the moon.

The astrologer stood,
stationary. Still. Serene.
And then the chart spoke.
"I am a map," it said,
"but not a compass. A guidebook,
but not a guide.

"In broad lines I sketch for you
a dozen aspects, roads
which you may travel,
but you alone must choose
which one to follow,
must fill out its form
with the footsteps of your own
experience.

"Some secrets I will never reveal.
I deflect your search,
frustrate you,
compel you to do your own
transmuting,
force you to move outward
through the myriad struggles
of your daily life,
allow you a moment
of silence at dawn
and then goad you on
deep into the recesses of your soul
toward the inner sun
which sustains you
which enables you
to provide your own
illumination.

"And there you will find
the outline unfolds, the whole chart
is written."

The astrologer stood,
stationary, turning direct.
"I have gazed through a narrow lens
at scribbled symbols," she said,
"discovered only microscopic truths,
blind to all telescopic truths.
But each opposition in my life
is a wide, wide angle lens,
a line of vision stretched across
infinity, two lines of energy
meeting at the center,
becoming one.

"Now, in the dawn,
I move toward the center
of the wheel;
I bridge the gap between night
and day, become the architect
of my soul, renovate
each of my houses, open
their windows,
translate light
into a life streaming with
the energies of each new dawn.

"I have reached
another angle in my life,"
she said.
"I will now begin to ascend
the horizon."

PART II

Twelfth House Planets & Signs

Introduction

In order to provide a thorough, in-depth discussion of twelfth house energies, I have included in this chapter lengthy twelfth house interpretations for the ten planets (and nodes), rather than briefer discussions of each of the planets and each of the signs. This chapter is therefore an exploration of planets in *and* ruling the twelfth house.

As you apply these interpretations to your chart, consider the uniqueness of your own twelfth house patterns. If, for example, you have a twelfth house Venus in Capricorn squaring Jupiter, you may find the interpretations for twelfth house Saturn (ruler of Capricorn) to be relevant to you; you may also relate to some of the meanings of twelfth house Jupiter. If your Venus rules your Taurean fourth house and your Libran ninth house, then the twelfth house meanings of your Venus will also influence these realms of your life.

If you have no planets in your twelfth house, look to the planetary rulers of your twelfth house signs. A planet which rules your twelfth house, but is not positioned within it, will manifest primarily in the house in which it is placed. However, it will be strongly influenced by twelfth house energies. (See the next section of this chapter for further information on twelfth house rulers.)

Whether or not you have twelfth house planets, you may also benefit by studying the interpretations of current transits and progressions passing through your twelfth house. These are temporary, rather than enduring twelfth house energies. But because progressions and outer planet transits in your twelfth house may influence you for many years, they function like natal twelfth house planets. (For example, transiting

Pluto may be there for fifteen years; a progressed outer planet entering your twelfth house during childhood will be there throughout your lifetime; a progressed inner planet may be there for thirty years.) The primary difference is that these transits and progressions will not express energies internalized in early childhood, and will therefore not have as deep a structural influence upon your personality.

Bear in mind as you read these interpretations that I have elucidated the major problems and conflicts which each planet symbolizes—struggles which are more likely to occur when your twelfth house energies have many squares and oppositions than when they make primarily trines and sextiles. Depending upon your chart, your life circumstances, and your psychological growth, you may or may not encounter many of these problems. Although I encourage you to confront your shadow self, I am not implying that you carry within yourself all possible negative (or all positive) manifestations of your twelfth house planets.

The lists of images included after the planetary discussions are meant to speak to your right brain (in the metaphorical language of the twelfth house) to help you attune yourself more deeply to twelfth house energies. The lists of famous people who have each of the twelfth house planets and signs are compiled from a variety of published books of charts. Only those which state the time of birth have been used; in some cases, the accuracy of the data may be questionable. For the lists of famous people who have planets in particular signs in their twelfth house, I have included only those who have two or more twelfth house planets in that particular sign.

Finally, quotations are included to further elucidate the meanings and experiences of each twelfth house energy. There is no known connection between the chart of the author of the quotation and each specific twelfth house position. Rather, I have sought to present quotes which humorously or inspirationally speak from the standpoint of each twelfth house energy. Since almost all quotations are from secondary sources (the original source unknown), I have not been able to document the precise origin of each quotation.

Planetary Rulers of the Twelfth House: By House Placement

The following brief interpretations will help you understand how rulers of your twelfth house signs channel twelfth house energies into the specific house placements.

Twelfth House Ruler in the First House (similar in meaning to the recurrence of the twelfth house cusp sign on the ascendant):

You are often unconscious of how you project yourself and may communicate mixed messages as a result of being out of touch with your twelfth house energies. Vulnerable to the influence of the outer world, and lacking strong defenses, you may be shy and retiring. Lacking a well-developed persona or a concern with outer image, you readily share your inner life, and outwardly express your ideals and spiritual aspirations. Identified with your inner self rather than your self-in-the-world, you live by the motto, "To thine own self be true."

Twelfth House Ruler in the Second House:

Subconscious energies influence your experience of your personal resources, your attitudes and behaviors in regard to money and possessions, and your orientation in regard to financial self-sufficiency and earning a living. Rather than face your feelings and insecurities, you worry about monetary issues, and can be compulsive in regard to earning or spending. Your sense of "not being enough" may become a preoccupation with "not having enough" money, or the objects and experiences which money can buy. You have a powerful emotional charge around financial issues and the possessions which help you to gain contact with your hidden self. The value which you place upon the inner life influences both your choice of work and your expenditures. Early conditioning, and possibly also past lives, deeply influence your attitudes in regard to your self-worth, your personal resources, and your relationship to the material world.

Twelfth House Ruler in the Third House:

You have a powerful and often compulsive need to express your thoughts and feelings, whether orally or in writing. Because subconscious influences from the past affect your communication, you may not be aware of the motivations behind your words, or the hidden messages which you reveal. Because of your receptivity and psychic sensitivity to the thoughts of others, you are likely to be a responsive listener, to whom other people turn for support in regard to their daily troubles. This placement also suggests that your relationships with brothers and sisters, other relatives and neighbors are emotionally charged for you, and that you frequently escape from problems by taking short trips, attending courses, and focusing upon your daily schedule and interactions. Early life experiences in school, with peers, and with siblings are likely to have had a profound impact upon you.

Twelfth House Ruler in the Fourth House:

Solitude and retreat into the privacy of your home are essential to you. You may live alone, or be particularly insistent in regard to maintaining your own space apart from your family, partner, or roommates. Deep-seated issues in regard to your family of origin influence your need to retreat and to remain in contact with your inner self, which, since early in life, you have sought to protect against outside intrusion. Family issues may be difficult for you. A major focus of your life may be your quest for your own psychological and spiritual roots, as well as your desire to construct or reconstruct more substantial inner foundations.

Twelfth House Ruler in the Fifth House:

You need to express yourself creatively, through imaginative pursuits which enable you to contact and give form to your inner experience; or, if you are not creatively inclined, you may become preoccupied with leisure pursuits which help you come to terms with emotional conflicts. Subconscious influences also lead you into love affairs (often secret) which both stir up and help you transcend your personal insecurities. Likewise, you may feel a compulsive desire to have children, or to relate to children, as a means of encountering and making peace with your own inner child and healing his/her past wounds.

Twelfth House Ruler in the Sixth House:

Your diet, exercise routines, and health-oriented activities are important to you, and are a means by which you maintain your psychological well-being. Frequently, you escape from your emotional conflicts by focusing upon your physical body, as well as by involving yourself in your work and in work relationships. Needing to be of service in your job, you are particularly drawn toward the psychological, social service, and medical (or holistic health) professions. Workaholic patterns, or tendencies to maintain an overly active schedule may be related to deep-seated emotional issues which you hesitate to face, but which fuel your desire to be productive, and to respond to the needs of others.

Twelfth House Ruler in the Seventh House:

You tend to attract and to choose partners who reflect your shadow self—the disowned portions of yourself, both positive and negative, which you are not able to express. Because of the subconscious influences upon your partnerships, you may repeatedly enact the same issues in your relationships, as you attempt to face and come to terms with facets of yourself which you encounter in others. As a result, you may be somewhat compulsive or obsessive in your relationship patterns. This connection between your twelfth and seventh houses may also catalyze your desire for a soulmate—someone with whom you feel a powerful emotional, spiritual, or karmic bond.

Twelfth House Ruler in the Eighth House:

Subconscious or karmic factors influence your attitudes toward sexuality, shared resources, and occult activities. Your inner conflicts may manifest outwardly as difficulties in regard to money received from outside sources (child support, inheritances, tax returns, etc.). Emotional complexes may inhibit or fuel your sexual expression, which may be influenced by unresolved past conflicts. This placement also suggests that you have both psychic and psychological capabilities, and are deeply attuned to the feelings and needs of others. You may also experience profound transformations as a result of metaphysical and spiritual pursuits, or altered states of consciousness.

Twelfth House Ruler in the Ninth House:

You need to be involved in educational and religious pursuits which reflect your inner life and enable you to find meaning in your personal conflicts. An explorer of distant horizons, you are drawn to make contact with yourself and to expand your consciousness through increasing your understanding, pursuing a spiritual path, or traveling to remote, peaceful locations which offer you a refuge from your daily routine. Your ninth house quest may be an escape from your emotional issues, or a means of resolving or transcending them.

Twelfth House Ruler in the Tenth House:

You seek to avoid your emotional conflicts by focusing, sometimes obsessively, upon your career and public activities. Yet subconscious factors fuel your motivation to succeed, and provide the personal resources which enable you to translate your inner promptings into concrete, outer expression. Motivated by high ideals and hesitant to enter the competitive marketplace, you may be drawn to a psychological or social service profession where you can quietly respond to the needs of others. Although fears and insecurities from the past influence your professional endeavors, you possess a wellspring of intuition, compassion, inspiration, spirituality, and psychological perceptiveness which can enable you to make a valuable contribution to humanity.

Twelfth House Ruler in the Eleventh House:

Through friendships and group activities, you encounter your disowned and hidden selves. Driven to focus on friends and group experiences as an escape from your problems, you nevertheless attract to you people who reflect your subliminal world. Because subconscious factors and complexes motivate your behaviors in these interactions, you may experience repetitive patterns and conflicts which require you to face yourself more deeply. Fortunately, the psychological and spiritual influence of the twelfth house inclines you to choose affiliations which aid this process. In friendships and group relationships, you seek to share your inner life and respond to the inner lives of others. You may also be drawn to active involvement in psychological, metaphysical, spiritual, or social service organizations.

Twelfth House Ruler in the Twelfth House:

This position reinforces the twelfth house meanings of the planet which both rules and inhabits your twelfth house. It also suggests that the energy of this planet and its sign may be so barricaded within your psyche that you have difficulty working through the emotional conflicts it symbolizes and discovering constructive outlets for its expression. Your sensitivity, intuition, inspiration, and humanitarian ideals in regard to this planetary energy are considerable, but you may be so influenced by repetitive, subconscious fears and insecurities that you are unable to liberate this imprisoned self from the bonds of the past. Aspects to this planet may help enlighten you about the issues which it represents and provide channels for its integration. You can also benefit from psychotherapy and spiritual pursuits which help you come to terms with this hidden facet of yourself.

Sun (Leo) in the Twelfth House

Your twelfth house Sun suggests that you are a sensitive person, highly vulnerable to the impact of your environment. Hesitant to share your inner experiences, you maintain a private sanctuary within yourself, to which you retreat from the demands of the outer world. As king or queen of your inner castle, you reign supreme. But managing and directing your earthly affairs is another matter. Because you feel that you do not belong to the world around you, you create a quiet, protective world of your own where you can be true to your inner voice and follow your path of psychological or spiritual development.

You need time alone for reflection, for attuning yourself to your thoughts, feelings, and fantasies, and for freeing yourself of the influences of others, which you too easily absorb. Because you feel connected to larger spiritual forces, you may practice a meditative discipline which helps you to gain the clarity you seek. Your inner resources are vast; by refueling yourself through turning inward, you revitalize yourself and open yourself to warm, radiant feelings which you may not otherwise experience.

One of your strengths is your capacity to create an intention, and then surrender to the flow of your experience. By focusing upon your intentions in regard to manifesting outer events, you attract such events into your life, without having to exert active effort in their behalf. Rather than forthrightly exercising your will, you inwardly orient yourself toward your aims, and then let go, allowing the universe to provide your means of attaining them. If your motives are clear and you feel worthy enough to receive what you seek, you may experience considerable success as a result of your inner capabilities.

A twelfth house Sun indicates humility, but it can also indicate inferiority feelings and poor self-esteem. Early in life, you may have received messages from your parents which led you to believe that you have no right to exist, that your personal desires are selfish and unimportant, and that you possess an innate badness or unworthiness for which you must atone. Perhaps nothing you did or said was considered good enough, or your parents were narcissistically absorbed in their own worlds, and provided little support for your fragile, developing ego. If, as a child, you harbored deep-seated guilt and often felt deserving of punishment, you may, as an adult, create situations in your life which make you feel guilty or which punish you for some real or imagined wrong.

Low self-esteem can fuel self-defeating behaviors. Ask yourself: What do you do to maintain internalized negative messages about your value, to prove that you are as unworthy as you believed yourself to be as a child? Do you sabotage your actions in the world, so that you have an excuse to retreat to your inner hiding place? Do you glory in a humble, virtuous self-image, and invite exploitation by putting yourself in subservient positions in relationships? Do you create situations of humiliation or failure in order to prove your inadequacy, and then alternately belittle yourself and self-righteously assert your bruised ego? Because you may feel powerless in the outer world, you need to be wary of self-defeating attempts to regain power in the inner world by shoring yourself up with images of martyrdom. Personal power and self-esteem do not result from the empty self-satisfactions of the victim role.

One of the difficulties for a twelfth house Sun is to maintain a realistic self-image. Because you often relate to a fantasy image of yourself developed in the past, your sense of who you are may be insubstantial. Like Alice in Wonderland, you experience yourself as painfully small one day, and uncomfortably large the next day— pumped up with grandiose conceptions of your virtues, achievements, and value. When you feel confident, you may become overconfident, and commit yourself to tasks which are beyond your capabilities; then when you fail to succeed, you may castigate yourself for your inadequacy.

Because of your vulnerable self-esteem, tolerating failure is not easy for you. If you are male, your sex-role identity may be threatened by your inability to live up to your impossible standards of maleness. Finding peace with yourself will necessarily involve revising your standards, and learning to embrace and even honor your own limitations. "The stronger the real ego is, the less egocentric or self-centered it will need to be," wrote Strephon Kaplan Williams.[1] The more you accept your true self, in all of its smallness, the less likely you are to suffer from the hidden egotism or arrogance which may lead you to defend yourself at all costs against threats to your fragile ego. The more substantial your experience of self, the less you will need to cling to and justify a self-image to prove your value.

One of the self-boosting mechanisms that you may have developed in times of self-doubt is reliance upon grandiose fantasies in regard to success, glory, or attention. Although you may be uncomfortable in the public eye, you may also crave being the center of attention. When you do have an audience, the thrill of many eyes focused upon you may be intoxicating. Sometimes, carried away with the satisfaction of long unmet needs, you may inappropriately cling to center stage; or, enamored with your newly found freedom of self-expression, you may dramatize yourself, revealing hidden talents for acting or role-playing.

More frequently, you are likely to hide rather than expose yourself to threats of too much visibility. Perhaps you had traumatic experiences involving exposure, self-revelation, or humiliation when you were younger; perhaps you carry with you deep-seated shames from the past; perhaps you feel embarrassed at the degree to which your ego exults in attention and recognition, when you so ardently espouse ethics of humility and self-sacrifice. Whatever the case, you may have decided early in life that it's dangerous to allow yourself out of your twelfth house, and that you feel happiest and safest "staying inside."

Your tendency to conceal yourself and retreat from the public eye is not likely to result merely from feelings of inadequacy. Your own spirituality and ethics incline you to value a life of humility and service. Although you sometimes crave honor and glory, you are usually content with the quiet satisfactions of meeting human needs, working behind the scenes with the disadvantaged, or otherwise helping people who need your support. Not only do you possess a remarkable ability to intuit other people's motivations and problems, but you are extremely sensitive to the plight of the underprivileged, the ill, or the handicapped. As a result, you may be drawn to work in a social service field, or to volunteer your time to charitable causes. On the one hand, you may boost your ego by surrounding yourself with people who are less capable than you, while atoning for the guilt you harbor; on the other hand, you experience real and heartfelt compassion for the suffering, the poor, the needy—for the underdogs with whom you can identify. Not only do you compensate for poor self-esteem through living a life of service, but you also create opportunities to express your love, and to live according to your humanitarian ideals and values.

If you are religious, your belief in God or spiritual forces may be a way you attune yourself to the father principle, which you never adequately experienced in terms of a personal father. Most likely, your real father was not an overt influence upon you. He may have been absent during many of your childhood years, he may have ignored you, or he may have influenced you in subtle, psychological ways, but failed to provide a strong model for you in regard to coping with reality. You may also have repressed many memories and feelings about him, thus preventing him from consciously influencing the course of your life.

Sometimes a twelfth house Sun indicates a father who was overly present outwardly, who dominated the household, but who was psychologically inaccessible because he treated you as if your existence had little value. If you are male, you may have felt squashed by your father during the "oedipal phase" of ages 4–6; then, you were beginning to develop your sex-role identity and attempting to separate from your mother by asserting your newly discovered power as a male.

Having a twelfth house Sun suggests the potential for an inner base of power from which you command your life. But it can also suggest a lack of power, if you have not adequately developed your Sun-self, opened your heart, or learned to draw from the energies of your solar plexus the courage and vitality you need to function effectively. If you have little sense of your personal power, then you are likely to attract into your life strong, potent male figures who easily command center stage. For some people, particularly those with weak or absent fathers, the opposite pattern prevails. If you learned to live without a strong male figure early in life and have experienced adequate nurturing from a mother figure, you may not need or desire close relationships with men; you developed a sense of your own completeness without such relationships.

Your twelfth house Sun may not incline you to a life of public display and recognition, but it does suggest the potential for psychological and spiritual development. Although you may not exhibit a high degree of courage in your encounters with the outer world, you certainly exhibit courage in your inner confrontations, in your capacity to confront yourself and to come to terms with the ghosts of the past.

Your growth may involve acceptance of your true self, and relinquishment of a false too-small and too-large self, an unrealistic ego ideal, or a fantasied self-image. As you learn to accept your limitations and honor your strengths, you may need to affirm, "I have value and worth in my own right. I have a right to exist." Because of your vulnerability in regard to self-expression and self-assertion, you may benefit from training in acting, psychodrama, public speaking, and other skills which help you to gain confidence. The more substantial your real sense of self, the more able you will be to confront and relinquish the unhealthy egotism, pride, or arrogance which secretly undermine you and prevent you from discovering your true value.

Twelfth House Sun (Leo) Images

cowardly lion	king of the sea	underdog
lion in captivity	backstage director	underwater stage
sun behind clouds	lord of the underworld	king in exile
ruler of Oz	hospital chief of staff	
captured prince	underground leader	

Famous People: Twelfth House Sun

Orson Welles	Anne Frank	Judy Garland
Henry Kissinger	Pearl Buck	Janis Joplin
Johnny Carson	Evangeline Adams	Liza Minnelli
Lynn Redgrave	Patricia Schroeder	Havelock Ellis
Jack Dempsey	Richard Wagner	U.S. Grant
Alan Leo	Mohandas Gandhi	Joseph Stalin

Famous People: Twelfth House Leo Planets

Rosalynn Carter	Indira Gandhi	Leonard Bernstein
Peter Sellers	O. J. Simpson	Ann Landers
Alan Leo	Arlo Guthrie	Arthur Schlesinger
Liza Minnelli	Elton John	Patricia Schroeder
Aubrey Beardsley	Annie Oakley	

Twelfth House Sun (Leo)

You've no idea what a poor opinion I have of myself—and how little I deserve it.
—W. S. Gilbert

She could be in the middle of a house full of people and still feel like she was locked up by herself.
—Carson McCullers

I give up the fight: let there be . . .
A privacy, an obscure nook for me.
—Robert Browning

Nowadays there are
Almost as many lions
In cages as out of them.
If offered a crown, refuse.
—Kenneth Rexroth

I closed my door to the world . . .
I remained within myself, magical, invisible . . .
I lighted myself within.
                    —Emilio Prado

Man is not made for life in the collective but is a solitary king in a dream
world of his own creation.
                    —Herman Hesse

I am Oz, the Great and Terrible, said the little man, in a trembling voice.
But don't strike me—please don't!—and I'll do anything you want me to.
                    —Frank Baum

It is not only for an exterior show or ostentation that our soul must play her
part, but inwardly within ourselves, where no eyes shine but ours.
                    —Montaigne

There is no need to run outside
For better seeing . . .
Rather abide
At the center of your being.
                    —Lao Tzu

Moon (Cancer) in the Twelfth House

Your twelfth house Moon suggests that you are a private person, hesitant to reveal your feelings and needs. Often, fearful of your vulnerability, you block awareness of your feelings; you seek refuge from your inner world in habitual activities which you may perform in an automatic manner. Contacting your hidden emotional self may be difficult for you, because you have developed a lifetime of defenses against primitive levels of need and dependency which frighten you. You may feel intense shame in regard to the child-self which is buried within you.

Repressed for a long time, your sadness and longing may sometimes burst forth as infantile tears, which seem regressive and inappropriate. Like Alice in Wonderland drowning in the flood of her tears, you feel overwhelmed, and seek to squelch future displays of feeling. "Be strong; don't cry," may be your motto. You are afraid not only of drowning in your feelings and your needs, but also of revealing your vulnerability to others, then being rejected or abandoned.

Perhaps because of traumatic experiences as a child, in which you experienced unbearable helplessness, need, and dependency in relationship to a parent who could not sensitively respond, you learned to turn to yourself early in life and to establish your self-sufficiency. "I must do it alone; I don't need anyone," you decided, as you withheld yourself emotionally in relationships, and learned how to engage with people without full involvement. Emotionally self-contained and insulated, you became a capable survivor, and learned how to effectively play the roles required of you. But often, as a result of your repression, you feel empty and depleted, out of contact with your source of inner sustenance.

If your Moon is deeply buried,[2] you may struggle against fear of the primitive infant locked within you, and against a desire to return to the womb or to escape into fantasies of total nurturance. Fearful of your passivity and your desire for motherly love, you compensate through cultivating your adult competencies and by becoming a caregiver. But although you are independent in the external world, you hold onto your established patterns of behavior and to whatever internal sources of security you have developed.

Forced to turn to yourself early in life, you learned how to take care of yourself, and how to substitute behaviors and activities for the nurturing from others you did not receive. You may as a result be compulsive about your self-caretaking rituals, particularly in regard to

food. Tendencies toward anorexia, adherence to strict diets, preoccupation with cooking, and fear of eating in restaurants are all
manifestations of a twelfth house Moon. Sometimes, you become ill
as a means of resting from the demands of your adult self, and in
order to allow yourself to receive the caretaking that you seek.

Your twelfth house Moon suggests that you never felt allowed to
be a child. Perhaps your mother was emotionally a child herself, and
wanted you to cater to her needs rather than become capable of
responding to yours. She may have been deeply troubled, psychologically or physically unavailable; she may have sacrificed herself
to involvements in the outer world at the expense of her family life.
Whatever your situation, her negative responses to your needs and
feelings, and her messages of "Don't cry," "Be strong," or "Do it
yourself," led you to believe that you had no right to have feelings.
The hurt or trauma you experienced then may have resulted in a deep-
seated decision never to make yourself vulnerable again. "I'd rather
die than need you," you may have inwardly said to your mother,
"because if I need you I will have to bear the intolerable pain of your
failure to meet my needs." As you grew older, fearing the restimulation and opening of earlier wounds, you may have said to yourself,
"I will not be dependent upon anyone ever again."

Often a twelfth house Moon signifies a failure in the early attachment bond with the mother, although a deep inner bond with her
exists. Such a bond (accompanied by idealization) persists in part
because you need to hold onto her psychically, as a result of not having received adequate nurturing. Frequently, a twelfth house Moon
suggests problems in the oral or suckling stage or lack of adequate
physical nurturance. If your mother was unable to respond to your
nonverbal (and verbal) signals, you learned to distrust closeness to
other persons, and failed to develop a healthy degree of trust.

Because of childhood trauma, you may have repressed your early
experiences, and remember little of your family life; you may also
have developed a lifestyle which involves minimal family contact.
Perhaps because you never had a secure home, or because you fear
experiencing your need for a home and family life, you may avoid
creating a home that could be truly nurturing for you. Sometimes,
people who have twelfth house Moons never develop roots anywhere;
they move frequently, unable to settle down, afraid of sinking into
the feelings and needs which they associate with attachment to home
and family.

Another influence of a twelfth house Moon is confusion in regard to female identity and to relationships with women. Lacking an adequate female role model, you may have distorted ideas about womanhood and motherhood. If you are female, you may be insecure about your identity as a woman, and inclined to equate female role behavior with self-sacrifice; you might then, in reaction, reject the traditionally feminine, and seek refuge in "male" values. Sometimes, women with twelfth house Moons deny the desire for motherhood; or, in contrast, allow themselves to become pregnant in order to recreate the mother/infant bond.

If you are male, you may feel insecure about the hidden female within you, which at times feels like overwhelming need and passivity. You may devalue the "feminine" realms of life, while simultaneously idealizing women, falling in love with inner images and fantasies, yearning for the perfect woman/mother/mate, or attracting clinging, dependent women who force you to make contact with the energies you project.

To the extent to which you fear your vulnerability and hunger for nurturance, you attract people who need you and become dependent upon you. Fleeing from relationships which awaken your own need, you are nevertheless quite capable of responding to need in others. In fact, you may even respond with a sensitivity and sympathy which you are incapable of giving to yourself. Psychically sensitive to others, you are attuned to their feelings and intuitively know what to say and do.

Because you are a natural caretaker, you are probably drawn to work in the service professions, where you can meet the needs of wounded or troubled humanity. Identifying with the troubled, ill or weak, you demonstrate your talent as a nurse, healer, or counselor. Having sacrificed your personal mother to the world, you may also sacrifice your personal mothering needs in order to mother humanity as a whole. You seek to give to others what you always wanted to receive. Such giving may not fill the empty space within you, but it does provide vicarious satisfaction and the experience of having made a significant social contribution.

Another advantage of your twelfth house Moon is your keen intuition and innate spirituality. Because of your sensitivity, you need to spend a considerable amount of time alone, reflecting upon aspects of your personal life which you do not share with others, and clearing yourself of the psychic overload you have accumulated as a result of too much contact. Your solitude may also be important to you because it helps you to regain contact with yourself, to connect with your feeling nature, and through meditation, music, or other pursuits, to let go of the walls you have created and surrender to forces greater than yourself.

Because you have preserved your true child self deep within you, in a form that is largely untouched by the world, you are capable of contacting and drawing from rich sources of inner nourishment which reside within that child. Because its boundaries are thin, it is capable of openness to spiritual realms. The more you are able to honor that archaic child within you, the more you will become attuned to your divine nature and be able to enrich yourself with the openness to higher energies which it can offer you.

You need to contact, accept, and embrace the child within you, to tolerate its terror of abandonment and its primitive feelings and needs, and to learn to soothe and reassure it. Feeling-oriented therapy, rebirthing, self-psychology, primal therapy, and past-lives therapy all may facilitate this process. As you begin to acknowledge and honor your inner child, you may also choose to create for yourself a home which is truly nourishing, and which helps you to feel warm, safe, and emotionally secure. Once you begin to hear, accept, and meet the real needs of your inner child, you will experience a sense of realness and wholeness which previously was inaccessible to you; you will also be able to give to others more effectively, to meet their real needs, rather than vicariously using them as a means for recovering your lost self.[3]

Twelfth House Moon (Cancer) Images

octopus in a tank	sorceress in captivity	cosmic cradle
oyster bed	home for orphans	abandoned child
child in a crib	waterlogged sponge	nursemaid
oceanic womb	dream house	private kitchen
underground stream	underwater sanctuary	secret well
psychic sponge	tidal wave	sacred meal
fetal position		
floating harbor		

Famous People: Twelfth House Moon

Adlai Stevenson	Alfred Lord Tennyson	William Blake
Antoine de St. Exupery	Shirley MacLaine	Paul Simon

Rudyard Kipling
Hermann Goering
Jackie Gleason
Piet Mondrian
Jose Feliciano
Henry David Thoreau
Hubert Humphrey
Gregory Peck

Arthur Rimbaud
Percy Bysshe Shelley
Abraham Lincoln
William Butler Yeats
Michael Dukakis
Thomas Hardy
George Bernard Shaw
Billy the Kid

Oscar Wilde
Liberace
Edgar Degas
Ronald Laing
Havelock Ellis
Claude Debussy
Erik Satie

Famous People: Twelfth House Cancer Planets

Maria Montessori
Judy Garland
Jane Russell
Iris Murdoch

Elbert Hubbard
Hedy Lamarr
Tokyo Rose
Paul Lynde

Tony Curtis
Galileo
Erik Satie

Twelfth House Moon (Cancer)

Man's security comes from within himself.
                    —Manly Hall

But what am I?
An infant crying in the night;
An infant crying for the light,
And with no language but a cry.
                    —Alfred Lord Tennyson

I wish I hadn't cried so much! I shall be punished for it now, I suppose, by being drowned in my own tears.
                    —Lewis Carroll

You only blinched inside, said Pooh, and that's the bravest way for a Very Small Animal not to blinch that there is.
                    —A. A. Milne

He sat up, looked about him, and tried to beat down the tremors, the yearnings, the old cravings that rose up and beset him and took possession of him entirely.
                    —Kenneth Grahame

I suppose the most absolutely delicious thing in life is to feel someone needs you.
                    —Olive Schreiner

I never ask the wounded person how he feels; I myself become the wounded person.
                    —Walt Whitman

The deepest feeling always shows itself/In silence.
                    —Marianne Moore

Mercury (Gemini, Virgo)
in the Twelfth House

Mercury's influence upon your twelfth house suggests that you are a reflective person, capable of providing your own mental stimulation and drawn to intellectual pursuits involving reading and writing. In the privacy of your home, you spend many hours introspecting, studying a variety of subjects, writing, or speaking on the phone, often in order to clarify your thinking about issues of personal concern. You are almost always communicating with yourself—dialoguing with your thoughts, talking aloud to yourself, and even talking in your sleep. Because you are self-critical, anxious, and prone to worrying, you may experience a high degree of nervous tension which may interfere with your ability to concentrate or focus your attention upon one project.

Your mind is always active, processing your inner experience and seeking to organize the vast amount of stimulation which threatens to overwhelm you. As a result, you can be compulsive about details— making lists, planning, and organizing your life. Some of your mental obsessiveness may be an unconscious attempt to control anxiety and keep threatening thoughts out of your consciousness. Frequently, twelfth house Mercury people experience considerable embarrassment, guilt, or shame in regard to thoughts they have which violate their moral code; yet their attempt to inhibit these thoughts only increases their anxiety and their compulsive mental behaviors.

One of the difficulties of a twelfth house Mercury is that your nervous tension, anxiety, worry, or negative thinking may lead you to suffer from psychosomatic symptoms or nervous disabilities which are not easy to diagnose or cure. As a result, examining your self-defeating thinking patterns and developing constructive patterns of self-talk may have significant ramifications in regard to your emotional and physical health. Forms of cognitive therapy such as rational-emotive therapy can help you to free yourself of debilitating thinking patterns from the past which helped you to survive in childhood, but which interfere now with effective adult functioning.

This placement of Mercury indicates that you are vulnerable in regard to your mental capacities. Squares to Mercury (especially from your third and ninth houses) and oppositions suggest trauma during your school years. Perhaps you suffered from reading disabilities or were humiliated for your inadequacies by insensitive teachers or peers. Perhaps you studied conscientiously, but could not live up to the standards of the adults who mattered. Like the Scarecrow in the Wizard of Oz ("If I only had a brain"), you may have doubted your mental abilities, although you may not have had intellectual deficits.

Sometimes, people with twelfth house Mercuries have overvalued rather than undervalued their minds. They seek refuge in their mental capacities or painstakingly struggle to prove their competence through achievement in school. But grandiose standards for yourself in regard to intellectual capacity may also lead you to feel mentally inferior, because you strive for impossible levels of brilliance in thinking, studying, and writing. High standards may fuel glorious fantasies of success and acclaim in an intellectual or communications field, but you may hesitate to publicly test your capacities by fully committing yourself to professional achievement in these areas.

Your vulnerability in regard to your thinking and intellectual ability is likely to extend to your attitudes about writing. A closet writer, you may fear revealing your writing to others, afraid that their critical standards will be as exacting as your own. Nevertheless, writing is a satisfying occupation for you; whether or not you write professionally, you are likely to find considerable satisfaction in journal writing and reflective forms of writing which help you to clarify your thinking.

You may have a natural bent for writing, because you have a subtle attunement to inner perceptions and a sensitivity to the emotional atmosphere which gives meaning to experience. Your deep-seated intuition, your continual quest for self-knowledge, and your interest in psychological processes enhance your perceptiveness in regard to human behavior and thought. Your capacity to block out the outer world and listen to the inner voice can enable you to draw from deep sources of insight within yourself.

Basically, you are a nonverbal thinker, perceiving the world in terms of feelings, images, and sensations. Translating these nonverbal impressions into words may be difficult for you, like being forced to swim up to the surface of the ocean after residing at the ocean's bottom. But because you live in these watery realms, you may have an innate poetic sense which enables you to use images, metaphors, and stories to evoke the deeper meanings of experience. Although you live in your mind, your mind is almost always influenced by feelings, intuitions, and past perceptions, all of which provide a rich reservoir of images and meanings which enhance all forms of your communication.

Because you live so deeply within yourself, you are keenly attuned to inner experience but absent-minded in regard to details in the outer world. You may be prone to daydream excessively, and even to confuse your fantasies with outer reality. Another difficulty of the close connection which exists between your conscious mind and your unconscious perceptions is that you may frequently be overwhelmed by feelings and sensations which interfere with your capacity to think clearly. As a result of this underwater breathing, your mind may be cloudy, your thinking distorted, and your decision-making capacities befuddled by unclear and ambiguous considerations.

Your struggle to make conscious sense of preverbal impressions, and the experience of being inwardly bombarded by many unwanted images and thoughts, may keep you in a state of confusion. Repetitive or circular thinking and patterns of rationalization may interfere with your capacity to find the clarity you seek. As a result, you may need to engage in regular activities which use your mind but free you from exercising your analytical, critical faculties in a self-defeating manner. Journal writing practices, poetry writing, meditation, and affirmation and visualization work might all be useful to you.

The same vulnerability and attunement to your unconscious which influences your thinking and writing also influences your communication with other people. A private person, afraid to speak openly and let people know your real thoughts, you may not always be straightforward and honest. Sometimes you keep your thoughts to yourself, and then burst forth with a long stream of words, monologuing rather than establishing dialogues with others. Making contact while communicating your thoughts may be difficult for you; the internal stimulation which sometimes overwhelms you may seek discharge, and lead you to use others as a sounding board, rather than establish two-way communication. Groups are likely to be particularly trying, because your attunement to inner signals at the expense of outer signals may inhibit your capacity to tune into the communication signals of social interaction. Being able to hear and respond to the cues appropriately, so that you neither keep silent nor unintentionally interrupt other people, is a skill you may need to develop.

But because you may feel inferior about your communication abilities or intelligence, you more frequently hide your thoughts than express them. Translating your subtle perceptions into words which others can understand may not be easy for you; you often feel as if you speak a private language, and that when you really do express yourself you are not heard or understood.

Because your thinking is subjective and often profound, you may not have developed the capacity for small talk, which helps to establish greater ease in social interaction. This social deficit interferes with your comfort in meeting people, starting conversations, and becoming involved in discussions of external matters which are of little concern to you. You may as a result shy away from many social situations, and limit your contact to people with whom you can more freely express your inner world.

Your tendency to retreat from the overstimulation of social encounters is also influenced by your psychic oversensitivity to other people's thoughts and feelings. Unknowingly, you absorb the thoughts and anxieties of the people around you; you pick up subtle innuendos and unconscious communications which most people miss. Inevitably then, you become psychologically overloaded, and may be confused in regard to whose thoughts and concerns you are carrying. On the other hand, your psychological sensitivity can serve you, because you so perceptively attune yourself to other people's motivations and needs, and respond to their hidden but very real messages with acute sensitivity and awareness.

Your twelfth house Mercury may incline you to make a contribution to society through the written word or through social service; you may wish to use your mental, organizational, and communication-oriented skills for a purpose which extends beyond that of your personal well-being. Because of your ability to perceive subliminal levels of experience and to mentally organize subtle perceptions, you may be drawn to literary, counselling, or spiritual professions, as writer, scholar, researcher, psychologist, or minister.

Your capacity to use your Mercury constructively may depend upon your ability to overcome the negative conditioning which influenced your thinking, communication, and social skills early in life. If your Mercury is troublesome, you may have frequently received such parental messages as, "Don't be stupid!"; "Be quiet!"; or "Children should be seen and not heard." Perhaps your parents insensitively teased you about your thinking or manner of speaking, or belittled your perceptions. As a result, you too easily absorbed your parents' way of thinking, and developed considerable insecurity and distrust of your own mental and verbal abilities. You may not have felt that you had a right to think for yourself or to voice your own thoughts.

Another early influence related to a twelfth house Mercury is a family which doesn't communicate about personal and interpersonal experiences. In such a situation, secrets prevail. Parents may monologue with each other and their children, rather than encourage dialogue or meaningful exchange of thoughts and experiences; other parents assume they know their child's thoughts, and they "mind read" or "mind rape," by telling the child what he thinks or by speaking for him in front of other people.

For you to harness the positive potential of your twelfth house Mercury, you need to be aware of the self-defeating attitudes and behaviors which you have developed, and to replace them with constructive beliefs, patterns, and actions. Doing so may involve not only examining your thought patterns, but also actively developing your thinking, writing, communication, and social skills, and consciously learning to value your capacities. Talk-oriented psychotherapy, particularly therapy with a cognitive focus, can help you reprogram negative thinking, learn to trust your perceptions and intelligence, and gain more confidence in regard to communication and social interaction.

Twelfth House Mercury (Gemini, Virgo) Images

parrot in a cage	nautical almanac	invisible ink
basement radio	reporter in prison	ghost writer
writer's retreat	carrier pigeon in fog	daydream
chameleon in hiding	underworld errandboy	monastery scribe
concealed beehive	speaking in tongues	soggy newspaper
underwater transmitter	underground reporter	

Famous People: Twelfth House Mercury

Richard Wagner	Rennie Davis	Judy Garland
Ernest Hemingway	Peter Sellers	John Cage
Evangeline Adams	Marc Edmund Jones	Lawrence Welk
Patricia Schroeder	Germaine Greer	Gertrude Stein
Henry Kissinger	Henry David Thoreau	Pearl Buck
Katherine Mansfield	Theodore Dreiser	Spiro Agnew

Famous People: Twelfth House Gemini Planets

Vincent Van Gogh	Greta Garbo	Cher
Rosemary Woods	Edward G. Robinson	Burl Ives
Arthur Conan Doyle	Henry Cabot Lodge	Richard Strauss
Edna St. Vincent Millay	Paul McCartney	Theodore Roosevelt
Arnold Schwarzenegger	Henry David Thoreau	Henry Kissinger

Famous People: Twelfth House Virgo Planets

Julie Andrews	Brooke Shields	Yoko Ono
Shirley MacLaine	Ira Progoff	Jay North

Twelfth House Mercury (Gemini, Virgo)

One learns in life to keep silent and draw one's own confusions.
—Cornelia Otis Skinner

He reads much; He is a great observer, and he looks Quite through the deeds of men.
—William Shakespeare

I am lost in a rubble of stampeding thoughts that can never be rounded up.
—Anonymous

It was hard to communicate with you. You were always communicating with yourself. The line was busy.
—Jean Kerr

She hides herself behind a busy brain.
—Brian Hooker

The real offense, as she ultimately perceived, was her having a mind of her own at all.
—Henry James

Till I was 13, I thought my name was 'Shut Up.'
—Joe Namath

Think twice before you speak—and you'll find everyone talking about something else.
—Francis Rodman

Mental activity is easy if it doesn't have to conform to reality.
—Marcel Proust

To treat your facts with imagination is one thing, but to imagine your facts is another.
—John Burroughs

We write to be able to transcend our life, to reach beyond it. We write to teach ourselves to speak with others, to record the journey into the labyrinth, we write to expand our world, when we feel strangled, constricted, lonely.
—Anaïs Nin

Venus (Taurus, Libra) in the Twelfth House

Your twelfth house Venus suggests that you enjoy solitude and easily turn within for emotional fulfillment when personal relationships are unsatisfying. Capable of being a partner to yourself, you create and live by your own values, cultivating your inner beauty and choosing to give yourself the love you also seek from outside. Because you are able to draw sustenance from inner resources and to experience profound levels of inner peace, you feel spiritually protected; your dreams, as well as your waking life, may reflect your attunement to higher realms.

To the extent to which you are unable to meet your emotional needs by yourself or in relationships, your twelfth house Venus may incline you to various forms of indulgence which boost your sense of well-being. Secretly, you may eat large quantities of sweets, or go on periodic shopping binges (usually buying beautiful clothes, jewelry, or aesthetic objects). If your Venus, or your chart as a whole, reflects the influence of Taurus more than of Libra, you may deny your own materialism, while nevertheless allowing yourself to become quite attached to your belongings. You may also be ashamed of your indulgent behavior, which may be excessive, but which is also a healthy attempt to love yourself and experience greater pleasure in life.

Your twelfth house Venus also indicates that you wish to transcend yourself through creative expression, particularly art or music. Vulnerable about your talent, you may be a closet artist, secretly painting or sculpting during leisure hours, but hesitant to reveal your work to others or make the compromises which would enable you to become a professional. Because you seek to contact the realm of ideal images through art, and because you apply ideal standards to your work, you may harshly denigrate your own talents. You may also possess grandiose fantasies in regard to artistic success—fantasies which interfere with your capacity to dedicate yourself fully to your art, since you are hoping for an impossible level of accomplishment.

Your creative life and your love life are suffused with longing for transcendent experience. You seek a love which extends beyond the personal, which embraces the godlike in all humanity. This desire may incline you to choose work of a service nature, to feel drawn to soothe the pain of wounded individuals, and to help them embrace the seeds of their potential. Because of your compassion and sympathy for people in need, you want to give; and your sincere interest in the welfare of others, more often than not, evokes a loving response in return. But your need to give, and your focus upon the spiritual potential of others may have adverse effects in personal relationships; you may not know how to choose a partner with whom you can create a viable life on earth.

You suffer from heart lust; you want a soul mate. In touch with your spiritual self, you want to commune with the highest self in another. Gazing into each other's eyes or gazing outward through the lens of common values and ideals, you wish to lose yourself in the experience of blissful oneness. Indeed, you are capable of such peak loving experiences, but these experiences may be insubstantial, since they often are created by your fantasy, rather than grounded in the reality of fully knowing the other person. You tend to fall in love with love, or to love an image or ideal rather than a whole person. Attracted to the inner qualities of a person and the fleeting glimmers you have of their soul and their soul's potential, you ignore external realities which would undercut the high romance. Your concept of love, which is likely to be unrealistic, may be so unconscious that you continually confuse fantasy and reality, deluding yourself about your partner, and making the same mistakes over and over again, without learning from past experience.

Yet you are a giver, capable of loving another, and of establishing a relationship in which deep mutual sharing occurs. However, receiving is likely to be much more difficult for you than giving. Because you may gain much sustenance from being in love, actual contact with your loved one may be secondary in importance to your inner experience of love; as a result, and because you are often uncomfortable receiving, you may love someone who is elusive, inaccessible, unable to respond to your needs. But when you are together, you seek to create a private world in which you can lose yourself in each other, before returning to the separate worlds which claim you.

In your intimate relationships, you are shy about publicly expressing affection, but are very affectionate in private, perhaps even sugary and sentimental. Your sense of privacy in regard to your love life may also influence your tendency to engage in secret infatuations, or to become involved in behind-the-scenes romances which fulfill your fantasy of idyllic retreat from the world, but which are not integrated into your daily life.

Often, people who have a twelfth house Venus go through phases in their lives in which they avoid love relationships. Fearful of losing themselves in another, feeling ashamed about the intensity of their needs, or suffering from the pain of continual disillusionment, they avoid intimate connections. They may alternate in their lives between intense all-consuming love relationships, and complete lack of involvement. If this is your pattern, you may find that the years you are without a partner are years in which you can learn to love yourself more effectively and prepare yourself for more satisfying future relationships. The danger, however, is that you will deny your needs for so long that when you do give into them, you fall back into the old patterns of intense infatuation. Because close relationships are the means by which you most fully encounter yourself, you need to develop a network of people with whom you experience deep and genuine sharing.

Apart from love relationships, your twelfth house Venus can enable you to create friendships and other kinds of platonic relationships which involve mutual expression of feelings and needs. Although you may lack the social graces which enable you to relate on conventional levels, you do not lack the attunement to inner realms which makes intimacy possible. For this reason, and because you value deep personal sharing, you are capable of developing enriching, loving relationships which can fulfill some of your partnership needs.

One other issue which may be problematic for you in your relationships is your confusion about femininity. Most likely, you were influenced in your concepts of women by a mother who did not provide an adequate role model. She may have been very giving, but she was likely to have given in a narcissistic manner, without awareness of your real needs; or she may have been completely incapable of giving or loving, so that you were forced to turn inward at an early age to find sources of love within yourself. If you are a woman, you may, as a result, be confused and insecure in regard to your female identity. If you are a heterosexual male, you may have unrealistic and overly idealistic images of what you can expect from a female partner, which may be an attempt to compensate for lack of love early in life.

Understanding the early childhood and family issues which influenced your twelfth house Venus may be helpful to you. Perhaps, love was not outwardly expressed in your family, or even experienced. Perhaps, your parents were unclear in regard to their values, their attitudes toward the material world, and their willingness to form genuine relationships. The oedipal phase (approximately ages 4-5) may have been particularly difficult for you, since your love for the opposite sex parent was probably frustrated, and you chose to turn to the world of ideal images within yourself rather than fully invest again in an outer person who could disappoint you. This choice contributes to the richness of your spiritual and artistic life, but may interfere in your capacity to develop substantial relationships.

Nevertheless, in relationships you find yourself. You need to be personally engaged with others. You also need a private life in which you can "follow your bliss"—experience your spiritual source and express your creativity. Artistic training may help you develop confidence in your talents; training in social skills and graces may benefit you socially. Finally, a caring bond with a skilled psychotherapist attuned to interpersonal issues may help you work through the fears and conflicts you experience in regard to intimacy.

Twelfth House Venus (Taurus, Libra) Images

closet artist	butterfly in a jar	secret garden
watercolors	dove in captivity	sweet dreams
lady-in-waiting	sacrificial lamb	mermaid
flood of perfume	second-hand rose	water ballet
backstage singer	queen of fantasyland	sleeping beauty
secret rainbow	basement florist	water lily
honey in a jar	secret wedding	sacred dove
underwater dancer		

Famous People: Twelfth House Venus

Isadora Duncan	Grandma Moses	Mia Farrow
Lyndon Johnson	Claude Debussy	Liza Minnelli
Jane Addams	Leonard Bernstein	James Hilton
Jerry Rubin	Arthur Rimbaud	Helen Hayes
Alan Watts	Camille St.-Saëns	Ethel Barrymore
Piet Mondrian	Barbra Streisand	Jimi Hendrix
Jane Fonda	Julie Andrews	Clara Barton
George Gershwin	Grace Kelly	Richard Wagner

Famous People: Twelfth House Taurus Planets

Hubert Humphrey	George Bernard Shaw	Orson Welles
Jack London	Laurence Olivier	O. Henry
Joe Namath	Teilhard de Chardin	Frank Baum
Ottorino Respighi	Gigi Perreau	Tom Snyder
Richard Wagner	Ulysses S. Grant	

Famous People: Twelfth House Libra Planets

Barbara Walters	Camille St.-Saëns	Arthur Rimbaud
Arthur Godfrey	Joan Fontaine	Ethel Barrymore
Greg Allman	Albert Eichmann	Dick Martin

Twelfth House Venus (Taurus, Libra)

Relationship is surely the mirror in which you discover yourself.
—Krishnamurti

Don't forget to love yourself.
—Sören Kierkegaard

I have spread my dreams under your feet;
Tread softly because you tread on my dreams.
—W. B. Yeats

One must love, say I, with all of one's self—or live a life of utter chastity.
—George Sand

You can always get someone to love you—even if you have to do it yourself.
—Thomas Masson

I pray thee, O God, that I may be beautiful within.
—Socrates

Love is a game—yes?
I think it is a drowning.
—Amy Lowell

What she wants is a live guru—someone to inspire her. . . . snatch her up
out of herself.
—Ruth Jhabvale

The cure of her melancholy lies
In melodies and loveliness.
—Alfred de Musset

And suddenly I was swept out of myself—knowing, knowing.
Feeling the love of God burning through creation, and an ecstasy
of bliss pouring through my spirit and down into every nerve.
—Loran Hurscott

Eleanor Rigby/ Picks up the rice in the church where a wedding
has been
Lives in a dream . . . All the lonely people.
—The Beatles

Love is an attempt to change a piece of a dream-world into reality.
—Henry David Thoreau

Mars (Aries) in the Twelfth House

Your twelfth house Mars indicates that you often lack physical energy and avoid strenuous exercise. When you are physically active, you prefer a solitary exercise regime to group activities or competitive sports. Ill at ease with your body, and often feeling clumsy, you may be somewhat unconscious in your movements and insecure in your capacity to direct and control your bodily energy. Sometimes you feel as if you live with your foot on the brakes, unable to accelerate; other times, you don't know how to brake, or stop your own acceleration.

Your insecurity in regard to your body may extend to mechanical objects, with which you are uncomfortable. To the extent to which you have weak physical boundaries, you experience your own psychological states through the machines and motor vehicles around you. For example, when you feel deflated, your car may have a flat tire; when you need to let off steam, your car's exhaust system may fail, and a noisy muffler may express your anger for you. This position of Mars also indicates that your emotional conflicts may be related to such physical problems as headaches, bleeding, inflammations, burns, fever, and high blood pressure. Carelessness in action may also cause you to be accident-prone.

Your twelfth house Mars suggests that you live in a constant state of internal excitement and restlessness, which may lead you into compulsive activities, or motivate you to continually generate personal projects which provide an outlet for your energy. Because you have difficulty keeping still, you keep busy; however, because you fear asserting yourself in the outer world, you may preoccupy yourself with activities which are solitary or behind-the-scenes.

This is a highly self-motivated and self-driving position for Mars, as long as you are able to initiate activities which awaken your enthusiasm. Often stimulated by grandiose fantasies of adventure and accomplishment, you invest yourself totally in each new interest, until your passion wanes and you seek another project. Alternating between overdoing and underdoing, you also experience long phases of disengagement from life, time periods during which you feel unable to experience the states of involvement and excitement which you crave.

To the extent to which you feel out of touch with your passion and energy, you suffer from too much repression and suppression of your wants or desires, as well as a nagging sense of incapacity or inadequacy, expressed through negative self-talk beginning with "I can't." Feeling defeated before you even try, you inhibit your desires for experiences which might satisfy you. Since you have difficulty handling the frustration of unmet longings, you may choose not to want rather than to want and be disappointed. Yet simultaneously, you become invested in desires which are substitutes for your real wants and needs, and which inevitably fail to result in fulfillment.

Unconsciously, you may be influenced by a deep inner taboo in regard to experiencing, expressing, and satisfying your desires. You may too easily confuse the healthy motivation to meet your needs with selfishness or self-centeredness. Because of your difficulty in acting on your own behalf, you do not always feel capable of taking responsibility for your life. As a result of failing to assert yourself appropriately, you feel helpless, and attract situations in which you are victimized. You may also expect others to do for you that which you are unwilling or unable to do for yourself.

Your twelfth house Mars is prone to generate a wide range of fears, sometimes expressed through nightmares of aggression, violence, or rape. You may be afraid of your impulses and of losing control, of your own and other people's anger, of sexuality or lack of sexual potency; you may also fear wild animals, fire, automobiles or other motor vehicles, and mechanical objects.

Although often afraid to venture into the outer world, you are a courageous explorer of inner worlds. You ruthlessly confront your own inner demons; you seek to plumb the depths of your psyche; you thrive on emotional challenges. Adept at probing the psyches of others, you have an innate talent for helping people uncover the roots of their conflicts. For this reason, and because of a desire to atone for past sins, as well as a genuine motivation to serve, you may be drawn to a social service profession in which you can use your psychological skills.

Most likely, the psychological field is of particular interest to you because of your own lifelong struggle with issues regarding anger and sexuality. Because of your difficulty in knowing your wants and asserting yourself effectively, you may not know what your desires are until they are frustrated, or until you feel violated; then, you become inordinately angry in reaction and defense. Other patterns in regard to anger which you may experience include: avoidance of conflict, fear of anger directed toward you, paranoia (often a projection of your own unrecognized anger), passive-aggressive behavior, feeling hurt instead of angry, delayed reactions of anger, overreactions of rage resulting from unresolved anger from the past, anger directed toward yourself instead of others, indirect expressions of anger, and displacement of your anger onto people or situations which feel safer for you to deal with than those which triggered your aggressive feelings.

Because of a deep-seated belief that your anger is bad and/or destructive, you repress it, and then eventually express it indirectly or inappropriately. Because of your desire for cooperation and harmony, and because of your spiritual values, you hesitate to hurt others. Usually, you would rather hurt yourself by giving yourself negative, depressing messages or engaging in self-defeating behaviors than risk upsetting and possibly losing the relationships which are important to you. Yet inwardly you may seethe, and seek revenge. Although you hesitate to acknowledge this part of you, you may experience a perverse pleasure in watching those who have hurt you squirm or suffer as a result of your behavior or their own misfortunes. You need to accept the reality that you will sometimes hurt others, and you need to become comfortable enough with your desires and aggressions that you learn to assert yourself consciously and constructively, rather than unconsciously and destructively.

Your twelfth house Mars also indicates that you are vulnerable about your sexuality and desirability. Sex for you may be more of an emotional than a physical experience. Uncomfortable with the lusty, animal dimensions of sex, and capable of transcendent sexuality, you seek to make love with your soul as well as your body. You tend to spiritualize sex and to long for those peak sexual experiences which allow you to surrender completely with a partner you love and trust.

Although you are able to surrender and respond fully to your sexual partner, you are likely to be inhibited about taking the aggressive role, or going after what you want sexually. Early taboos in regard to assertion, as well as your right to be a fully sexual being, may influence you. Sexual traumas occurring during childhood and adolescence may have left you with underlying feelings of guilt, shame, and fear in regard to sexual experience and your adequacy as a sexual partner—as well as an attachment to experiences of intense excitement and desire. These influences may lead to off/on patterns in regard to sex—long periods of celibacy alternating with indulgence. Fearful of exposing to another your own conflicting blend of sexual desire and fear, you may satisfy your sexual urges through masturbation or fantasy, rather than risk the vulnerability of sexual contact.

This position of Mars inclines you to merge psychically as well as sexually with your partner, and to have difficulty separating emotionally after sexual contact. Once you have begun a sexual relationship, you may slip into an unconscious constellation of romantic fantasy which interferes with your capacity to realistically assess your experience. Because you are more likely to be turned on by the inner rather than outer characteristics of another, you are unwittingly attracted to partners who psychically trigger the same feelings and complexes you experienced early in life. Through secret infatuations and behind-the-scenes relationships, you maintain a level of protective fantasy which enables you to reenact experiences of the past. In such reenactments, you need to be wary of allowing your fear and guilt to sabotage precisely what you desire. Consider Rapunzel, who loved and desired her prince, but sabotaged her escape with him by revealing to the witch who had imprisoned her that he had been secretly climbing up to her tower each evening!

Your sexual identity, as well as your behavior, is influenced by your twelfth house Mars. Most likely, you are affected by early childhood definitions of femininity and masculinity by which you unconsciously measure yourself. If you are female, you may doubt your femininity because you are aware of a strong inner male force which runs you and can easily control your relationships; you are afraid of your capacity to dominate men—of failing to be "womanly," and of threatening those you love and desire. If you are male, you suffer because of your inability to live up to traditional images of masculinity; you doubt your adequacy as a male, as well as your sexual desirability and potency. Whether male or female, you need to redefine your images of masculinity and femininity and to honor both your active/assertive and passive/responsive qualities.

To the extent to which you are out of touch with your aggressive and sexual nature, you attract into your life circumstances and people which express these energies for you. Fearful of your inner persecutor, you may project your "badness" outside yourself and feel persecuted by others. In your relationships, you defend against the intense desire energy of Mars by hesitating to make demands upon others or to be imposing. Afraid of being invaded or violated, you wear a "keep out" sign to protect yourself from intrusion. Although fearful of conflict, you nevertheless fight wholeheartedly against those people who trespass without permission, and who get too close to the vulnerability of your inner sanctuary.

Most of these conflicts have their roots in childhood. Parental messages such as "Smile," and "Be feminine," as well as a multitude of "don'ts" beginning with "Don't be selfish," "Don't touch yourself," and "Don't be angry" influenced you to repress your healthy Martian energy. Early in life, rather than rejoicing in your newly discovered initiative, you may have been shamed for your impulses and for your urges toward autonomous action. Expressions of desire, will, and self-initiated activity were slapped down by your parents, to such an extent that you learned to quietly obey and to suppress your urges toward self-expression. But unconsciously, you translated your parents' behavior into the painful realization, "I have no right to exist."

Admonitions against impulse, desire, and action also pertained to anger. Ever since you were an infant, your aggressive, biting energy may have been so threatening to your parents that they scared you into submission. Whether your parents avoided conflict, or expressed only the ugliest and most destructive qualities of Martian energy, they failed to provide role models in regard to constructive assertion and expression of anger; as a result, you learned to inhibit your aggression and to oppose your parents only in subtle, indirect ways. But simultaneously, you built up a reservoir of unexpressed resentment and rage.

Finally, your conflicts in regard to sexuality have their origins in early life. Most likely, you experienced a confusing blend of judgment in regard to sexuality, combined with the unwanted but nevertheless titillating sexual stimulation or intrusiveness of a parent or relative. Early sexual traumas, and conscious or unconscious guilt in regard to your desires, contributed to your vulnerability about sex, and to the embarrassment or humiliation (often accompanied by blushing) which you sometimes experience in regard to sexual issues.

Although Mars in the twelfth house can be problematic, it does suggest that you possess a vast reservoir of psychological resources which are most available to you in times of crisis. You thrive on challenge; you have an extraordinary capacity to begin anew; you are capable of self-motivated and inspired action.

In order to liberate your Mars from the self-defeating bonds of the twelfth house, you may need to establish a healthier relationship with your body. Yoga, karate, rolfing, or physical therapy may enable you to experience and come to terms with your physical, aggressive, and sexual energy. Bioenergetics, in particular, can help you to increase your capacity to tolerate excitation, to cope with frustration, and to ground your energy.

You may also benefit from overhauling your belief system in regard to self-interest, assertion, and sexuality so that you feel more comfortable acting on your own behalf, experiencing and expressing your desires, and affirming your sexual identity and behavior. Assertiveness training may be useful, as may forms of psychotherapy which help you to experience and express sexual and aggressive feelings and desires. As you become comfortable with your desires, aware of what you want, and confident asserting yourself, you will honor your Martian energy, which enables you to feel more empowered, more fulfilled, and more alive.

Twelfth House Mars (Aries) Images

crocodile in a swamp	driving through fog	soggy match
dynamite in a locker	buried hatchet	getaway car
guerrilla warfare	fire in a cave	flooded accelerator
gymnasium of the soul	crusade	security guard
underground explosion	fantasyland engineer	hospital surgeon
martial arts	sacred battle	resistance fighter
forbidden fire	backseat driver	pressure cooker
ice-skating	steam bath	boat engine
hot water	water sports	

Famous People: Twelfth House Mars

Walt Whitman	Harry Belafonte	Johnny Carson
Igor Stravinsky	Vincent Van Gogh	Cat Stevens
Eleanor Roosevelt	Mary Tyler Moore	John Lennon
James Hoffa	John Denver	Rollo May
Brooke Shields	Patricia Schroeder	Paul Gauguin
Neil Armstrong	Sri Aurobindo	

Famous People: Twelfth House Aries Planets

Pearl Bailey	Adolph Eichmann	Liza Minnelli
Isadora Duncan	Saint Teresa of Avila	Queen Victoria
Pancho Gonzalez	Johannes Brahms	Sarah Bernhardt

Twelfth House Mars (Aries)

There was never a war that was not inward; I must fight till I have conquered in myself what causes war.
— Marianne Moore

If you would keep your soul/ From spotted sight or sound,/ Live like the velvet mole;/ Go burrow underground.
— Elinor Wylie

There is knocking in the skull/ An endless silent shout Of something beating on the wall,/ And crying, Let me out.
— Ogden Nash

Anyone can become angry—that is easy, but to be angry with the right person, to the right degree, at the right time, for the right purpose, and in the right way—this is not easy.
                    —Aristotle

A man deep-wounded may feel too much pain to feel much anger.
                    —George Eliot

I am the wound and the knife!
The victim and the executioner.
                    —Charles Baudelaire

We have met the enemy and he is us.
                    —Pogo, Walt Kelly

Anguish is always there, lurking at night,
Wakes us like a scourge, the creeping sweat
As rage is remembered, self-inflicted blight.
What is it in us we have not mastered yet?
                    —May Sarton

Desire. Desire. The nebula/ opens in space, unseen/
your heart utters its great beats/ in solitude.
                    —Adrienne Rich

And all had yet been well, but now arose
All her interior and forgotten foes—
A revolutionary army led
By Passion, with a red cap on his head—
Who now, throughout the poor beleaguered town,
Formed their wild ranks, and shouted Conscience down . . .
And each imprisoned vagabond desire
Rushed madly forth, and set her heart on fire.
                    —James Laver

Jupiter (Sagittarius)
in the Twelfth House

The influence of Jupiter upon your twelfth house suggests that you are an inner explorer and an appreciator of the wealth of the psychological/spiritual world. Your abiding faith in the value of the inner life and of your inner resources enriches you; you may even feel protected by a spiritual guide who contributes to your well-being and facilitates your personal development. Because you seek to grow inwardly and are continually questing for the meaning and purpose of each experience, you are likely to possess considerable wisdom and to be attuned to keen intuition which you trust far more than the precepts of the outer world.

Motivated to ''follow your own bliss,'' you thrive upon the inward journey, but may not trust the world outside yourself. Your abundance of dreams and images expands you, in contrast to the constriction you may feel adapting to a society which does not honor the values you hold dear. As a result, you may split off your inner and outer self, hesitant to expand outwardly because you do not know how to create a bridge between these two facets of life. Likewise, you give generously of your inner resources, but may not be giving in external or material ways, which are not important to you, and which threaten your identification with the inner life.

Your twelfth house Jupiter indicates that you are very much influenced by philosophical and/or religious beliefs which relate to your personal experience, but that you do not subscribe to organized philosophical and religious systems, which may have been imposed upon you in the past. Because your inner life was not supported by society, you learned early to be protective and even secretive in regard to your beliefs, as well as the spiritual awakenings or peak experiences which transformed you.

Your vulnerability and caution in regard to your beliefs may both help and hinder you. On the one hand, you preserve within yourself a sustaining faith; on the other hand, because you do not expose your assumptions and attitudes to the test of reality, you may operate from a distorted belief system which undermines your effective functioning. You unwittingly mistake your beliefs for reality and lose objectivity about your experiences; you may also be fixed and dogmatic in viewpoint, considering your way of thinking to be the only way, and stubbornly holding onto your attitudes as a means of preserving your identity.

Another result of maintaining an inner sanctuary is that you may alternate between having expectations and hopes which are ungrounded and unlikely to be fulfilled, and, on the other hand, holding to a pessimistic outlook which refuses to hope and is fearful of disappointment. When you do experience your Jupiterian energy, you may not have any sense of realistic limits; your Jupiterian exuberance expands in all directions and believes in unlimited possibility. Inevitably, disillusionment occurs; you then retreat inwardly and convince yourself that you are incapable of outwardly manifesting what you seek. This pattern may also be influenced by deep-seated assumptions that the outer world cannot support your well-being, and that you cannot and should not expect to feel happy about your outer life.

Your tendency to find fault with the world outside yourself, and to suppress your capacity for happiness, has its origins in your childhood experiences. Enthusiasm, optimism, expansiveness, and other Jupiterian expressions of outreaching, abundant energy were not encouraged by your parents, who may have given up on many of the rewards of life, and could not bear to see their children reaching toward what they could not have. Although your Jupiter suggests that you had a blissful experience within the womb and were eager to be born, you may have learned early in life that the world outside the womb was untrustworthy. Perhaps your parents were always making promises, but never following through. As a result, you became hesitant to invest yourself in hopes and aims which might never be fulfilled.

Your twelfth house Jupiter can also indicate that you did not feel allowed to have your own beliefs or goals, or even to think for yourself in your family. Because your parents might have dictated their world view (which you introjected) and assumed that you were an extension of themselves, you may have learned to distrust your own perceptions and opinions about the world around you. Trauma in regard to asserting your own beliefs during your school years may also have influenced you to retreat into yourself and to create a personal refuge which none could violate.

Another manifestation of your inner retreat may be a tendency developed early in life to melodramatize your emotions and attitudes. Because your subjective views took precedence over the objective world, you easily lose perspective about your experience. As if expecting the world to thwart your aims, you may react strongly to minor disappointments, which become magnified by your voluminous imagination. As a result, although you actively reach out to experiences which support your inner growth, you may hesitate to reach out to new outer experiences, and to develop a bridge between your inner and outer lives.

Frequently, you deny yourself the fulfillment which you could create, perhaps because you fear your greed, your lack of limits, your laziness, self-indulgence, or your tendency to overdo or overextend yourself when external barriers are removed. Being happy, having richness or abundance, allowing yourself to fully expand and open are threatening to you, at odds with the script you internalized from your parents. In order to develop your identity, you may have defined prosperity in radically different terms than they did, but in doing so may have limited your capacity to create for yourself a fully prosperous life.

Usually, you feel prosperous when you have time for inner exploration. Solitude to you is not synonymous with loneliness; you spend many private hours reading, studying, planning for the future, or immersing yourself in your thoughts and fantasies. Self-taught, you may avoid obtaining undergraduate or graduate degrees unless you find a curriculum which accords with your personal development needs; likewise, you may be hesitant to travel, except to places which enhance your communion with your soul and provide a refuge from the demands of daily life. You need time alone to replenish your spirit, to connect with your internal source, and to assimilate the vast amount of stimulation which you take in but do not easily process.

Your Jupiter also suggests that your ability to find peace within yourself is evident to other people who are often inspired by your presence, who offer their support, and who express their confidence in you. Although you may not appear to be an outgoing, generous person, you do give from deep recesses of well-being within yourself and are particularly responsive to people in need. For this reason, you may work professionally or as a volunteer in a social service field where your reflective approach to life can help other people transcend their own conflicts. Since you are a natural explorer of the psyche and have the ability to confront and understand your psychological process and behavior, you are likely to be a talented guide to others who are likewise pursuing their inner journeys.

Your twelfth house Jupiter suggests that you could benefit from examining the unconscious assumptions and expectations from the past which limit you, and which prevent you from finding the fulfillment and abundance that you desire. Can you allow yourself to be happy? To have what you (secretly) want? To create a bridge between your inner and outer selves, in order to use your talents in the world and thereby enrich yourself? Can you develop and commit yourself to goals which satisfy the inner questor, and enable you to experience success within society? Further pursuit of education, cognitive or rational-emotive psychotherapy (which examines beliefs and assumptions), or a spiritual therapy such as psychosynthesis (which honors inner wisdom) may be beneficial to you, as well as experiences of community with kindred spirits pursuing similar quests and sharing similar values.

Twelfth House Jupiter (Sagittarius) Images

forbidden journey	internal telescope	seaplane
backstage philosopher	astral travel	water pageant
prophet in exile	meditating preacher	sacred diploma
underwater explorer	educational cruise	guardian angel
the impossible dream	archer in a fog	high tide
explorer of the interior	closet professor	navigator

Famous People: Twelfth House Jupiter

Ram Dass	Immanuel Kant	Buzz Aldrin
Lord Byron	Carol Channing	Phyllis Diller
Paul Cezanne	Vincent Van Gogh	Mario Cuomo
Henry Miller	Alan Leo	Johannes Brahms
Hans Christian Andersen	Emile Zola	

Famous People: Twelfth House Sagittarius Planets

Jimi Hendrix	Caroline Kennedy	Henry Mancini
Pope John Paul I	Alan Alda	Ethel Waters

Twelfth House Jupiter (Sagittarius)

The longest journey/Is the journey inwards
To the source of being.
                    —Dag Hammarskjöld

You must make your own religion, and it is only what you make yourself
which will be of any use to you.
                    —Mark Rutherford

I will hew great windows for my soul.
                    —Angela Morgan

He loved his dreams and cultivated them.
                    —Colette

I am my own Universe. I am my own Professor.
               —Sylvia Ashton-Warner

Your pain is the breaking of the shell that encloses your understanding.
               —Kahlil Gibran

A lively understanding spirit/Once entertained you.
It will come again./Be still. Wait.
               —Theodore Roethke

He is a man who expands with joy in the heart of an enchanted isolation.
               —Henry A. Murray

In your longing for your giant self lies your goodness: and that longing is
in all of you.
               —Kahlil Gibran

If I held all truths in my hand, I would beware of opening it to men.
               —Bernard de Fontenelle

Truth is within ourselves; it takes no rise
From outward things. . . .
There is an inmost centre in us all
Where truth abides in fullness.
               —Robert Browning

Saturn (Capricorn) in the Twelfth House

Your twelfth house Saturn indicates that you control and organize your inner life so that you are not overwhelmed by chaotic feelings. Afraid to surrender to your inner flow and experience the fears which threaten you, you discipline your emotions by pushing them out of consciousness, and involving yourself in scheduled tasks and activities. Although your self-control helps you manage your life and handle crises, it also restricts you. Feeling out of contact with the deeper realms of your psyche, you block access to the feelings, images, dreams, and fantasies which could nourish you. To the extent to which you experience a frozen sea within yourself or an inner rigidity which prevents you from relaxing, you may be unable to receive from others and to make real contact with the people around you.

You are afraid of your inner life—understandably so, since you harbor deep-seated fears and struggle against feelings of discouragement and despair. You fear isolation, suffocation, entrapment, aging, rejection, and being left or abandoned. You fear letting go and melting the ice within yourself which gives you a sense of internal structure and contributes to your effective functioning. Lacking faith and trust in yourself and the world, you hold onto yourself and the sources of security you have developed, although outwardly you appear to be adaptable and flexible. Basically, you exhibit a high degree of self-sufficiency and inner strength; however, such strength may be brittle, derived from the denial of your vulnerability and needs, rather than their integration and fulfillment.

In order to cope with early deprivation, you developed a strong defense system capable of keeping threatening feelings and needs from upsetting your equilibrium. But because you often felt rejected and inadequate, your self-esteem is fragile, and you easily feel undermined by feelings of self-doubt, inferiority, worthlessness, and guilt. Hard on yourself, and unable to accept your limitations, you have difficulty tolerating failure and affirming your value as an individual when you are not living up to the standards you have set for yourself.

Solitude may be difficult for you, because without the stimulation of interpersonal contact, you encounter your fears and negativity. You may therefore battle with the pull inward, which feels necessary, but which also cuts you off from the external stimulation which feeds and replenishes you. However, once you do move through your resistance to being alone, you may enjoy your own company, particularly when you are focused on a personal project or work interest which engages you. A twelfth house Saturn does give the capacity to work alone and to follow through on the tasks to which you have committed yourself.

One psychological effect of a twelfth house Saturn is an all-or-nothing oscillation between ungrounded fantasy and a pessimistic view of reality. When your Saturn rules you, you dare not dream or hope for fulfillment, nor believe in your capacity for success in the outer world. Your vision is bleak, and elicits depressive feelings which you wish to avoid. As a result, you may block the Saturnian voices, not only the fear, pessimism, and self-doubt, but also the wise, cautionary reality principle which can help you to see, accept, and prepare for limitations within and around you. When you dare to dream, you dream without Saturnian grounding; when your dreams fail to materialize, you hesitate to desire or dream again, rather than to learn how to create and pursue dreams which can be actualized. Confronting reality is difficult for you, because your reality lens is fogged with feelings of anxiety and hopelessness which threaten you rather than help you to concretely manifest your aims.

You may be attached to the intoxicating, boundless states of life without Saturn, to the sense of unlimited potential and possibility which you experience when you are able to completely block Saturnian fears and doubts. Such an attachment can interfere with your capacity to make commitments to real life aims, since doing so means relinquishing some sense of possibility in order to focus yourself and test yourself in one area of achievement. Because you hesitate to relinquish the boundless ideal, because you fear entrapment and failure, and because you also fear success (which threatens the script you learned to live in your family) you may prefer to live in the moment, rather than dedicate yourself to long-term goals or relationships.

Intimacy is threatening; you fear being known, then judged or abandoned, as you have been in the past. Therefore, you are slow to trust and may withhold your real feelings within a relationship in order to protect yourself and maintain control. Sensitive to rejection and invalidation, you guard against such experiences. But because you may not feel worthy of receiving love, you may unconsciously choose partners who treat you as you treat yourself, rather than affirm you and compassionately accept your weaknesses and vulnerabilities.

One advantage of having a twelfth house Saturn is that you are an enjoyable, uplifting companion, since you hide your negativity from others and present the jovial, life-affirming facet of yourself which thrives without Saturnian oppression. Directing oppressive, restrictive energy toward yourself rather than others, you may be outgoing, sociable, and accepting of other's limitations, while unable to tolerate your own. People are attracted to your positive spirit and heartfelt support of their endeavors; yet to the extent to which you wall off your troublesome feelings in order to encourage and uplift others, you may be haunted by the sense of inner emptiness or isolation experienced by the self which you barricaded from your awareness.

In your family, you were most likely supported when you "put on a happy face" and enthusiastically reached out to life around you, rather than brooding upon your disappointments or burdening your parents with fears and upsets which they were not able or willing to hear. Unable to come to terms with the limitations of their own lives, they did not know how to soothe your anxieties or impart balanced realistic attitudes in regard to functioning successfully in the world. Absorbing their own despair and sense of failure, you internalized their feelings and experienced them as your own. Because of their tendencies toward denial, as well as their patterns of disillusionment and giving up on fulfilling their aims, you likewise learned to deny your own needs and desires. Since having long-term goals and making commitments appeared to be unsatisfying, you hesitated to develop your own goals and to commit yourself to values important to you.

Your twelfth house Saturn suggests that your father in particular was rejecting and restrictive, and probably neither emotionally nor physically available. You lacked both the protection and security which a healthy, stable father figure could provide, and also missed having a viable role model for developing competence and the ability to successfully advance in the work world.

Because twelfth house repressed emotions from the past distort the awareness of a planetary energy, you may have a distorted conception of your father, based more on fantasy than reality, and may battle against the oppression of your inner father archetype at least as much as that of your real father who never responded to your needs. To the extent that you rejected your father, you are likely to reject traditional religion, with its patriarchal father god; on the other hand, you may seek a spiritual father figure who is responsive to and protective of human weakness.

Because your own father was a poor model in regard to work, and possibly because you had traumatic experiences in regard to your competence in school, you may struggle with feelings of inadequacy in regard to your professional capabilities. Afraid of competition, uncomfortable with authority figures, and feeling double-binded by both your fear of failure and the family influences which conditioned you against success, you constantly battle anxiety when you attempt to create a fulfilling work situation. Devaluing your competency, you may settle for work which is beneath your capabilities rather than risk the challenge of a more advanced position.

Experiencing and expressing your personal power in the work setting is difficult for you, not only because you are more comfortable keeping a low profile, but also because you have inner images of power and success as exploitative, corrupt, or otherwise undesirable. Although you excel in controlling your inner life, you may feel anxious and disorganized in regard to controlling, organizing, and managing work activities, particularly when you are in a position of responsibility or leadership.

Taking on professional responsibility may also be difficult for you because you already, often unconsciously, feel a personal responsibility for the people important to you, and a universal responsibility to minister to the needs of humanity. When you witness suffering and deprivation, you feel called upon to do something about it; you may even experience a sense of mission in regard to work which expresses your humanitarian values. For this reason, you may be drawn to the social service field, or to a behind-the-scenes profession where you can respond to legitimate human needs, as well as exercise your own capability to work productively on your own.

In order to come to terms with your twelfth house Saturn, you may need to confront the unresolved grief over past losses which may be freezing you emotionally and preventing you from feeling in touch with the potential richness of your inner life. Such losses may be actual deaths or separations, or may be emotional losses—mourning the father you never had, or the unlived facets of yourself which stifled since childhood. Because of your need for control, surrendering to tears is an experience of dissolution which threatens your identity. Yet you may gain a more substantial and stronger sense of internal control by opening more fully to your vulnerability and learning how to soothe the fears of your inner child.

According to Strephon Kaplan Williams, "You do not get over fear by living only love. You deal with fear by accepting and experiencing it fully."[4] You might be afraid to confront your fears because you often become mired within them, paralyzed by the voices of your negative tapes, immobilized in regard to action, and inclined to escape into sleep. Learning how to tolerate and move through the experience of fear is particularly important for you, as is coming to terms with specific fears such as isolation or abandonment.

Rather than alternate between an optimistic, unrealistic, outreaching self and a secret self which is fear-laden and self-condemning, you need to develop attitudes which embrace and honor the wounded child within you and the dark places of the soul which frighten but also provide deep sources of nourishment. You also need to take on difficult challenges in your work life, and to affirm yourself even when you fail to perform adequately, simply because you have been courageous enough to risk, to push through your fear, and to overcome your conditioning.

Psychotherapy which helps you to experience and express fears, guilt, and self-condemnations and to develop new attitudes in relationship to yourself can be particularly useful for you. Reality therapy and rational-emotive therapy (which counters negative assumptions and internal messages) may be beneficial, as may career counseling and professional workshops which help you develop vocational skills that will increase your sense of competence.

Finally, you are likely to make peace with your twelfth house Saturn as you learn the value of commitment to tasks, jobs, relationships, and long-range goals. You need to know that you can turn away not only from past sources of security, but also from the enthrallment of unlived potential; you need to discover that by narrowing your options, and making choices and commitments which you sustain over time, you can experience fulfillment and a growing sense of confidence in your own capabilities.

Twelfth House Saturn (Capricorn) Images

underwater fortress	closet entrepreneur	coral reef
scapegoat	underwater architect	boat anchor
desert places of	interior construction	exiled politician
the soul	backbone of a fish	desert island
monastery walls	foundations of sand	monastery politics
sacred tree	cliff over the sea	prison fence
sealed door	underwater rocks	frozen pipes

Famous People: Twelfth House Saturn

Robert DeNiro	Franz Schubert	Arlo Guthrie
Ann Landers	John Galsworthy	Chris Evert

Leonard Nimoy	Sylvia Plath	Robert Redford
Benjamin Spock	Walt Whitman	Sissy Spacek
Indira Gandhi	Hubert Humphrey	Spencer Tracy
Annie Besant	Ulysses S. Grant	Conrad Adenauer
Wyatt Earp	William McKinley	Leslie Caron

Famous People: Twelfth House Capricorn Planets

| Margaret Mead | Desi Arnaz Jr. | John Ruskin |
| Rudolph Bing | Spencer Tracy | Joseph Stalin |

Twelfth House Saturn (Capricorn)

When one has not had a good father, one must create one.
—Friedrich Nietzsche

The only thing we have to fear is fear itself.
—F. D. Roosevelt

They cannot scare me with their empty spaces between stars.
I have it in me so much near home
To scare myself with my own desert places.
—Robert Frost

As far as your self-control goes, as far goes your freedom.
—Maria Ebner von Eschenbach

True success is overcoming the fear of being unsuccessful.
—Paul Sweeney

And her heart is lonely . . . and like a spectre of an age departed,
She glides alone—the solitary-hearted.
—Hartley Coleridge

Inside every clown is a sad sack who emerges only in private.
—Anonymous

I, a stranger and afraid/In a world I never made.
—A. E. Housman

What we achieve inwardly will change outer reality.
—Otto Rank

Fear is static that prevents me from hearing my intuition.
—Hugh Prather

Are not enough things prohibited you in the Law? Must you prohibit yourself
still others?
—The Talmud

A winter's day in a deep and dark December-
I am alone, gazing from my window to the street below
On a freshly fallen silent shroud of snow.
I am a rock; I am an island.
                    —Simon and Garfunkel

If I could I would always work in silence and obscurity, and let my ef-
forts be known by their results.
                    —Emily Brontë

Uranus (Aquarius) in the Twelfth House

Your twelfth house Uranus suggests that although you appear conventional, you are quite individualistic in private. Fearful of revealing your personal idiosyncrasies and of being perceived as different, abnormal, or crazy, you hide your nonconformist tendencies. Your vulnerability in regard to your public image may be related to a family background in which unconventionality and extremism were discouraged or even actively denigrated. As a result, you fear that your deviant interests and behavior will not only make you anxious and prone to rejection, but will also lead to outright condemnation. Yet secretly, you fantasize being totally unconventional, independent, and even outrageous in your behavior.

Behind the scenes, you express interest in astrology, psychic phenomena, radical philosophies, and other intuitive or progressive forms of knowledge. Mentally active, you pursue a variety of unusual activities which stimulate you and expand your outlook on life. Although you may be quick to change your focus of attention, and although you have difficulty concentrating upon one activity for any length of time, you nevertheless become fascinated with each new pursuit. In spite of, or indeed because of your outward conformity, you enjoy the thrill of being involved in unique or avant garde interests, especially intellectual interests which help you to uncover the hidden dynamics of the psyche or of reality.

One troublesome characteristic of a twelfth house Uranus is that you are constantly in a state of internal excitement. Your restless, nervous energy interferes with your sleep; you may have bizarre, disconnected dreams from which you suddenly wake, sometimes as a result of electrical charges buzzing through your body. By day, you are tempted to secretly engage in lawbreaking behaviors, to express your self-will in unexpected ways, and to rebel against rules and regulations, particularly those which you create for yourself; you also may be driven to make sudden, unforeseen changes in your life, which do not always benefit you. Because your inner world is often chaotic and unpredictable, you may at times feel like a split personality, or you may fear that your intense, disorganized emotional states are indications that you are going crazy. Your sudden dramatic shifts of consciousness and behavior frequently disorient you; yet they also account for your psychological flexibility and your capacity for coping with the contradictions and incongruencies of life.

Another benefit of your highly charged nervous system is that the unsettling states of mind that you experience contribute to your acute intuitive and psychic faculties. Sudden flashes of insight, moments of genius, transformative experiences, glimpses of ideas and possibilities which are progressive even by New Age standards occur frequently for you. The internal energy which may be so disruptive also awakens you to new and significant modes of being, enables you to liberate yourself from past influences, and fuels your dedication to the process of inner awakening. This placement of Uranus is an excellent one for a metaphysical truthseeker or for anyone who wishes to listen to and follow the guidance of the inner self.

A related dimension of your Aquarian internal life is your attraction to New Age, humanitarian philosophies and lifestyles. But because your Uranus is in your twelfth house, you may hesitate to join social and political movements, or to act on behalf of a cause in which you believe. Deeply identified with the misfits of society, you feel alienated from the mainstream and choose to pursue your own path, rather than become involved in group and community activities. Although capable of playing the roles society requires of you, you are not invested in those roles; you prefer to cultivate your private life and a company of kindred spirits with whom you can express your individuality.

This placement of Uranus suggests that your friendships are of considerable importance to you. Your intuition, which is keen, is an asset in helping you to understand your friends and to relate to their life issues. They, in turn, provide a hidden support to you, particularly in times of stress. The more open you are to your inner world, the more likely you are to benefit from friendships, since you are not inclined to seek relationships which are based upon superficial or external matters. If, however, you fear the instability of your psyche and hesitate to share yourself intimately with another person, you may tap into the "loner" expression of Uranus and avoid forming friendships at all.

Because you need to safeguard your autonomy, you may maintain psychological distance or detachment in relationships. Although you share yourself and commit yourself to others, you fear emotional closeness and intrusion upon your carefully guarded independence. On the one hand you invite intimacy, but on the other hand you subtly impart messages of "Don't get too close. Don't intrude upon my space." Your erratic emotional temperament may also create barriers which threaten intimacy.

Another facet of your relationship life is your attraction to individualistic or eccentric people who are less inhibited than you about revealing their idiosyncrasies. In their company, you feel free to express yourself, to be "crazy." You also experience a secret delight in shocking others. Because you sometimes have volatile, erratic, strange and inappropriate outbursts, people are likely to be aware of your "secret self" and to both appreciate you and be wary of you. After all, even you are not sure who you will be when you wake up in the morning.

Making peace with your twelfth house Uranus involves fully owning and embracing your individuality, and finding constructive outlets for your unique talents, so that you do not need to unduly disrupt your life in order to express your Uranian energy. You need to create structures and relationships which enable you to periodically break free of convention and to risk acting crazy or outrageous. Only by accepting and valuing your uniqueness as a human being are you likely to tune into the remarkable degree of originality and inspiration which lies just beneath the surface of your consciousness.

You may also find that dedication to metaphysical study or to a humanitarian cause provides opportunities for you to demonstrate your mental agility and your progressive ideas and attitudes. The restless mental energy within you needs a focus or outlet in the world, where you can make a contribution and experience your connection to humanity.

Because of your high degree of nervous tension, you also need to develop your tolerance for excitation, to engage in physical activities through which you discharge excess energy, and to periodically calm yourself through some form of meditation which enables you to rest your active mind.

Twelfth House Uranus (Aquarius) Images

a private madness	lunatic's hideaway	rebellious monk
lightning over water	underground tremors	mutant fish
acupuncture of the soul	hidden genius	captive wizard
underground electricity	hydroelectric power	underground agitator
internal electricity	internal revolution	secret rebel
moving against the current	inner tornado	

Famous People: Twelfth House Uranus

Adolf Hitler	Peter Fonda	Burt Reynolds
John Denver	Phoebe Snow	John Travolta

Rainer Maria Rilke	Edgar Cayce	Fred Astaire
Michael Dukakis	Rex Harrison	Jimmy Hoffa
Norman Mailer	Robert Kennedy	Nostradamus
Brooke Shields	Farrah Fawcett-Majors	Elvis Presley
George Gershwin	John D. Rockefeller	James Barrie
Theodore Roosevelt	Sri Aurobindo	Frank Baum
George Bernard Shaw	Harry Truman	Erik Satie

Famous People: Twelfth House Aquarius Planets

Janis Joplin	Gertrude Stein	Piet Mondrian
Immanuel Kant	Jimmy Hoffa	Konrad Adenauer
Havelock Ellis	Ramakrishna	

Twelfth House Uranus (Aquarius)

A hidden self rebels, its slumber broken.
—Walter de la Mare

We must always change, renew, rejuvenate ourselves; otherwise we harden.
—Goethe

I know my own best friend is me.
—Ogden Nash

Who are you? said the Caterpillar.
Alice replied, rather shyly, 'I—I hardly know, Sir, just at present—at least I know who I was when I got up this morning, but I think I must have changed several times since then.'
—Lewis Carroll

She tried to be respectable because respectability kept away the chaos that sometimes overwhelmed her, causing her to call out in sleep, screaming wild sounds.
—Anne Richardson Roiphe

Revolutions begin with the self, in the self.
—Toni Cade

When I am crazy you all seem perfectly sane, but when I am sane you all seem perfectly crazy.
—Ogden Nash

My personality is not split; it's shredded.
—Jack Paar

And he, that yearns the truth to know
Still further inwardly may go.
—Lewis Carroll

Neptune (Pisces) in the Twelfth House

Your twelfth house Neptune indicates that you possess an innate sensitivity which contributes to your responsiveness to people in need. Deeply compassionate, you are drawn to the vulnerability of others, which you seek to nurture and protect. Yet because your Neptune is buried within your twelfth house, you are able to wall off your sensitivity from your personal life and to keep yourself from undue emotional involvement. Your Neptune is deceptive, because although your empathy and caring are real, you do not easily attach it to specific individuals, and you are most comfortable responding to the needs of people with whom you are not personally entangled.

Because you are so protective of your vulnerability, you may hesitate to let down your walls and surrender to the feelings of love and need which emerge in close relationships. Perhaps because you did not feel safe expressing your sensitivity in your family, you learned to barricade your true self behind a strong defense system, so that it would not be unduly hurt and corrupted by the outer world. Your resulting difficulty is that although you may be receptive to others, you are often out of touch with your own heart and spirit. Your well often feels empty; although you may give to others, you may be unfulfilled and yearning, unable to relax within the soft, warm, soothing Neptunian energies within you.

In solitude, often overwhelmed by the energies you have absorbed from others, you may feel directionless and internally disorganized. You need time to yourself to sort out your inner confusion and to attune yourself to dimensions of consciousness which bring you clarity and inner peace. Taking showers or baths and being near the water, as well as listening to music or expressing your creativity, help you to regain contact with your self. Often, you escape into daydreams or fantasies which comfort you; you may also be tempted to use drugs or alcohol in order to transcend the concerns of your daily life. Neptune for you is often an all-or-nothing experience; either you are lost in inner space and intoxicated with the heights, or you feel barren and empty, beset with vague yearnings for a fulfillment which appears completely out of reach.

Having a twelfth house Neptune indicates potential for channelling your imagination into satisfying creative pursuits. Yet because your creative self never received much encouragement, and because you are fearful of your own inner chaos, you may refrain from developing your creative talents. A closet musician or poet, you may be insecure and vulnerable in regard to personal expression and hesitant to share your work with others. Because your Neptunian sensitivity is so deeply buried, you may require long periods of solitude or retreats from a demanding schedule in order to hear the voice of your muse and express your creative impulse.

Within yourself, Neptune yearns for unconsciousness, union, and transcendence. At night, you sleep deeply, often so deeply that you do not remember your dreams. By day, you may resist surrendering to your urge to "get high" or to find wombs to which you can return; nonetheless, the nameless yearning within you may draw you to a spiritual path by which you can attune yourself to your lost soul. A secret mystic, you both desire and fear the sublime; you wish to transcend yourself and to experience the boundlessness of infinite love, but you are terrified of losing your sense of identity and your groundedness in the world. Spiritual study and meditation can nonetheless help you to fulfill your inner quest and find the connection with divine energies which you seek and need. The practice of visualization can also benefit you, because you have an uncanny power to use your imagination to influence reality.

One difficulty of your twelfth house Neptune is the tendency of Neptune's vague and often indecipherable energy to hinder your ability to be honest with yourself, and as a result, you might not speak and act in a straightforward manner with others. You do not mean to be elusive or deceptive, but your own confusions and illusions influence your behavior. Sometimes, denying your vulnerability and need, you may hesitate to act directly, not because you are trying to protect others but because you fear their responses.

You are ashamed of your weakness, your helplessness or impotence, your sensitivity, your need for solace, and your desire to be rescued; as a result, you defend yourself against these feelings. But because you carry within yourself a small vulnerable child who constantly influences you, you act in ways which reinforce your experience of smallness. Tough on the outside but soft within, you too easily take on the role of victim and allow yourself to be exploited.

One advantage of your inner sense of smallness is that it contributes to your identification with the underdog and your attraction to social service work. Through service to others, you express your compassion, you respond to the vulnerability in others rather than reveal your own vulnerability, and you fulfill your ideals in regard to serving humanity.

Although you may not consciously focus upon your ideals, they subliminally influence you. In contrast to your humble and small self, your Neptune also manufactures for you an often unconscious degree of grandiosity. Perhaps you daydream of being a great healer, creator, or spiritual leader; perhaps you refrain from developing your potential in many areas in order to avoid testing your capabilities and challenging the fantasized image which sustains you. On the one hand, your high ideals motivate you to altruistic behavior and selfless devotion; on the other hand, they contribute to an often distorted sense of your own potential, at the expense of developing your power in the world.

In relationships as well as work, you are motivated by unconscious fantasies. Sometime in the past, in early childhood or in previous lives, your consciousness was imprinted with the image of blissful union or the merging of souls. As a result, you are relentlessly searching for an experience which reflects this inner ideal; inevitably, unable to embrace the limitations of real human relationships, you are disappointed. This divine angst often feeds your ambivalence in personal relationships; although you may in rare, treasured moments experience the soul connection you seek, no one ever feeds your soul's hunger. Constantly, you struggle to embrace the real person before you, while hesitating to turn away from the inner image which you love and hold onto at the expense of reality.

In your personal relationships, you are nonetheless responsive to the needs of others and attract to yourself sensitive, creative, or spiritual people who overtly manifest your latent Neptunian self. A psychic sponge, you often absorb their feelings and confuse them with your own. Because of your confusion, you can be indirect, elusive, and act from mixed motives. People are likely to be drawn to the deepseated sensitivity and innocence they sense within you, but to the extent to which you are unclear or incongruent in your words and behaviors, they may distrust you.

Many of the conflicts you experience within yourself and with the outer world are likely to be influenced by your early experiences. Your soul may not have wanted to be born; it may have refused to relinquish its attachment to celestial realms. Perhaps your parents were threatened by your childish innocence, purity of spirit, sensitivity, and creativity, and sought to block the expression of your true and beautiful self. Deeply hurt, the divine child within you retreated to almost inaccessible realms, but never far enough to erase its own memory. Meanwhile, your conscious ego absorbed the messages of your parents that creative, spiritual, and altruistic values were unimportant or were values that you were not expected to manifest.

To make peace with your twelfth house Neptune, you need to find a spiritual or creative path which helps you to experience your soul energy, and to renew yourself by drawing from the vast reservoir of radiant love existing within you. You need to discover your dream, to follow your bliss, and to open the channels which allow you to bring that energy into your daily life. Instead of endlessly searching for the divine in life, you need to find the connection with the divine within yourself and direct it into your life, so that you can more fully embrace the world around you.[5]

But in order to know and express your inner divinity, you must first unlock the doors which have sealed off the deeply vulnerable child within you. Allowing him/her to reveal himself is difficult, because the harshness of the world threatens to assault his weaknesses and corrupt his innocence. Such forms of psychotherapy as psychosynthesis, which utilizes visualization, and which honors the spiritual and the creative may inspire and help you. But you are likely to benefit from any psychotherapy or healing relationship with someone who has a rare sensitivity and tenderness, who embraces and loves the vulnerable, scared, exquisitely beautiful child within you, and encourages him to emerge and find his place within the world.

Twelfth House Neptune (Pisces) Images

guardian angel	soul in exile	internal tidal wave
dream within a dream	cosmic fantasy	dolphin
internal music	internal beacon	unicorn in captivity
forbidden magic	closet alchemist	waters of the soul
erosion by water	private mission	sacrificial lamb
hospital nurse	backstage dancer	secret mystic
mirage	inner vision	hidden spring

Famous People: Twelfth House Neptune

Greg Allman	Herbert Hoover	Warren Beatty
Leonard Bernstein	George Bush	Ann Landers
John Mitchell	Edgar Degas	Fritz Perls
John Lennon	J. P. Morgan	Roberto Assagioli
Rudyard Kipling	Joan of Arc	Shirley MacLaine
Edna St. Vincent Millay	Edward G. Robinson	Doris Day

Famous People: Twelfth House Pisces Planets

Evangeline Adams	Johnny Cash	Sandy Koufax
Alexander Graham Bell	Walt Whitman	Jim Backus
Mary Tyler Moore	Lynn Redgrave	Wyatt Earp

Twelfth House Neptune (Pisces)

It is in the ability to deceive one's self that the greatest talent is shown.
—Anatole France

I have a temple I do not
Visit, a heart I have forgot,
A self that I have never met,
A secret shrine.
—Charles Sorlay

Preserve, within. . . . a sanctuary, an inaccessible valley of reveries.
—Ellen Glasgow

I see myself as a sieve. Everyone's feelings flow through me.
—Liv Ullmann

If you wander around in enough confusion, you will soon find
enlightenment.
—Dicky Diehl

"This is serious," said Pooh. "I must have an escape."
—A. A. Milne

Where is your Self to be found? Always in the deepest enchantment that
you have experienced.
—Hugo von Hofmannsthal

When peace and hope and dreams were high
We followed inner visions and touched the sky.
Now we who still believe won't let them die.
—Carole King

We walk by faith, not by sight.
—Corinthians, the Bible

My kindness has always/been my curse
a tender heart is the cross I bear.
—Don Marquis

To find your own way is to follow your own bliss.
—Joseph Campbell

Pluto (Scorpio)
in the Twelfth House

Pluto's influence upon your twelfth house suggests that although you possess an internal reservoir of remarkable energy and power, you frequently feel powerless and at the mercy of the outer world. Because you fear your primal energy, you have developed a defense system which blocks your access to the deeply buried resources within you. Split off from your consciousness, this Plutonian energy may be terrifying to you, particularly because it is not integrated into your conscious self, has not become tamed or civilized through the process of socialization, and has become distorted by years of repression.

Sexual urges, passions, resentments, and hatreds from the past may all fester within you, threatening to overcome your self-control and overwhelm your consciousness. Because of the accumulated emotional charge of such energies and their threat to your sense of self, you may not be able to allow them into consciousness enough to discover the constructive power source, the aliveness, the regenerative and healing capabilities, and the inner strength which they can provide you once acknowledged, worked through, and integrated into your life.

But unless your Pluto is completely unaspected, these energies do emerge in your life. The planets which Pluto aspects carry the intense emotional charge and desire energy of Pluto. When transits aspect your Pluto, you experience periods of intense, explosive energy, as your volcanic unconscious self erupts into your consciousness. At such times, you may feel out of control, possessed, obsessed, driven by desires which you do not understand. But you also feel alive, motivated, powerful, and capable of taking charge of your life.

The twelfth house is a difficult place for Pluto, which threatens to overpower the ego wherever it occurs in the chart and to compel us to confront the dark, shadowy facets of ourselves which we would rather forget. Those of us who have twelfth house Plutos may be bearers of humanity's collective shadow. Through encountering the dark, demonic forces within ourselves, not only our own unfinished business of the past, but also the "sewage" we have absorbed and introjected from the outer world, we may be making a significant contribution to maintaining the psychic equilibrium of the collective.

But on a personal level, you may suffer from Pluto, particularly when you turn its harsh, uncompromising energy against yourself. Squares to a twelfth house Pluto can be especially tormenting, because they force you to confront your shadow energies. Although you may appear to be easygoing on the surface, inside you fight a constant battle. You judge yourself cruelly and attempt to whip yourself into shape; you deny yourself satisfactions which would ease your burdens; you feel haunted by past sins, guilts, and shames which you have never transcended. Bouts of self-hatred may lead you, against your will, to engage in self-destructive behaviors or to morbidly preoccupy yourself with thoughts of death or suicide.

To the extent that you are able to channel this Plutonian energy into physical exercise or into activities (related to the signs and houses of aspecting planets, and the house Pluto rules), you may be able to harness its constructive power and conquer obstacles in the outer world. Certainly, oppositions from Pluto to the sixth house provide outlets for accomplishment in work and health arenas. But to channel Pluto most successfully, you must first allow its energies into your consciousness.

If you block your inner life, you may avoid solitude, reflection, and quiet, relaxing activities which loosen your defenses. When alone, you engage in obsessive-compulsive rituals or demanding projects which require your full attention, and which silence the inner voices. Nevertheless, you feel pulled into states of withdrawal, as well as deep sleep. Because your dreams often portray shadow energies which disturb and haunt you, you rarely remember them. You may be too threatened by your unconscious to want to access its primal images.

On the other hand, your twelfth house Pluto may incline you to take an opposite approach to your inner life. Unable to block the turbulent forces within you, you may become a courageous, determined, ruthless explorer of your shadow self. Able to regenerate yourself through periods of solitude, you plunge into the depths your psyche, confront the angels and demons which reside there, and harness their energy for your conscious purposes. You possess unlimited resources for self-renewal, both physically and emotionally. Your life is an ongoing process of self-therapy, frequently supplemented by experiences of psychotherapy to which you commit yourself wholeheartedly in an attempt to uncover the sources of your conflicts and heal yourself of past wounds. More than most people, you are capable of profound and enduring self-transformations.

The advantages of a twelfth house Pluto are as dramatic as its liabilities. Although unable to experience sufficient energy and power in your daily life, you discover deep resources of energy, capability, stamina, and strength in crisis. For this reason, you may test yourself by involving yourself in challenging situations. You may adopt a lifestyle which forces you to confront Plutonian energies outside yourself (for example, joining the military or engaging in underworld activities); you may be drawn to work which involves helping people in crisis. Because your capacities for psychologically and physically healing yourself and others are truly remarkable, you can benefit from exercising and cultivating these talents.

"Most people live, whether physically, intellectually, or morally, in a very restricted circle of their potential being," wrote William James. "Great emergencies and crises show us how much greater our vital resources are than we had supposed." Your twelfth house Pluto indicates that your hidden resourcefulness is greater than that of the average person, who does not have such a reservoir of inner power to draw upon in times of stress.

Another talent indicated by your twelfth house Pluto is your psychological perceptiveness. Because of your access to the primal depths within yourself, you have an uncanny ability to perceive the subliminal energies within others. As a result, as you become capable of encountering shadow material, you may choose to enter a psychological field. Another alternative is work involving investigation or research.

Your twelfth house Pluto suggests that emotional turmoil early in childhood influenced you to turn your energy inward and to block from your awareness the pain, desire, or anger you were experiencing. Perhaps you were deeply shamed by your family; your parents may have communicated to you that your aggression and sexuality were unacceptable. During adolescence, you may have been so tormented by sexual impulses that you further restricted your access to the primitive but potent forces within yourself.

Sometimes, a twelfth house Pluto indicates a history of physical or emotional abuse. A Plutonian parent may have tormented you mercilessly, dominating the household, and castrating you, insuring that you would not threaten his/her power. Unable to find acceptance or constructive outlets for your desire, passion, hatred, and rage, which your parents could not cope with, you kept those emotions buried. Unable to assert your power, you developed behavior patterns which expressed your powerlessness.

Because your parents disowned their shadow selves and projected their negative qualities onto their children, you may have introjected many of their unacknowledged feelings and conflicts. Therefore, as carrier of the family shadow, you suffer not only from your own repressed desires and emotions, but also from those of your parents. Unable to handle their primitive energies, they may have needed a receptacle for their rejected selves and a target for their blame. Part of your own process of psychological integration may, as a result, involve separating out their shadow from your shadow. You need to develop compassion for yourself, to refuse to flagellate yourself for sins and crimes which were never yours, or which were the result of your parents' unresolved conflicts.

Inevitably, your family relationships formed the blueprint for your personal relationships later in life. Because you learned to hide so deeply within yourself, or hide so deeply from yourself, you may have developed a persona which is distinctly different from the intense, tumultuous Plutonian self within you. Private and withholding, you may vicariously experience the turbulence of your inner life through attracting to you people who are more emotionally expressive than you are and whose psychological conflicts are more overtly recognizable.

In your personal relationships, you are often motivated by forces which you do not acknowledge or understand. Fearful of asserting your power, you may act indirectly, manipulating others, or secretly acting out feelings of revenge through sabotaging behaviors. Afraid of being dominated, you may struggle with paranoia or anxieties of persecution, and you may fear that the other person, like your parents, will act destructively toward you. Repeating scenarios of the past, you may invite persons into your life who treat you as harshly as you treat yourself.

Coming to terms with a twelfth house Pluto is a demanding process. Sometimes, unable to access your buried energies, you attract traumatic life circumstances as a means of forcing yourself to mobilize your resources; you may, like Persephone, require abduction and rape from Pluto in order to enter the next stage of development. But the more conscious you are of your primal energies, and the more dedicated to self-development, the more likely you are to create nontraumatic situations which challenge you to discover and utilize your personal power.

"If you want to love, express hate," wrote Strephon Kaplan Williams. "If you want to hate, express love."[6] This guidance is especially useful for you, because you need to honor, own, and express the dark facets of yourself before you can recover your constructive, healing power. You need a philosophy of life which honors the darkness, and a self-image which accepts human limitation, weakness, and evil. Clinging to virtuous ideals only pushes the dark passions further down into the basement, where they fester and secretly subvert you. Through psychotherapy and trusting relationships with people who are accepting of your shadow energies, you can begin to redeem yourself and transmute the darkest, most twisted forces within you into sources of strength and potency.

The devils of the psyche grow large in the darkness of unconsciousness. You need to let your inner devil out into the open in order to observe him, discover how he feels and what he wants, and allow the open air of consciousness and the waters of compassion to transform him into a valued inner guide.[7] In order to do so, you must, however, become large enough in yourself that you can contain his terrifying energy. You may need to strengthen yourself physically through a regime of arduous exercise; you may benefit by such physical disciplines as yoga, the martial arts, rolfing; you may attain greater integration through psychotherapies such as bioenergetics or Reichian therapy, which loosen your bodily armor and help you to increase your tolerance for excitation, terror, rage, and passion.

But before you can begin the process of reowning your physical/ emotional energies, you may need to alter your attitudes. What rationalizations do you use to keep yourself powerless? What ideals do you live by which disempower you? What are the secondary gains you experience as a result of your powerlessness or victimization? What will enable you to relinquish them and create more substantial means of fulfillment and self-esteem?[8] Only by looking at your investment in keeping Pluto locked up within your twelfth house can you begin to assess the issues involved in recovering your disowned energies and in more fully experiencing and expressing your personal power.

Twelfth House Pluto (Scorpio) Images

undercover detective	bomb on a subway	dragon's cave
healer's sanctuary	basement furnace	oil well
archaeological excavation	pits of hell	volcano
hibernating dragon	outlaw in hiding	ocean bottom
archaeologist of the spirit	haunted basement	shaman
eve of destruction	underground tunnel	underwater treasure
dawn of resurrection	backseat dictator	time bomb
	phoenix in underbrush	tap root
	dream power	

Famous People: Twelfth House Pluto

Anita Bryant   Patty Hearst   Anne Frank
Muhammed Ali   Phil Berrigan   George Wallace
James Earl Ray   Margaret Mead   Patricia Schroeder
Mario Cuomo   Peter Ustinov   Mark Spitz
Roberto Assagioli   George Patton   Clara Barton
Brooke Shields   Judy Garland   Peter Hurkos
Edna St. Vincent Millay Marilyn Monroe   Salvador Dali
Jonathan Winters   Ava Gardner

Famous People: Twelfth House Scorpio Planets

Hermann Goering   Benjamin Disraeli   Chris Evert
Marc Edmund Jones   Katherine Mansfield

Twelfth House Pluto (Scorpio)

Out of the night that covers me,
Black as the pit from pole to pole,
I thank whatever gods may be
For my unconquerable soul.
                        —W. E. Henley

If there is faith that can move mountains, it is faith in your
own power.
                        —Maria Ebner von Eschenbach

And fire and ice within me fight
Beneath the suffocating night.
                        —A. E. Housman

What other dungeon is so dark as one's own heart! What jailer so
inexorable as one's self?
                        —Nathaniel Hawthorne

If these great patient/ dyings—all these agonies/
and woundbearings and blood shed/ can teach us how to live,
these dyings were not wasted.
                        —Marianne Moore

She had to live not in the passing world but in her own deeps.
                        —Pearl Buck

Hell is empty/ And all the devils are here.
                        —William Shakespeare

He imagines his worst enemy in front of him, yet carries the enemy within himself—a deadly longing for the abyss, longing to drown in his own source, to be sucked down to the realm of the Mothers. His life is a constant struggle against extinction, a violent yet fleeting deliverance from ever-lurking night.
—Carl Jung

I have been deeply aware of men's weakness. I have made myself less powerful, concealed my powers . . . If you cannot control your demons, you do harm to others. I found the way to cage mine, that was all. Anger, jealousy, revengefulness, vanity. I locked them up.
—Anaïs Nin

I know the bottom . . . I know it with my great tap root. . . . I have been there.
—Sylvia Plath

Some have named this space where we are rooted a place of death. We fix them with our callous eyes and call it, rather, a terrain of resurrection.
—Robin Morgan

For Further Understanding . . . Read Myths

Mythology records the collective unconscious of humanity, symbolically portraying the identifications and themes which we enact in our lives. We can further attune ourselves to our twelfth house energies by reading and reflecting upon myths which reveal the scripts we may live. The following myths are recommended reading for each of the following planets and signs:

Sun: Semele, Phaethon, Parsifal
Moon: Niobe, Alcestis, Artemis, Tantalus, Demeter, Io
Mercury: Philomela, Electra (in relation to Orestes)
Venus: Psyche, Arachne, Hero, Clytie
Mars: Clytemnestra, Daphne, Pasiphae, Deinara, Iphigenia, Prometheus (and Beauty from the fairy tale "Beauty and the Beast")
Jupiter: Icarus, Phaethon, Cassandra, Antigone, Ocyrhoe, Chiron
Saturn: Ariadne, Iphigenia
Uranus: Antigone, Hippolyta, the Sibyl, Prometheus
Neptune: Dionysius, Hephaistos, Orpheus, Ariadne, Salmacis, Iphigenia
Pluto: Medusa, Medea, Phaedra, Clytemnestra, Kali, Pele

Although Liz Greene, in *The Astrology of Fate*,[9] does not discuss the twelfth house, her interpretation of myths which are relevant to the signs is an inspirational and helpful guide to uncovering the deep psychological issues and complexes related to each sign and planetary ruler.

The Lunar Nodes in the Twelfth House

Not only the twelfth house, but also the South Node of the Moon indicate the strengths and weaknesses which we have brought into this incarnation. The South Node is our line of least resistance; we tend to retreat into expressing its sign and house because we feel secure functioning on that level and because we so naturally express its energies and pay attention to that area of our lives. However, in this lifetime, we are not meant to focus unduly upon our South Node qualities and interests, because doing so leads us to regress and eventually limits the opportunities open to us.

We need to use our South Node (our innate talent) rather than be used by it. Emphasizing this facet of ourselves to the detriment of our other qualities and interests may keep us bound to the past, frustrated, and unsatisfied. Rather, our task is to learn to use our South Node abilities in order to fulfill the meaning of the North Node in our charts, according to its placement by sign and house, and also according to the placement of its dispositor.

Developing our North Node is not usually easy for us, particularly if it squares or opposes planets in our chart; we feel drawn continually back to the sign and house of the South Node. But by actively expressing the energies of the North Node's sign and by developing the capacity to operate effectively in the area of life denoted by the North Node's house, we open a cosmic channel. We attract helping, healing energies to ourselves, awaken the talents and strengths which we were born to manifest, and experience the immeasurable satisfaction of having fulfilled our personal life task.[10]

The South Node in the Twelfth House

Your placement of the South Node in the twelfth house indicates that you are drawn into the cloudy, chaotic realms of your subconscious. You tend to retreat from the world and lose yourself in the pleasures and pains of your emotions, dreams, and fantasies. Solitude is comfortable for you; you would rather be alone and attune yourself to your inner world than focus upon the often threatening demands and activities of the world around you.

Most likely, you meditate or seek self-transcendence or wisdom in a religion or spiritual path which is meaningful to you. You may also feel the call to serve humanity, perhaps by working with the disturbed, the ill, or the handicapped. But whether or not you are able to help them become attuned to their internal sources of strength and nourishment will depend upon whether or not you yourself have become mired in your own psychological dross, surrendering yourself completely to its illusions and confusions. You need to learn to regulate the valve that leads to your subconscious, turning inward to become aware of your feelings and fantasies, accepting them, and then channelling that energy outward into loving, inspired action.

Your North Node in the sixth house requires you to turn your attention outward. You, least of all, need to swim throughout your life in murky psychological waters. Your task is that of acting upon your ideals and visions in a practical way, as well as maintaining your physical well-being, and promoting the health of the people around you. What, after all, does your spirituality mean if you are unwilling to empty a bedpan? What satisfaction do your fantasies really provide you if you are unwell, or unable to apply yourself to your job or daily tasks? You need to be of use, to provide some essential service, to order your thinking, to structure your time, to relate sensitively to co-workers, and to assume responsibility on the job. Even the most menial work can be spiritually satisfying to you if you bring to it the attitudes of humility and compassion.

Because you need to remain aware of the interconnectedness between mind and body, you may benefit from working in the health professions, particularly in the holistic health field. An important focus of your life should be cultivation of a healthy body/mind relationship—developing habits of constructive, realistic thinking, monitoring your diet, and getting sufficient exercise. Even when you are ill, you are likely to experience opportunities for growth and chances to learn to cope more effectively with your thoughts, feelings, and physical being. Through these experiences you will be gaining the insight necessary to help the people in your daily life overcome their psychological or physical problems.

The North Node in the Twelfth House

With the North Node in the twelfth house and the South Node in the sixth house, you are naturally inclined to be of service in a job and are usually organized, efficient, and responsible in fulfilling your duties. Particularly at home in a health profession, you are willing to perform menial tasks, provided that you feel that the work you are doing is useful to other people. You may, however, tend to lose yourself in some of the details of your daily routine and you may worry or brood about the facets of your job which are unsatisfying to you.

Your South Node in the sixth house also indicates that you may be prone to a variety of minor illnesses, or that you may overreact to aches and pains and focus unduly upon the state of your body. Nevertheless, you are likely to be attentive to your diet and conscientious about exercising regularly. You may even be vegetarian or attracted to alternative health practices such as acupuncture or spiritual healing.

Because your North Node is located in your twelfth house, you can particularly benefit from holistic or spiritual health practices. You need to pay attention to the interaction of your mind and body, as well as to delve into your psyche and discover your own healing resources. Periods of solitude are essential for you, because they allow you to contact your repressed emotions and thoughts and to experience your inner fullness.

Your task in this lifetime is not to adapt yourself to a demanding work schedule, but rather to attune yourself to your subconscious and superconscious energies—the anguish of past hurts, humiliations, and resentments, and the ecstasy or serene contentment of creative inspiration, meditation, or transcendent experience. You need to learn to let go, to be less preoccupied with the external aspects of your work and responsibilities, to begin to flow with and trust your experience, and to develop the compassion and love for humanity which will enable you to enrich people in psychological, spiritual, or creative ways.

You, more than anyone, need to explore your psyche, to listen to your dreams and personal guidance, and to periodically retreat from the world in order to contact your inner source. Your twelfth house journeys may lead you on meandering paths through dense jungles and barren plains, but they will also open you to ethereal heights and wellsprings of contentment. Because you gain through inward exploration, you are also likely to inspire others to develop the inner strength and clarity they need to overcome their physical or psychological problems, and to discover their true, essential selves.

PART III

The Psychodynamics of Twelfth House Conflicts & the Process of Integration

The Disowned Self

Many of us who have twelfth house planets suffer from psychological maladies related to disowned facets of ourselves. We feel incomplete; we know that something important is missing in our lives, beyond the right relationship or right job or right amount of money in the bank. We act in predetermined ways, driven by past patterns, powerless to create the kind of change and fulfillment we long for. Often, we do not even know what is missing, or what we are seeking; nor do we, accustomed to the familiarity of our suffering and disillusionment, dare to hope for more than we already have.

When we have disowned parts of ourselves, we experience an emptiness at the core of our being, a lack of vitality and life energy. We struggle with depression, with lack of passion for life, or we direct our passion toward persons and experiences which do no more than momentarily fill the inner void. Compulsions, obsessions, addictions of all kinds—alcohol, food, sex, work, spending, housecleaning, (and yes, even astrology)—can then preoccupy us. We become attached to activities which keep us from feeling our real needs, fears, desires, and pain, and which provide us with the immediate gratification which enables us to get through the day.

Most of the time, we are not conscious of our real feelings and needs. We live by "shoulds" and "oughts," unassimilated introjects from our parents and from society, proscriptions for life which influence our choices and behaviors, and prevent us from hearing the voice of our true selves. Damaged by childhood trauma, we may have developed a split within ourselves in regard to thought, feeling, and action, so that we are not able to function as congruent, empowered individuals. Instead of feeling, we emotionalize; instead of thinking, we intellectualize; instead of acting wisely, we act by impulse or compulsion, or avoid action altogether.

When we are out of touch with important facets of ourselves, we become smaller and our problems become larger. We develop physical and emotional armor which keeps the repressed feelings and thoughts out of awareness. Yet the more rigid we become, the less capable we are of handling the feelings and frustrations of daily life. We cannot take responsibility for what is out of our awareness; we cannot make realistic choices about parts of ourselves we are unable to encounter. We find ourselves acting out of subconscious motivation, rationalizing our actions according to beliefs and principles we only half believe, and justifying ourselves when our behaviors prove to be self-defeating. Attempting to build our self-esteem by boosting our self-image, we become diminished, because we are unable to maintain our self-worth in the face of a reality which proves to us again and again that we have little power to shape our lives.

The more we disown facets of ourselves, the more frightening the disowned energy becomes. Locked in the dark closet of the twelfth house, away from the light of consciousness and the air of human interaction, it grows distorted over time. When, triggered by transits and progressions, it momentarily bursts out of hiding, it appalls us to such an extent that we exert more energy to keep the closet door closed, and the unwelcome intruder out of our awareness.

But disowned parts of ourselves cannot be locked away. They accumulate energy around themselves. They create compulsions, obsessions, addictions, and symptoms. They attract people and circumstances which require us to encounter their energy in projected form. Whatever we attempt to push aside returns in disguised apparel, threatening us, demanding our attention. In our dreams, invaders and intruders appear, indications of personalities within us that have become hostile in their attempts to gain our attention, because we have been hostile toward them. We have ignored them, belittled them, harassed them, and disdainfully pushed them away. We have done to ourselves what our parents did to our vulnerable, emerging true selves when we were young, which was all they knew how to do, because their selves were shaped by parents who did the same to them.

Although this process may have its origin in past lives, and is imprinted upon us through our horoscopes before we have interacted with our parents, our early childhood experience inevitably reflects the psychodynamics of our dissociation. We may need to blame our parents, in order to experience and work through our anger, but we also need to realize not only that they too have been influenced by subconscious forces, but also that we have been born with inner filters that selectively perceive and process our experience. We are most aware of, and most influenced by, those events which express our planetary energies.

How does this process of disowning a part of ourselves occur? How does a part of ourselves, a planetary energy, become a not-me, an unconscious self, with a life of its own outside of our awareness?

Family Dynamics

The family scenario is as follows: Our parents have developed defense systems in order to cope with anxiety and maintain a tolerable level of self-esteem. They are stressed by the demands of work, marriage, and the pain of their own disappointments and unmet needs. Then we enter the world and begin to express a wide range of feelings, impulses, needs, and thoughts. Inevitably, some facets of ourselves grate against the armor our parents have erected. Blocking awareness of feelings and experiences which threaten them, they push us aside with the same ruthlessness, the same unconsciousness, with which they push aside their own inner demons.

Most of our parents are guilty of emotional child abuse—often unintentional, and often unacknowledged. When their attitudes and behaviors were antithetical to our emerging child selves, when they rejected and humiliated us for expressing parts of ourselves which they did not like, we felt beaten, threatened, negated. Totally dependent upon our parents, and craving their love, approval, and protection, we could not afford to alienate them. We learned to hide the feelings, needs, and impulses which led to the trauma of rejection or punishment. Unable to express themselves, these parts of ourselves soon burrowed deep within us, and disappeared from our consciousness.

Meanwhile, we outwardly expressed those facets of ourselves which elicited our parents' acceptance and approval. We developed a persona, an outer self, which, if too separate and distinct from our true inner selves, became a false self. To the extent to which we as adults identify with our false self, and have lost the feelings and needs of our true self, we lack vitality and the capacity to touch and be touched by the world around us.

Perhaps our mothers never really felt loved, and experienced such overwhelming pain when encountering loving feelings that they could not tolerate our affection. When we expressed our innocent love and adoration, they may have slapped us aside, fearful of receiving what they had always wanted, because in order to take it in, they would have to feel and let go of the pain that had filled their empty spaces. We learn that our love is undesirable. We learn that to love is to be rejected. We become afraid of, and ashamed of, our need to give and receive love. We learn to live with our Venus in hiding, in the twelfth house.

When a parent is unable to acknowledge or express a particular energy and belittles that energy in us, we bear not only the burden of our own wounded self, but also the burden of carrying the energy of the planet which our parent has projected onto us. We carry our parents' shadow selves.

Consider the following: Perhaps our parents feel incomplete and powerless. By having children—small, helpless creatures who are dependent upon them—they can experience their power to impact reality. Unable to bear weakness or vulnerability, they disdain our weakness and vulnerability. But simultaneously, they act in ways to keep us weak, infantile, and dependent. They convince us that we are stupid, incompetent, unable to manage our own affairs. They starve us emotionally, indulge us with sweets, then berate us for overeating. They create double-binds which make us feel that we are crazy, and all the more dependent upon them to protect us from our own incapacities.

When we attempt to be assertive, capable, independent, or self-sufficient, they belittle us, just as they belittle us for being weak and needy. But they need us to express their own despised inner child, so that they do not have to encounter within themselves that which most threatens them. They require that we carry their rejected shadow, that we live with our Sun or Mars or Uranus or Pluto in the twelfth house, unable to fully experience and develop our individuality and power.

Consider also: Our parent has a monopoly on a particular planetary energy. Daddy has a t-square to Mars in Aries. Only Daddy can yell, only Daddy can express anger, only Daddy can demand that his needs be satisfied. There is no room for our Mars to exist in a monopolistic family. Or perhaps Mommy has Mercury in Leo rising and wants an appreciative audience. She melodramatizes her thoughts and feelings. She tells us all her problems. She does not want to hear our experience, because we exist for her only as ears, a sounding board, through which she can come to terms with her unheard inner child. There is no room for our twelfth house Mercury in Cancer, except as a mirror to her Mercury. As a result, we learn to listen, but we never learn to express ourselves. We never adequately develop or trust our own ability to communicate.

What happens to the parts of the true self which burrow within us, which dive deep beneath the waters of our twelfth house? Many possibilities exist. Sometimes an energy, when completely repudiated, becomes fixated in the "id," our storehouse of repressed primal energy. We experience "horizontal splitting"—one facet of ourselves becomes completely inaccessible, and retreats into the engine room of our twelfth house, secretly directing our lives. All our choices and behaviors may then be motivated by hidden fear (Saturn), anger (Mars), desire for glory (Sun), or need for caretaking (Moon). Yet we remain completely unaware of, and defended against, these particular energies.

More frequently, we experience "vertical splitting." A part of ourselves does not become completely inaccessible, but appears and disappears from our consciousness without warning. We are somewhat dissociated or fragmented. For example, we may live without awareness of our twelfth house Neptune and feel trapped in mundane reality, until Neptune bursts forth and unexpectedly intoxicates us with liquor, with fantasy, with devotion to a guru, or with creative inspiration. Then once again, we lose awareness of Neptune and make choices which do not take our twelfth house Neptunian needs into consideration.

Early traumas may result in fixations. The earlier the trauma, the more likely it is to become part of our psychological structure, which is malleable when we are infants, but progressively rigidifies. Fixations that develop in order to cope with traumatic feelings early in life may persist, although we have forgotten the original trauma. They may be unrelated to that trauma, a means of keeping it out of consciousness (for example, we read incessantly, glorifying the life of the mind in order to keep from feeling), or they may be a more direct means of insuring that the painful original experience (or series of experiences) will not recur.

Perhaps we stole our brother's teddy bear and ripped it up, and were unfairly punished when Daddy gave all our Christmas gifts to the little creep on Christmas morning. What a cruel punishment for a Taurus child! What intolerable pain and deprivation we felt that day, such terrible pain that we decided never again, never never again would we suffer the loss of the material possessions which we so dearly wanted.

The next week, in spite of freezing weather, we sold lemonade on the street, attempting to earn enough money to buy ourselves out of our inner poverty. Influenced by our twelfth house Pluto in Leo square Jupiter in Scorpio on the second/third house cusp, we decided that the most important thing in life was to make money, or to convince other people to give us material goods, or to symbolically return to ourselves the Christmas gifts that were taken from us so many years ago. Twenty years later, we are operating our own retail store, receiving deliveries every day, obsessed with the business, still attempting to undo the damage of that half-remembered Christmas morning.

Some fixations, compulsions, and obsessions are "ego-syntonic." This means they are not at odds with our self-image, our values, our aims. They can help us to earn a living, attract a partner, develop a skill. Because they work for us and seem constructive, we remain unaware of the wound which festers beneath them, which may bleed internally, and even become a real physical wound or illness if too severe. Often, we develop a self-image, a value system, and a set of goals in order to support our fixation, or to avoid the reexperience of an unbearable trauma. In order to uncover and heal the hidden wound, we must then dismantle the self-structure and life-structure we have erected in order to keep it hidden. Most of us are not willing to allow such dissolution to occur, unless the pain of our life circumstances is so intolerable that we begin to "break down" in order to "break through."

Defense Mechanisms

Our character structure develops early in life. To the extent that we have lost parts of our true selves, and have developed false selves, we construct inner images and ideals to compensate for our missing pieces. "I have no right to exist outwardly, in reality," our true self tells us, "So I will compensate inwardly, in fantasy." Unable to relinquish our infantile grandiosity by discovering and exercising our true powers, we secretly maintain it. We erect an inflated self-image to cloak our stunted limbs, to conceal our wounds, to boost our flagging self-esteem. We glorify one facet of ourselves, and demean another. Not having enough self, we become attached to our self-image, identifying with certain facets of ourselves which we value, and repressing their opposite. What we repress becomes part of our shadow self, relegated to twelfth house unconsciousness.

The inflated, ideal self-image and the demeaned self are related. When we are loved for who we are, in our totality, we become capable of expressing and valuing all facets of ourselves. We do not need to develop an inflated self-image to compensate, or to hold inwardly to an ideal self which is worthy of love. We develop our self-esteem through being and developing our true selves. But when parts of ourselves are rejected, when we are loved only when we are perfect (or believe that we might be loved if only we were more perfect), we learn that all hope of meeting our needs lies in holding to and actualizing the ideal, rather than being who we really are. We seek satisfaction in life by rigorously shaping ourselves to fit our ideal images, or by seeking refuge in fantasies of future possibilities and potentials. To test those fantasies in reality is threatening, because our self may not be substantial enough to risk failure and the collapse of the inner images which sustain us.

Thus, if we have a twelfth house Moon, we may hold onto our fantasies of becoming the perfect caregiver, the dedicated social worker, the universal mother, available to all the hospitalized patients who need us, rather than risk letting our needs be known in an intimate relationship, and allowing ourselves to give and receive the personal nurturance we desire. How deep, how infantile, how insatiable our real need might be, if we allow it to surface! How much safer to meet it vicariously, to create substitute experiences, to boost ourselves with fantasy, rather than feel the hunger of our inner child, rather than risk exposing her again to a world which might not be able to tolerate her need.

Therefore, at an early age, we begin to distort reality by constructing defenses which preserve our self-image, maintain self-esteem, and protect ourselves from traumatic feelings. Intellectualizations and rationalizations support our self-structure and our behaviors. "Projection" allows us to encounter rejected facets of ourselves in the world outside of ourselves, rather than experience the intolerable threat to our self-image of confronting facets of ourselves we are not yet able to assimilate. Through "symptom-formation"—obsessions, compulsions, fixations, somatizations (bodily expressions of emotional conflicts)—we focus the intense energy of our conflicts onto arenas where we can reenact the original traumas in ways which we can tolerate. Through "reaction formation," we maintain our self-esteem by convincing ourselves that we feel the opposite of what we actually feel. Denying our twelfth house Mars, we act lovingly toward those we hate. Denying our twelfth house Saturn, we pretend to desire that which we fear.

The nature of our defense mechanisms can often be surmised from the astrological chart. A woman with three Gemini planets and a twelfth house Moon may be prone to intellectualize about her feelings. A man with a twelfth house Venus in Aries, which rules both his first and sixth houses, may translate his Venusian conflicts into physical form, perhaps by becoming a diabetic. A Libran woman with Moon in Pisces and a twelfth house Mars/Pluto conjunction may be prone to reaction formation, driving herself to win the approval of those she hates, but thinks she loves. A man with his twelfth house ruler, Uranus, positioned within his seventh house may project his erratic, individualistic hidden self onto a partner, and never encounter his own Uranian nature.

Many defense mechanisms contribute to our lives. The displacement of our traumas in regard to emotional deprivation may motivate us to develop our professional capacities in order to feel the adult satisfactions of productive work and achieve financial security. Sublimating emotional conflicts into artistic expression may be emotionally fulfilling and may result in art work which wins us acclaim and inspires others. Seeking to atone for our guilt, for real or imagined sins of the past, may provide motivation for social work, and enable us to feel the self-esteem which results from making a viable social contribution.

We need our defense mechanisms. But we need defense mechanisms which minimally distort our reality, and which provide constructive outlets through which we can work through our emotional conflicts. The less we repress important facets of ourselves, the more likely we are to make choices which meet our needs and which contribute to our well-being.

On Repression

We repress feelings, impulses, needs, desires, and thoughts which were unacceptable in childhood, and which we fear would be unacceptable today. We repress those facets of ourselves which might threaten relationships which are important to us, and upon which we depend. We repress that which threatens our identity or self-image, which causes intolerable fear or pain, or which might result in shame or humiliation. If we have poor impulse control, we repress desires which might become uncontrollable impulses and result in loss of control. We also repress parts of ourselves which are so at odds with other parts of ourselves that we are unable to tolerate the anxiety of the inner conflict.

Our capacity to regain awareness of repressed twelfth house energy may depend upon the relationship in our charts between the kinds of energies in the twelfth house and those energies outside it. Can our conscious selves, our egos, absorb and assimilate these twelfth house energies without breaking?

Certainly, if we have a Pisces Sun, Mercury, and Venus, we may be able to recover the disowned energies of our twelfth house Neptune, since we are already identified with many facets of our Neptunian self. But what if we have a Libra stellium and a Pisces Moon, and what if our Mars/Jupiter conjunction in Scorpio in the twelfth house squares Pluto in Leo? What if we have erected a self-image, value system, lifestyle, and relationship network to support the values of love, harmony, and symbiotic unity with all life? How do we account for our Mars/Jupiter in Scorpio? What happens when transiting Pluto crosses this conjunction, and we discover the degree of our hatred and rage (before we can awaken to our constructive power)?

Not only do we develop self-systems and life-systems to maintain our repressions, but we also repress experiences which threaten the inner and outer structures we have created—structures which are especially precarious when they are built upon one dimension of ourselves, at the expense of its opposite. The more we identify with one facet of ourselves, and need that identification in order to have an identity and maintain our self-esteem, the more we need to repress the opposite qualities.

Maintaining our identity and our self-esteem are not necessarily related. Some of us may indeed have negative or diffuse identities, based upon absorbing the dark shadow energies our parents projected upon us, therefore making us unable to acknowledge the light. Our parents, mired in their own pain and disillusionment, may not have been able to tolerate the life-affirming energies of our Sun, Jupiter, or Venus, which are relegated to the twelfth house. We may have discovered early in life that expressing the intellectual genius of our twelfth house Uranus aroused the jealousy and resentment of our parents and peers, whose scorn contributed to our sense of isolation and alienation.

Perhaps our innate talents were at odds with our sex role conditioning or our religious upbringing. A five year old daughter's wrestling skills are not likely to be valued by a Cancerian mother who wears lace dresses and upholds the "sugar and spice" theory of femininity. Inevitably, the daughter will then wrestle all her life with her twelfth house Arian Mars. What about the Pisces boy with Moon in the twelfth house, who grew up on a military base, with a father who espoused macho values? What is he to do with his sensitivity, his responsiveness to others, his spirituality, and his creative talents? What about the dynamic, passionate young girl with a twelfth house Venus/Mars conjunction in Scorpio, sent by her parents to a Catholic boarding school? To what extent will the nuns and priests who raise her help her to value her passion and her emerging sexuality? To what extent will two self-effacing missionaries honor the exhibitionistic, dramatic talents of their son, who has a twelfth house Leo stellium?

If we are not grounded in our bodies, if we are emotionally unstable, we may fear owning our positive qualities. Better to feel low and remain close to the ground than risk becoming manic or egotistical. Better to refrain from flying than be tempted to fly too high with our newly discovered talents and risk the inevitable fall from the heights.

Inner Persecutors & Demons

Our "light shadow," the positive dimensions of qualities which we repress, may exist in our twelfth houses as internal helpers, guides, or rescuers which support us in times of crisis. On the other hand, our "dark shadow," the negative dimensions of those qualities, may absorb the self-hatred of our internal repressor and contribute to self-defeating behaviors.

When we repress a facet of ourselves, at least two parts of ourselves are involved in the repression—the guardian of the gate of the twelfth house, who is our inner repressor/persecutor/protector, and the part of ourselves (the internal personality) that we repress. The degree of anger, hatred, or fear involved in the repressing process is related to the degree of anger, hatred, and fear we experienced from our parents and other adults who emotionally impacted us, as well as the anger, hatred, and fear we felt in response and may not have been able to express. We direct toward ourselves the feelings which were directed toward us, or which we were not able to direct toward them. We usually are not able to let go of these feelings toward ourselves until we can translate the intrapsychic process back into the original interpersonal process which occurred—until we can experience the voices of the repressors and respond to them in their original form.

Often, these voices become internal persecutors. Their voice is the voice of hatred. The negative messages they give us are debilitating not merely because of their content ("You're no good," "No one will ever love you," "There you go again, acting like a jerk," "What's wrong with you that you can't hold a job?" "You can't do anything right," "What's the point of taking the risk? Nothing you do ever works, anyway," etc.) but also because of the degree of hatred which they direct toward us. Although the judgment we proclaim upon ourselves and our lives is usually distorted, generalized, and catastrophic, sometimes it may even be correct. The problem may be not only the nature of the judgment, but the underlying hatred with which it is proclaimed.

At times, a cautionary voice may need to hold us back from unwise behaviors. We need to repress, or to suppress, many of our impulses. But where is the concern for our well-being, the compassion, the love, the forgiveness with which we could restrain and warn ourselves? Why must we whip ourselves into submission, destroying our confidence, our hope, our vitality?

Often, the voice of the inner persecutor is not our own voice at all, but the introjected voice of a parent, distorted and intensified over time by fear and by our own unexpressed anger. The voice is judgmental, condescending, critical, overbearing, unforgiving. It has no tolerance for human limitations, for mistakes, for imperfection, for weakness. Sometimes it is contradictory, urging us to restrain from action and then condemning us for holding back.

Although internal persecutors may be associated with any twelfth house energies, they are most apparent when Mars, Pluto, or Saturn are associated with the twelfth house. In these cases, the energy of the repressor and the energy of the repressed personality are integrally related. We may not even be able to differentiate them. Ruthlessly, we rage against our rage; or we panic, terrified that we will subvert ourselves with our fear.

Understanding the nature of our twelfth house persecutors raises important philosophical questions about good and evil. Are our introjected persecutors merely an expression of our own fear and our parents' fear? Are the distorted personalities residing in our twelfth house distorted merely because the healthy, natural impulses of our inner child have been unduly restrained, and our integrity violated? Are we naturally good and life-affirming, but inclined to develop evil or life-denying propensities when our basic instincts are severely frustrated? Or are the twisted energies locked within our twelfth house a testimony of our innate evil, our death instinct, our hatred for life? Are we to believe, like Freud, that we human beings are a hotbed of seething destructive impulses—or that we are guilty of original sin? How do we account for the reality that our internal persecutors and our distorted twelfth house personalities may indeed seem to be (and may sometimes express themselves in ways that are) terrifyingly demonic?

I cannot assume to answer questions which philosophers and psychologists have never been able to answer sufficiently. I can only tentatively state my beliefs. Once I believed I knew the answers: Love reigns supreme; we are all, at our core, beings of light. But a decade of post-Saturn return confrontations with the dark side of life has tempered my Sagittarian optimism. I now believe in the reality of evil, but not that it is an innate and inevitable human propensity. I also believe in the reality of good. Basic human instincts may be neither good nor evil, but perhaps are neutral energies which when nurtured with love, respect, and wise, compassionate limit-setting become vehicles of the good forces which exist in the universe. When unduly frustrated, deprived, and violated, such instincts may attract and express the evil which indeed may exist as a real, terrifying, and autonomous dimension of life.

Within our twelfth house, particularly when it is tenanted or ruled by Mars, Pluto, or Saturn, evil may reside. Demonic energies may occasionally burst into consciousness. But this does not mean that our basic nature is evil or demonic. What it means is that intense suffering and deprivation have deformed us and attracted to us demonic energies which we can harness and transmute—preserving the life-affirming, dynamic, vital, creative energy that exists within the demonic, while overthrowing, dissolving, or banishing its destructive, life-denying, evil propensities.

If as children we experienced more frustration, deprivation, and trauma than we could handle, if we were placed continually in double-bind situations in which we were powerless to impact reality or meet our needs, if we repeatedly felt terror of annihilation (loss of self) or isolation (loss of other), we may have, in our terror, developed a reservoir of archaic rage, a blind urge to destroy, and a hatred for life. Our twelfth house soil may have fertilized demonic impulses at least as much as it nurtured our true selves.

To the extent to which our parents bore within themselves the seeds of the demonic, and disowned their own cruel or aggressive impulses, we became a viable planting ground for their shadow selves. But the demonic or destructive energies which we carry are not indications of either their innate evil or our innate evil. Rather, these demonic qualities indicate wounded, twisted, distorted energies which have aligned themselves with destructive forces, only because they have not had sufficient opportunity to grow and be healed in the presence of life-affirming energies.

Do we carry the unassimilated demons of our parents, as they carry the demons transmitted by their parents, and ad infinitum back into the past, back to Adam and Eve? Are we once again proposing the doctrine of original sin, transmitted from family to family through the generations? I am no theologian. But rather than support the doctrines of Christianity, or the doctrines of Judaism, I am inclined to view the roots of the good/evil dilemma we experience as related to the mind/body, spirit/flesh, dark/light split that permeates Western (and many Eastern) religious traditions. If God is all good, then Satan must exist to bear God's shadow self. If we honor certain qualities as virtues, then other qualities must become vices, and become relegated to the shadow dimension of life. Whenever we consciously identify with one quality, we unconsciously express or attract its opposite. Lucifer the lightbearer aimed for too much goodness, and became evil. We likewise, rejecting unpleasant facets of ourselves and aspiring to too much goodness, become that which we reject.

The Dynamics of Shame

Let us return once more to the family dynamics which contribute to our patterns of repression and self-rejection. In order to understand and begin to transcend the self-negating facets of our twelfth house dynamics, we may need to be willing to uncover our shame. Often, twelfth house energies are twisted by the pain of deep-seated shame and humiliation, against which we must aggressively defend.

When we are shamed, we feel inferior, diminished, and insufficient as human beings. Our sense of self is trampled. We lose personal dignity and suffer a blow to our self-esteem. We feel ourselves to be bad, unworthy, perhaps even less than human. We experience shame not when we choose to act against our best interests or our parents' wishes (actions more likely to elicit guilt), but rather when we are humiliated, or fear humiliation for feelings and behaviors over which we experience little control.

We are ashamed of our forbidden appetites, wishes, and desires. We are ashamed of being unable to restrain our impulses, of failing to control our bodies, of being carried away with unacceptable emotions. We are ashamed of not living up to the standards of our sex role identity, or of not mastering developmental tasks at the expected time. We are ashamed of regressing, of remaining dependent, of holding onto childish behaviors when we are supposed to be mature or independent.

Usually, we experience shame when we unwittingly break parental and social taboos. We have not lived up to the standards of behavior which our parents and which society have demanded of us. We are not behaving in a civilized manner. Too great a disparity exists between our actual self and our self-ideal, particularly in regard to the facets of ourselves indicated by our twelfth house energies.

As adults, we feel ashamed of feelings, thoughts, and behaviors for which we were shamed as children. A twelfth house Moon may indicate traumatic experiences of being shamed for our weakness, vulnerability, or need. A twelfth house Pluto suggests shame in regard to toilet training (issues of holding and letting go), our sexuality, our aggression. A twelfth house Saturn suggests that we were shamed for our fears and for our attempts to prove our competence through schoolwork or chores.

Recently, psychological literature has been focusing upon the dynamics of shame-based families—families in which parents frequently and cruelly shame their children. Shame-based families are often addictive-families, in which members seek solace from the traumatic feelings induced by shame and humiliation. According to Merle Fossum and Marilyn Mason,[1] shame-based families are often characterized by: rigid rules, perfectionism, patterns of blame and denial, lack of empathy and compassion, focus on image and standards rather than reality, treating each other as things rather than persons, boundary invasion, lack of authenticity, and addictive or compulsive behaviors developed in order to control anxiety and avoid the real, painful issues. Often, in order to maintain the family system, parents subtly encourage in their children the very behaviors which they also shame.

In *Facing Shame: Families in Recovery*, Fossum and Mason present "Eight Rules in Shame-based Families":

1. CONTROL. Be in control of all behaviors and interactions.

2. PERFECTION. Always be "right." Do the "right" thing.

3. BLAME. If something doesn't happen as you planned, blame someone (self or other).

4. DENIAL. Deny feelings, especially the negative or vulnerable ones like anxiety, fear, loneliness, grief, rejection, need.
5. UNRELIABILITY. Don't expect reliability or constancy in relationships. Watch for the unpredictable.
6. INCOMPLETENESS. Don't bring transactions to completion or resolution.
7. NO TALK. Don't talk openly and directly about shameful, abusive or compulsive behavior.
8. DISQUALIFICATION. When disrespectful, shameful, abusive or compulsive behavior occurs, disqualify it, deny it, or disguise it.[2]

The level of emotional trauma which we may have experienced if we grew up in a shame-based family may be so deep that we must utilize all our survival and defense mechanisms to prevent the restimulation of our shame-based wounds. Yet simultaneously, we keep repeating the behaviors for which we were shamed as children, and for which we feel ashamed as adults.

Maintaining the Family System

Whatever patterns of behavior contributed to our survival, our sense of security, and our defense mechanisms as children become a part of our character structure. Our sense of self develops, to some extent, through introjecting our parents' attitudes and behaviors. As adults, we continue to parent ourselves in similar ways, relying upon internal messages, outer objects, and life experiences in order to preserve the familiar reality of childhood. If a parent, who has a t-square to a ninth house Mercury, lectures us repeatedly about good and evil, and obsesses about the future, we unconsciously express our twelfth house Jupiter by lecturing ourselves, delivering lectures to our students, and focusing upon tomorrow's potentials rather than today's realities. If we have learned how to subtly rebel against a parent who has Sun in Aquarius opposing Saturn, and who condemns us for our rebellious, nonconformist impulses, then we find ways to secretly rebel against our own internalized standards, while simultaneously judging ourselves for our unreliability and erratic behavior.

The greater the rejection we experienced, and the greater the separation anxiety we felt as a result of our parents' emotional or physical absence, the more we cling to the internalized images and ideals which provide for us the security of parental protection. The less our true selves experienced the support necessary for growth and for developing a solid base of self-esteem, the more we learned to rely upon the internalized parent and its attitudes, standards, and judgments. Although as adolescents we may have perceived and exaggerated our parents' imperfections, as young children we needed to idealize and depend upon them in order to survive. The badness we perceived in them we usually relegated to our own selves (with the help of their judgments), since being bad, helpless children who are dependent upon good, reliable parents was less anxiety-provoking than being good, helpless children dependent upon bad, unreliable parents.

As adults, not fully differentiated from our parents, we remain invested in maintaining our inner child's reality in order to preserve the security of the parent/child bond. When we attempt to change attitudes and behaviors which threaten our inner reality system, we may experience the primitive, overwhelming terror of the inner child who feels abandoned in a large, frightening world without parental protection. Opening ourselves to fulfilling, strengthening, and ego-building experiences may awaken high degrees of anxiety if those experiences threaten the internalized attitudes, messages, and behaviors which have contributed to our parent/child dynamics and to our lifelong sense of self. To defy the familiar inner voices of the introjected parents may arouse such separation anxiety and guilt that we punish ourselves by defeating the very actions which would support our growth and sense of well-being.

According to Robert W. Firestone, author of *Voice Therapy: A Psychotherapeutic Approach to Self-Destructive Behavior*:

> In actuality, real gratification disturbs the fantasy process of self-gratification. Therefore, once the fantasized connection is formed and the parent introjects well established, people have strong resistance to investing emotionally in genuine, satisfying associations with others. Their principal goal is to maintain the imagined safety and security of the illusory connection with the internal parent. . . . The more the person depends on an illusion of pseudo-independence, the more *dependent* in reality he becomes.[3]

Because of our need to maintain the parental introject, and because of our desire to perceive ourselves as independent adults, we deny our process of internal dependence. We then rationalize our actions in order to support the self-image we wish to uphold, and to quiet the anxiety and guilt which bursts forth whenever we approach real individuation. Although we wage battles in the inner and outer worlds which we interpret as conflicts about money, relationships, jobs, etc.

(usually in accordance with houses ruled by our twelfth house planets and areas of life represented by their aspects), often the real battles are the battles with our fear and with our guilt.

Guilt, Suffering, & Self-Defeating Behavior

Neurotic guilt is the guilt we experience when we attempt to separate from the familiar patterns of our childhood, and to act in ways which would elicit our parents' disapproval. Our conscience threatens us, and seeks to punish us for our misbehavior by sabotaging our actions, withdrawing support to our self-esteem, making us suffer for breaking family taboos.

Existential guilt, on the other hand, is the guilt we experience when we retreat into fantasy, prevent ourselves from actualizing our potential and using our powers, or otherwise fail to grow in the ways we need to grow. When we hold back, we encounter existential guilt; when we move forward, we confront neurotic guilt. Only by supporting and strengthening our urge for self-esteem, growth, and fulfillment, and by battling the voices of neurotic guilt and anxiety, can we begin to actualize our true selves and discover our real capabilities.

But many of us are addicted to suffering. As if we possess within ourselves a happiness/unhappiness thermostat which we must maintain at a temperature set in our childhood, we keep creating experiences guaranteed to reestablish the initial setting. If our thermostat was set at 38 degrees, and we allow ourselves for weeks to experience the warmth of 75 degree inner weather, then the inner child, afraid of unfamiliar temperatures, will create a deep freeze in order to bring the average temperature for the month or year to a level closer to our 38 degree requirement. How relentlessly, how secretly, how cleverly that frightened child within us manipulates the controls! How little power we have to regulate that thermostat until we are able to encounter her, to hear her fear, and learn to soothe her anxiety; until we are able to create for her enough fulfilling, ego-building, life-affirming, growthful experiences which become more desirable than the old, familiar securities she has known.

Meanwhile, we choose to suffer. We suffer in order to feel alive when we are dead to our true feelings and energies. We suffer because our internal Furies must punish us for real and imagined wrongdoings. We suffer in order to maintain our unworthy, unredeemable self-image, in order to elicit sympathy and help, in order to keep from turning our anger against others, and in order to control the threats of loss and disillusionment by doing to ourselves what we fear others will do to us. We keep ourselves inadequate and incompetent because we fear our aggression and power, we fear others' resentment and envy, and above all, we fear surpassing our parents and experiencing the inner parents' rage, rejection, or abandonment of our inner child.

We give ourselves negative messages; we become addicted; we involve ourselves in hurtful love affairs; we choose jobs which will not satisfy us or allow us to experience our real capacities. We deny ourselves pleasure, sexual satisfaction, meaningful relationships. We refrain from pursuing goals we value, and utilizing talents which fulfill us and build our self-esteem. We choose to repeat self-defeating behaviors and to maintain our stance as victims—helpless children in a crazy world ruled by oppressive parental voices.[4]

Why? Because we are afraid. Because we are too identified with the fearful, helpless inner child and the rejecting inner parent. Because we have not fully experienced and internalized role models for other ways of being. Because we have not yet developed a compassionate, wise internal parent, which can help us to uncover, discover, and raise our true self, so that he/she grows into a competent and healthy adult.

If we had indulgent parents, who too easily encouraged our weaknesses, inflated our budding egos, encouraged dependency, and led us to believe that we were entitled to special treatment and care, we may not be plagued by rejecting inner voices. Yet we may nevertheless be mired in self-defeating patterns which undermine us, and we may lack confidence in our adult selves. The indulgent parent may have been just as detrimental to our well-being as a rejecting parent might have been. Both types approach parenting according to their narcissistic needs, rather than our needs as children both to be children, and to develop the capacities which will enable us to become integrated, well-functioning, and reasonably happy adults.

We may hold onto our suffering and our self-defeating patterns for many reasons. We may fear separating from the security of our parental voices. We may fear relinquishing the gratification of our internalized indulgent parent voice. We may also be unwilling to let go of our anger—our anger toward our parents, which we turn against ourselves, and which we use as a subtle means of maintaining inner power and of wreaking a secret revenge. "Victory through defeat" may be our motto. By keeping ourselves inadequate and victimized, we may disappoint the parts of our parents which are legitimately invested in our growth; we may refuse to give them and others the satisfaction of having contributed to our well-being; we may feel entitled to attention, special treatment, sympathy, and above all, freedom from the responsibility of functioning as an autonomous adult.

We cannot begin to rework the patterns of the past until we are conscious of our anger and learn to redirect it. We cannot begin to create the life satisfactions we seek until we are conscious of our fear, and learn to quiet it, move through it, and maintain our commitment to supporting and developing our true selves.

On Fear & Anxiety

Often we are afraid, but remain unaware of our fear. We structure our lives in order to avoid unfamiliar situations which would create intolerable anxiety, or all-too-familiar situations which would reawaken traumatic feelings. Afraid of losing ourselves in others, we choose partners who are unable to be fully intimate. Afraid of losing the other and being alone with ourselves, we choose partners who need us so deeply and offer such symbiotic security that we never have to feel our terror of isolation and abandonment.

We turn our fear into addictions, compulsions, and obsessions with sex, money, food, or work. We develop psychosomatic symptoms and focus upon our ailments. We convert fear into anger, and anger into an aggressive drive for success or financial security, which we rationalize as commitment to our ideals of family and productive service. We turn fear into impulse, excitement, passion, as well as frequent and unpredictable desires for change.

When fear is fluid, it energizes us. Aware of our fear, we are able to experience it, define it, assess it realistically, and make choices which honor it or transcend it. But most of the time, we tense against our fear and develop muscular rigidities and body armor which keep fear out of consciousness. Our emotional life becomes narrow and restricted. When we do not feel our fear, we do not feel the wide range of our joys and sufferings. We become less alive. When we do not feel our fear, we too easily rationalize our actions, inhibit our risk-taking, and make choices which keep us revolving in the same circular patterns. We feel increasingly powerless, empty, unfulfilled.

Anxiety is fear which is diffuse, abstract, undefined, and which results from threatening psychological or emotional experience. Anxiety is paralyzing, immobilizing; we do not know the enemy which threatens us, or how to respond to it. Fear is generally more specific and concrete. Once we define our anxiety, and know it as fear, we feel more empowered. Aware of the enemy, we can choose the nature of our encounter, confrontation, or battle. We can allow our fear to inhibit action or moderate it, or we can choose to transcend our fear, and realistically or unrealistically take action.

Sometimes, we develop specific or concrete fears which disguise our real sources of anxiety—sources of anxiety which are common to all of us. We are afraid of unacceptable thoughts, feelings, and impulses. We are afraid of threats to our self-image, our moral standards, our sex-role identity. We are afraid of regression, experiences of shame and loss of control, of being overwhelmed by instinct and feeling. We are afraid of our own anger, aggression, and destructive tendencies. We are afraid of the suffering other people can inflict upon us—of being hurt, criticized, rejected, invalidated, deprived, humiliated, exposed, abandoned, smothered, invaded. Often, in relationships, we oscillate between our fears of too much closeness (merging, loss of self) and too much isolation (loss of other). Sometimes, we are afraid of having what we want, not only because such fulfillment directly contradicts our life script, but because we fear the pain of having and then losing what is most dear. Unmet needs may be less frightening than needs which are only temporarily met.

The greatest fears are fears of threats to our physical body and to our core psychological identity. We fear losing sources of security which help us maintain our sense of self, meet our most basic needs, and live by the values we hold dear. We fear reexperiencing the traumas which wounded us as children and adults, especially those which triggered our terror of annihilation, and may have led to a splitting or fragmentation of our core self. To the extent that we hold onto parental introjects to compensate for an incomplete sense of self, we fear whatever will threaten the existence of those introjects or inner voices, and could plunge us into the terrifying world of the abandoned, isolated, and rejected child.

Planets and signs in our twelfth house can pinpoint the kinds of experiences which give rise to our deepest fears and anxieties. Vulnerable and insecure in regard to those energies, we fear the stimulation of old wounds, the exposure of our damaged selves, the sense of being out of control and overwhelmed by parts of ourselves which we and other people have condemned, and might condemn again. Our inner repressor, the guardian of the gate of our twelfth house, ardently defends us from the pain and anxiety of reexperiencing our twelfth house wounds.

Our twelfth house Sun especially fears humiliation, exposure, and loss of self-esteem. Our twelfth house Moon is terrified of need, vulnerability, and dependency. Mercury here is sensitive about our mental and verbal capacities; Venus, our attachment to money or possessions, or our ability to give and receive love. Our twelfth house Mars defends against painful experiences involving assertion, anger, impulse control, sexuality, and physical capability. Our Jupiter fears confrontation with our patterns of excess, with greed and indulgence, with our hopes and expectations, and our philosophical or religious beliefs.

Our twelfth house Saturn fears both incompetence and competence in work, isolation, rejection, abandonment, and depression. Uranus here is anxious about eccentricity, nonconformity, unreliability, and indications of madness or genius. Twelfth house Neptune is afraid of revealing its deep-seated vulnerabilities, its spiritual or creative inspirations, its ideals and fantasies. Finally, our twelfth house Pluto is terrified of its dark primal energies—its desires, passions, destructiveness, drive for power, and preoccupation with death.

Only by acknowledging, experiencing, and confronting these fears can we transcend them. Only by opening past wounds can we heal ourselves and discover our hidden resources. Only by bearing the anxiety of separating from internalized parents and refusing to enact past scripts can we develop our true selves. Only then are we likely to make peace with ourselves, for only then will we have selves with which we can make peace.

Our Shadow Selves I

*Every man casts a shadow; not his body only, but his imperfectly
mingled spirit.*
                    —Henry David Thoreau

*A man's hatred is always concentrated on the thing that makes
him conscious of his bad qualities.*
                    —Carl Jung

*Today humanity, as never before, is split into two apparently irreconcilable
halves. The psychological rule says that when an inner situation is not made
conscious, it happens outside, as fate . . . when the individual remains un-
divided and does not become conscious of his inner opposite, the world must
perforce act out the conflict and be torn into opposing halves.*
                    —Carl Jung

*We cannot stand the sight of our dark side, so we repress it, push it under,
thinking we have thereby disposed of it. But we have not. We have simply
pushed it into a place where it both has us in its grip and automatically
projects itself on the person or the nation we do not like: so the tension and
strife and anguish we will not stand in ourselves is carelessly and irresponsibly cast out to increase the tension and strife and anguish of our world.*
                    —Charles B. Hanna

The Process of Integration: Twelfth House Liberation

The Commitment to Wholeness

When we are out of contact with our twelfth house energies, or unable to express them constructively, we often feel empty, impoverished, or powerless. We may be driven to atone for real or imagined sins of the past by taking on the role of the giver in personal and professional relationships; yet because our actions do not address the core issues, we never overcome our sense of guilt, badness, or inadequacy. If we are reasonably satisfied with our lives, and functioning adequately, if not ideally, in our roles, we may not be motivated to plumb the depths of our twelfth house, seeking to recover lost energies and to heal past wounds. But when our suffering passes our level of tolerance, and when our motivation toward growth and wholeness becomes as great or greater than our desire to cling to familiar ways, we may seek psychotherapy and/or begin the courageous process of confronting our shadow selves.

The question arises: what relationship do we want to establish with our twelfth house energies? Surely, we wish to know what they are, to be able to recognize them and define them, and to more freely choose their manner of expression. But since they are in our twelfth house, are we really supposed to express them overtly, as if they were in other houses of our chart?

Because our twelfth house planets rule other houses of the chart, as well as aspect other planets, and because our twelfth house ruler is likely to be positioned in another house, these planets do demand outer expression. When outer planet transits sextile, square, trine, or oppose twelfth house planets, we are also required to channel their energies into other realms of our lives. When a twelfth house planet, by progression, crosses our ascendant, we begin to liberate that energy from its unconscious and self-defeating patterns, and to express it more consciously and more overtly.

Twelfth house *outer* planets, which by progression remain in our twelfth house throughout our lives, may never manifest as outwardly or as consciously as planets which eventually cross the ascendant. We may always experience them in subtle ways, or express them in a solitary or spiritualized manner. But we can begin to free ourselves of the outmoded, detrimental patterns of fear, guilt, repression, and self-defeating behavior which they, and all twelfth house energies, may influence, and which have thus far undermined our sense of well-being and our capacity to function effectively.

The first step in making peace with our twelfth house energies is to increase our motivation to overcome past patterns and to experience wholeness, and also to build our sense of trust in our true selves. First we have to *want* to get the "rooms" of our twelfth house, and all our houses, in order. We have to *want* to relinquish our victim stance and the secondary gains which provide satisfaction: a self-righteous sense of virtue, the sympathy or help we feel entitled to elicit from others, the ability to locate the enemy outside of ourselves and have a definable target upon whom we can direct our anger and blame. We have to *want* to take charge of our lives, to feel empowered, to increase our self-esteem, to experience greater satisfaction, and to achieve our aims. We need to be able to create images of ourselves constructively expressing the energies of our twelfth house, and of the life we could live if we could access more of our inner resources. We have to feel our passion and to *want* the kinds of experiences which will nourish us. As we build our intention, the energy of our desire for change grows, and eventually becomes greater than the fear which prevents change. For this to happen, we need to believe that we *can* change, and that we *deserve* greater fulfillment.

Another motivating factor is understanding that we are prisoners of the energies in ourselves which we fail to acknowledge and integrate. Without our awareness, they undermine us. As long as we disown them, we block our access to our true selves, our real selves, which are the source of satisfaction. According to James Bugental, author of *The Search for Authenticity*[1], any facet of ourselves which we reown, no matter how unpleasant it may initially appear to be, contributes to our empowerment and well-being. Holding onto a virtuous or competent self-image does not feed our self-esteem if that self-image inaccurately reflects our relationship to ourselves. As we regain disowned facets of ourselves, we gain self, and are less invested in our self-image. As a result, we feel more complete, more open to pleasure and love; we gain power that we have previously invested in others; we become larger.

We need to be committed to our own wholeness, more so than to our own goodness. The Judeo-Christian ethic has influenced us to repress qualities in ourselves which do not reflect our religious and social ideals. Yet by attempting to be overly good, we relegate facets of ourselves to the dark closet of our unconscious, where, without the light of consciousness, they become twisted and distorted. Those of us who are most identified with our virtuous personas may even, unknowingly, act out the evil that we so actively defend ourselves against acknowledging.

According to Strephon Kaplan Williams,

Love is not the absence of fear.
Love is not the absence of hatred.
Love is the embracing of each aspect of life to transform it by
integrating it within the whole[2]

The paradox of our commitment to wholeness and our willingness to embrace our shadow self, is that as a result, the light of consciousness and compassion transforms these dark pieces of ourselves, and enables us to become more capable of love. By owning our shadow, by refusing to project our evil into the world at large, we not only develop greater empathy for suffering humanity, but we also contribute to socio-political change. Wars are based upon projection; environmental pollution is based upon the repression and denial of our connection to the world around us and of the long-term consequences of our actions.

Our commitment to the process of self-integration is a contribution to society. What we own and integrate within ourselves benefits the larger community; yet at the same time, we also need that community in order to grow and change. What was wounded in ourselves through early relationships must be repaired in relationship. We can't let go of our parental introjects until we have established new relationships and found more constructive role models which we can internalize and integrate into our developing selves. The more isolated we are, the more open we are to feeling possessed by the negative forces within us which have contributed to our self-defeating behavior.

As we relinquish our false selves and recover our true selves, we may not at first be large enough to encompass the newly experienced energies without the help of others. Nor are we likely to be able to be compassionate with ourselves unless we have experienced such compassion from others. The twisted, unredeemed facets of ourselves and the evil that may, for some of us, lurk within us, can only be countered through warm relatedness, through the healing power of love.

The Process of Change

"Give light, and the darkness will disappear of itself," wrote Coleridge.[3] Change begins with increasing the light of consciousness. Self-awareness leads to greater freedom of action, increased responsibility for ourselves, and self-empowerment. Yet the development of consciousness is often a painful process. In the myth of Cupid and Psyche, Psyche disobeyed her lover Cupid's demand that she refrain from seeing his form. Because she lighted a candle (discovering then that Cupid was a god), he fled, and she faced many trials and experienced considerable despair before she was reunited with him.[4] Often, the light of consciousness destroys the reality we have known, confronting us with unredeemed facets of ourselves, awakening the despair and trauma which follow loss of our illusions.

When we become more conscious, we become more aware of our shadow. It looms larger. As we step into the light, we may no longer see the light, although we increase our capacity to reflect it to others. What we see at first is darkness. Only by learning to hold both the light and darkness, our goodness and our evil, can we become integrated. In the anxiety and tension of the warring polarities, a new force, a third synthesizing force, eventually emerges which heals the split within us.

Our "superego" (our ideals and judgments, and the guardian of the gate of our twelfth house) battles our "id" (our repressed primal energies, often reflected by twelfth house planets and signs) until a healthy ego develops which can reconcile the conflict. We need our egos, but egos which are related to our real selves and real energies, not false selves, images, and personas which do not truly express who we are. As we alternate between repressing twelfth house energies and struggling with their unexpected outbreaks from the bonds of the twelfth house, we can begin to consciously embrace these energies and to discover and strengthen our true selves, which in time become capable of integrating these energies.

The first step is to experience our previously repressed feelings and needs—to acknowledge them, identify them, and define them. Only with the attitude of acceptance and compassion can we create the psychological space by which these feelings evolve and transform. According to Williams, "We must first accept the compulsion we are in before we can transform it. We must often live it fully before we can become released from it."[5] This paradox may be difficult to put into practice, because to attempt to accept a facet of ourselves in order to change it is not sufficient. We must truly and compassionately embrace a wounded part of ourselves, accept it as it is, and be willing to live with it as it is, before it can heal. Self-rejection inhibits growth, whereas acceptance frees our internal growth process.

Consider Robin, who has a twelfth house Moon in Pisces forming a t-square to a ninth house Sagittarian Sun and a third house Saturn in Gemini. Consciously, Robin embraces ideals of rational behavior and self-sufficiency, and seeks to excel in the emotionally repressed, competitive world of academia. But her wounded Moon, craving the nurturance she never received as a child, needs as part of its healing process to experience deep-seated hurt and longing, to express itself irrationally and emotionally, and to allow the necessary merging and dependency which will enable her Moon in Pisces self to emerge and develop. As long as she judges this part of herself with her Sun/Saturn standards, she is not likely to create the attitude of acceptance which she needs to create.

Therapeutic help might be necessary. As a caring and understanding therapist appreciates the beauty of Robin's vulnerability, perceives the spiritual, creative, and loving capacities that lie buried within that Moon, and understands the repression of her Moon as a necessary and honorable survival mechanism given Robin's painful childhood, Robin can begin to internalize her therapist's attitude, and nurture her Moon with the same compassionate acceptance she has now received.

Developing this accepting attitude often involves understanding the roots of our problems in the past and how we are needlessly repeating the past in the present. This process involves reexperiencing the reality of the child within us—the feelings and needs we still carry from the past, our parents' responses to them, the assumptions and attitudes we developed about life, the behaviors expected of us, and the coping mechanisms we learned. Through such reexperiencing, we begin to honor the survival mechanisms and the ingenuity of our inner child, who learned to live in an environment which did not allow him/her to fully unfold.

Consider Robin again. Her workaholic father, a science professor, had no patience for the emotional needs of his daughter. Her histrionic, alcoholic mother, frequently institutionalized, was such a poor role model that Robin quite early in life rejected the model of femininity and adulthood that her mother provided. She sought her father's acceptance, which was only available in response to her academic achievement. Because she experienced inadequate symbiosis and mothering early in life, she learned to repress the pain and despair of her unmet needs, and to compensate through accomplishment in school.

If Robin had remained in touch with her twelfth house Moon in Pisces, she might have been so overwhelmed with emotional need and pain that she would not have been able to develop herself intellectually, or to experience the self-esteem that her achievement did provide. If she had identified more fully with her mother, she might have drowned in her own emotional chaos, and resorted to such escape routes as alcohol or drugs. Her own workaholic escapism, modeled on her father's behavior, and the self-image and life philosophy which she created to maintain her sense of self, was a constructive alternative, given Robin's life situation. But now, as an adult, she needs to look at the assumptions and beliefs which keep her Moon in the twelfth house, and contribute to the emptiness and despair she experiences. She needs to ask herself if the attitudes she has developed in regard to feelings, needs, and dependency are truly necessary in all facets of her adult life.

The story of the last Wallenda brother is relevant to Robin's dilemma, and to the dilemmas of all of us who are holding onto outmoded attitudes and behaviors. The Wallenda brothers were famous tightrope walkers in the early twentieth century. All but one died in a famous tightrope accident. The remaining brother retired from public life, but years later staged a comeback, performing his remarkable feats of balance hundreds of yards above city streets.

This Wallenda brother had always, when walking the tightrope, held a small pole in his hand to aid his balance. During this performance, without a net to protect him from a fall, he stumbled, and remained hanging by one hand from the tightrope far above the ground. When a helper appeared, and reached out a hand to Wallenda in order to save him, Wallenda would not relinquish the pole he held in his other hand, in order to clasp the hand that would pull him to safety. As a result, he hung there, swinging from the tightrope, until he fell to his death. Whereas throughout most of his life, his pole had helped him to survive, now his survival required that he relinquish that pole. But he could not and would not let go of this survival mechanism.

Usually, the process of separating the past from the present involves a willingness and ability to enter the reality of the inner child, which is likely to occur when we are in the grip of overwhelming fear, pain, or anger in regard to a circumstance in our lives which is related to past trauma. Such situations enable us to reconnect with the original traumas, since we are reacting to our current reality through the lens of these unfinished past experiences. As we become more aware of the past situation, and able to differentiate it from the present, we become more capable of soothing the intense emotions of the inner child. We are able to reassure ourselves that our survival isn't at stake now, and that we have more resources available to us than we did in the past.

Perhaps we have a twelfth house Mars, and when we were young, our father had a stroke after we, in a fit of temper, expressed hatred toward him. We may now be terrified of expressing our anger toward those we love (particularly when they are ill), afraid that they may die as a result, that we will be abandoned, and that we will deserve the blame. So afraid are we of our anger, that we may have learned to repress our awareness of it; as we begin to allow this anger to surface, we experience it in the context of the survival terror, guilt, rage, and shame of the child we once were.

We need to speak to that inner child, to let him or her know that his/her feelings are real and valid. We must communicate that the current circumstances are different, and that learning how to feel and express our anger now is life-enhancing rather than life-destroying. We need to compassionately accept and honor the instinctive feeling reactions of our inner child, while simultaneously helping him/her awaken to current reality, secure in the knowledge that an inner adult now exists who is capable of handling each of our life obstacles.

But does the inner adult exist who can heal the wounded child and liberate twelfth house energies? For most of us, that adult develops as the child emerges and requires us to learn new responses to his/her feelings, attitudes, and actions. That inner adult is slowly learning new assumptions and attitudes, creating new patterns of self-talk for dealing with inner messages, developing new intentions, and experimenting with new behaviors.

How, apart from relying upon psychotherapists and other role models for direction (i.e., people we know and admire, people we don't know but whose autobiographies we read), can we facilitate the development of our adult? How can we build within ourselves a guardian of the gate of our twelfth house who is not so much concerned with keeping our energy in as he/she is concerned with helping us to find safe and viable methods of expression?

On an astrological level, we can begin by studying the constructive meanings of the planets and signs associated with our twelfth house, as well as the constructive meanings of the relationships between our twelfth house planets and planets they aspect. (If we don't know how Mars square Saturn can be constructive, then we can consider the traditional meanings of Mars sextile or trine Saturn in order to conceptualize how these two energies can work cooperatively.)

We can develop new assumptions and affirmations to replace the old ones: "Expressing my anger, with awareness of others' needs, will enable me to feel more empowered, and to receive the respect of others" rather than "My anger is so terrible that it will destroy my relationships." Sometimes, examining each of the negative assumptions we have carried from the past, and rethinking or rewriting them in an affirmative manner can help us to develop new thinking patterns.

As part of this process, we need to honor the possibility that at least a grain of truth and of wise caution may exist within our inner child's reality, which we may want to heed. Our anger may be destructive. Learning how to express it, when to express it, and to whom to express it is an important part of our integration process. As Howard Sasportas points out, the new assumptions and beliefs that we create may not necessarily counter the old ones; they must often include and yet also transcend the old reality.[6] We may, for example, learn to tell ourselves, "If I express my anger as I feel it when I feel it, it may have destructive results. But I am capable of learning how to ventilate it on my own and finding a form of expression which will benefit my relationships with others, rather than threaten them."

Richard Bandler and John Grinder, the founders of neurolinguistic programming utilize a "reframing" method which involves communication with our subpersonalities (planetary selves). In his synthesis of psychotherapeutic techniques for "healing the hated child," Stephen Johnson summarizes Bandler and Grinder's approach, which begins with helping a person contact the part of himself which is creating a particular problem:

> Having established communication, he is then asked to discover the positive intentions of that part. Following this, he is asked to contact that part of him which is creative and ingenious. Using all the resources of his creative part, he is asked to generate new ways of accomplishing the intentions just discovered. Next, the part in charge of generating the problematic pattern is asked to examine, correct, or assist the creative part in perfecting those new solutions until they are acceptable . . . When all new solutions are acceptable, the part in charge of generating the former problematic pattern is asked to take responsibility for generating these new solutions.[7]

Such an approach to reowning latent facets of ourselves, an extension of the subpersonality work of psychosynthesis and the dialoging of gestalt therapy, can be quite valuable.

Coping with Anxiety & Fear

According to the existential philosopher Sören Kierkegaard and the existential psychologist Rollo May, the development of the self is related to the capacity to confront anxiety and to move through it into new, growthful experiences. "To venture causes anxiety, but not to venture is to lose oneself," wrote Kierkegaard. The more we individuate, the more we break free of the instinctive, familiar pull of parental reality, the more anxiety we experience. We are continually poised between the existential anxiety of betraying ourselves which we experience when we cling to the past, and the neurotic anxiety of losing our secure foothold in past reality, which we experience when we attempt to move forward.

Many of us do not experience our anxiety. It remains locked within the muscular armor of our bodies, converted into physical symptoms, or channelled into addictions or other obsessive-compulsive behaviors. Frozen anxiety and fear create invisible walls or barriers, which keep us from experiencing our aliveness and creating fulfillment in our lives. Rather than knowing what we feel, we revert to automatic behaviors, or listen to the negative messages and rationalizations of our intellect, which prevents us from meeting the challenge ahead. When we are not aware of our anxiety, we have little choice in regard to opportunities and action. Awareness and the capacity to tolerate anxiety expand our freedom of choice.

In order to move through our anxiety, we may first need to melt some of the physical barriers and defenses which prevent us from experiencing it. In doing so, we become more capable of defining our fear, of specifying its nature, and experiencing the fluidity which enables us to move through it into new territory.

Anxiety is fear of the unknown; once the source of our anxiety is defined, we fear the known, which is easier to experience and confront. Our experience of anxiety or fear changes as we are able to be with it, and to find words to describe the emotional and physical sensations which accompany it. Our fear at first may seem overwhelming, and may threaten our sense of control, because the fear-ruled self is small, and feelings we keep pent-up inside ourselves seem larger and more threatening than those which we are able to fully experience, define, and express. But as we push through our fear, we become larger and our fear becomes smaller.

When we fully experience whatever is happening inside of us, whether it be fear, pain, or anger, we inwardly shift and move into a new dimension of being. "Face it, go into it, experience it—the process will set you free," wrote Jeanne Segal. "Ride the wild horse,"[8] she urges us. Likewise, Werner Erhard advises, "What you resist, persists. What you experience, disappears."[9]

Learning to increase our capacity to experience fear, as well as other unwanted emotions, may at first be difficult. We may need to allow ourselves to be carried away with these feelings first, before we trust them; we may have to come apart before we put ourselves together; we may fear breakdown before we experience breakthrough. Those of us who are physically blocked may need first to unlock our muscular armor, before we can experience deeper levels of feeling. To unblock the body is to strengthen our groundedness with the earth, to increase our capacity to tolerate excitation, and to unblock consciousness. The bioenergetics work of Alexander Lowen is of immense value in this process of physical and emotional liberation.[10]

As we increase our ability to experience fear, and the emotions which lie behind our fear, we need to expand our inner space by breathing deeply (which creates energy) and maintaining our contact with the ground. Simultaneously, we can benefit by affirming our ability to tolerate feelings which are (only initially) unpleasant. We become more capable of facing our fear and our life obstacles when we tell ourselves, "I AM large enough to handle this feeling, I CAN handle it, I WANT to handle it." Keeping in our awareness the vision of our ultimate aims can also facilitate this process.

Consider Robert, whose twelfth house Sun/Mercury/Mars conjunction in Gemini in square to Saturn in Virgo in the third house has inhibited his ability to express himself ever since grade school. Two years younger than a talented brother who excelled in his studies and later became a noteworthy television interviewer, Robert has always felt intellectually inadequate. His feelings were compounded by a stuttering habit and by insensitive teachers who had little patience with his learning blocks, his negative attitude, and his lack of cooperation.

As an adult, Robert has satisfied his Gemini planets by overcoming many of his early verbal difficulties, and by becoming a newspaper writer. But after twelve years at a desk, he is bored, and yearns to be more involved in reporting or interviewing—work which requires one-to-one communication skills, and which could be enhanced by his seventh house Capricorn Moon. Indeed, Robert has been presented with several opportunities to develop these facets of himself, but has turned them down, purportedly because he doesn't have the talent.

Discussing his sense of inadequacy in psychotherapy, Robert becomes aware that he holds himself back out of fear—fear of challenging his lifelong self-image, fear of failing, fear of being humiliated, fear of competing with his successful brother. Only as he allows himself to acknowledge and experience his fear is he able to let go of the rationalizations which block his career advancement, and begin to slowly risk fine-tuning his interviewing skills. Because of his fear and vulnerability, Robert learns not to "jump into the fire" too soon, which might result in proving his incompetency. He commits himself to sessions of deep massage which loosen his physical armor, and allow him to more deeply experience his fears and desires. He attends a communication skills course, as well as seminars in interviewing; he begins slowly to take on new projects at work which utilize his developing capacities. Two years later he leaves newspaper work altogether, for a challenging and satisfying job as an interviewer for an employment agency.

For us, as well as for Robert, the gains of confronting and moving through fear, and acting in spite of fear, are considerably greater than those of flight. As we become more capable of facing our twelfth house fears and risking new behaviors, we grow like the protagonist Peer in Ibsen's drama, *Peer Gynt*. At the end of the play, when the trolls sing, "Go back! Go around!," Peer cries out to them, "Ah! No! This time straight through!"[11]

Encountering our Shadow Selves

As we attempt to pursue our aims and recover facets of ourselves which have previously been unavailable, we encounter considerable inner (and often outer) resistance. The pull of our past attitudes and beliefs, both conscious and unconscious, holds us back. In order to overcome our resistances to change, we need to get those resistances out in the open, to give them a voice. Frequently, a real and important part of ourselves is resisting, afraid that its legitimate needs will not be met by the change we are envisioning.

This situation is most likely to occur if our twelfth house planets or rulers square or oppose other planets in our charts, or if their energy differs significantly from that of the more conscious personal planets outside our twelfth house. A Libran man will particularly resist expressing his twelfth house Mars/Pluto conjunction, which he does not know how to integrate into his deep-seated desire for harmonious relationships. A Virgo/Capricorn woman may not know how to create space in her earthy reality for the flowing, imaginative, chaotic energy of her twelfth house Neptune. A traveling salesman whose Aries stellium on the midheaven squares his twelfth house Cancer Moon is likely to have difficulty integrating that soft, vulnerable, domestic Moon into his adventuresome life.

When we resist change, we are not only afraid to relinquish the past. We may also be angry at having to take responsibility for our lives, and afraid that as we learn to meet unfulfilled needs, other viable needs will be frustrated. As we encounter parts of ourselves which resist change, we can discover what real needs they are attempting to fulfill, and seek to develop a plan of action which allows the new to unfold, without unduly threatening other facets of ourselves which seek expression.

Janine, the Virgo/Capricorn woman with a twelfth house Neptune, may experience absent-mindedness, confusion, and victimization in her daily life if she is not giving her Neptune conscious attention. Alternatively, she may find herself unconsciously motivated to overuse drugs or alcohol. As she learns to honor Neptune, to create space every day to listen to music, to write poetry, or meditate, she learns that Neptune is a trusting guide who contributes to her ability to function effectively, rather than undermines her earthy values.

Janine, like all of us, needs to honor her twelfth house energies. The planets, as archetypes, are like gods or goddesses within us, who curse us when they feel rejected, as Sleeping Beauty's family was cursed with unconsiousness by the evil fairy who was not invited to her birth celebration. Inviting the rejected god or goddess into our lives may at first require tolerating the distorted form of this wounded, and often enraged, energy. But slowly, as we learn to befriend it, it befriends us. Often, inviting it involves breaking a familial or social taboo—daring to light a candle to see our lover as Psyche did, or as in the tale of Bluebeard, entering the forbidden room.

Consider now Paula, a Sagittarius/Pisces with a twelfth house Saturn. In her yearly moves from one underpaid job to another, she has never learned the satisfaction of choosing one professional goal and committing herself to it. Seeking love, she has been inclined to say yes to others, and has not learned how or when to say no or set limits which would enable her to meet her needs and build more viable relationships.

If we, like Paula, have a twelfth house Saturn, we might want to study the constructive meanings of Saturn and to envision how a consciously validated Saturn might contribute to our lives. We might also observe how people we know have developed a positive relationship to their own Saturnian or Capricornian energy (or whatever energy is within our twelfth house). How have they learned to express it? How has this planet or sign benefitted them?

Often, we make choices which do not meet the real needs of our twelfth house energies, because we do not know what those real needs are. In order to satisfy them, we must first make contact with them, and enter into dialogue. Who, for example, is the planetary personality or subpersonality that represents our twelfth house Mercury? What does he/she want from us? Once we have established the inner relationship, we can begin to restructure our lives so that we express that energy more frequently, as well as make choices which include consideration of its needs.

Paula, in envisioning and dialoguing with her Saturn subpersonality, discovered that he was an uptight, crotchety, miserly old man who didn't want to give anything to anybody, and expressed his anger at being ignored by secretly withholding and withdrawing from involvement in work and relationships. Paula, as a Sagittarius/Pisces, was appalled to encounter this facet of herself, so at odds with her own self-image and her values. But as she entered into dialogue with her Saturn, she discovered that she had been playing the role of giver most of her life, while nevertheless failing to invest herself completely in any of her involvements, because she feared losing a self she did not have.

Consciously, Paula had always told herself that the current job or relationship was not "the right one," and that she would commit herself when "the right one" appeared. But Saturn was making sure that "the right one," never would appear, since the right job or right relationship had more to do with Paula's willingness to commit herself fully and create that rightness, rather than wait for it to happen.

As Paula established a relationship with her rejected Saturn subpersonality and learned to tolerate his negativity and judgment, he began to soften and transform. In their dialogues (sometimes on paper and sometimes through visualization during therapy sessions), he began to let her know his real needs. He wanted her to commit herself to an interest of her own, rather than exist as a respondent to others. Indeed, he wanted her to listen to and respond to him, to have his fears heard and soothed, and for her to provide for herself the solitary time necessary to make this possible.

Paula needed to hear her Saturn self, and eventually, to identify with it. We likewise need to "try on" our disowned selves and practice viewing our lives through their eyes. "I am afraid; I am withholding; I am lonely," we may say, as we become our twelfth house Saturn. But we may also learn to say and believe, "I am capable of commitment; I am loyal and reliable; I am capable of determining my goals, and achieving them."

The Yoruba tribe is one of many little-known Indian tribes which ritualized the idea of being one's shadow self. If a Yoruba were to dream of a wolf, the next day he would enact that wolf. If he were to dream of being lame or impotent, he would then enact his lame, impotent self, in order to reown and integrate it. Only through identification with the negative dimension of that self could he discover its virtues.

In her profound and poetic novel, *A Wizard of Earthsea*, Ursula LeGuin wrote about a young wizard, Ged, who flees from his own shadow until he is capable of confronting it, and calling it by his own name:

> Ged saw . . . a pair of clouded, staring eyes, and then suddenly a fearful face he did not know, man or monster, with writhing lips and eyes that were like pits going back into black emptiness . . . In silence, man and shadow met face to face, and stopped.
>
> Aloud and clearly, breaking that old silence, Ged spoke the shadow's name and in the same moment the shadow spoke without lips or tongue, saying the same word: "Ged." And the two voices were one voice.

Ged reached out his hands, dropping his staff, and took hold of his shadow, of the black self that reached out to him. Light and darkness met, and joined, and were one. . . . "Look, it is done. It is over . . . The wound is healed," he said, "I am whole, I am free."[12]

As Ged learned, only by encountering and embracing our disowned selves can we be healed.

Accepting Our Shadow Selves

When we identify with one archetype or one quality in ourselves, we constellate its opposite. According to Erich Neumann, the Christian ethic based upon a one-dimensional virtuous God inevitably leads to the projection of evil; it needs to be replaced with a new ethic, which involves a multidimensional God who encompasses both good and evil, and also requires each individual to take into himself all the ugly, distorted, and evil qualities he previously has rejected. In *Depth Psychology and the New Ethic*, Neumann wrote:

> The old idealised image of the ego has to go, and its place is shaken by a perilous insight into the ambiguity and many-sidedness of one's own nature. . . The ego is compelled to recognize that it is evil and sick in mind, antisocial and prey to neurotic suffering, ugly and narrow-minded. . . infantile and maladjusted, miserable and ugly . . . In the end, the individual is brought face to face with the necessity of accepting his own evil.[13]

Through such acknowledgement and acceptance, the forces of evil within us are transformed.

According to W. W. Firestone, author of *Voice Therapy*, the destructive facets of ourselves often take the form of persecuting inner voices, which berate us with such first person messages as "I'm no good," and "I'll never succeed," or with such second person messages as "You're no good," and "You'll never succeed." These attacking inner voices are usually introjects of our parents, which we need to identify and separate out from our own views before we can overcome them. In working with inner persecuting voices in psychotherapy, Firestone discovered:

> Articulating the self-attacks in the second person facilitates the process of separating the patient's own point of view from the hostile thought patterns that make up the alien point of view toward self. Prior to actually articulating the voice, most patients generally accepted their negative thoughts as true evaluations of themselves and implicitly believed them.[14]

Firestone also notes that attacks of the inner voice usually precede self-defeating behavior. Because the presence of the voice represents the presence of a parent from whom we have not fully separated, attempting to overcome the voice by directly opposing it usually elicits separation anxiety. He suggests that those of us struggling with inner persecutors make them more conscious, verbalize them aloud, and begin to develop new, corrective messages and experiences which strengthen our true selves and eventually weaken the power of the persecuting voice. Pamela Butler, in *Talking to Yourself: Learning the Language of Self-Support*, also addresses the process of countering negative self-talk and creating self-affirming inner voices.[15] The darkness within ourselves cannot be overcome directly, but must be transformed through dialogue with the light.

We need to aim not for light, but for the integration of dark and light. Our goal needs to be wholeness, not goodness, not happiness, not the maintenance of our self-system. As the roots of a tree extend beneath the earth while its branches extend into the air, so we, in order to attain balance individually and collectively, must extend ourselves deep into our own depths, and find the sustenance which lies buried deep within ourselves.

In another profound allegory, *Darkchild*, Sydney Van Scyoc tells the story of a girl who befriended an alien boy who had unknowingly been programmed with an inner guide whose purpose is to infiltrate and destroy the girl's society. The girl Khira loves all facets of the boy except the evil inner guide, against which he struggles as he makes friends in this new world. Her mentor, Kadura, advises her that the only way she can help the boy, Darkchild, to overcome his negative programming is to accept him in his totality. Kadura tells her:

> "The other—the one you despise. . . . You can have some tenderness for him too. You can begin growing by examining that tenderness, by fostering it. Your friend has trouble within himself. If you support him, even that aspect of him you like least, you will strengthen him to deal with his inner difficulty. . . . if you can bring yourself to care for him whichever face he presents—certainly that support will make him stronger."
>
> Khira drew back from the fire, shrinking from Kadura's suggestion. Care for the guide? When his very presence meant Darkchild had left her? . . . . How could she care for the guide when she felt angry at the very sight of him?
>
> "It is really very simple," Kadura answered her. . . . You must learn to put on the face you want him to see—the accepting face. . . . After

a time it will no longer be a face. . . . Eventually the act becomes the
reality, Khira. If you behave in an accepting manner toward the guide,
soon you will accept him.''[16]

Paradoxically, the process of psychological and spiritual growth
often involves lessening our attachment to our ideal selves (and the
ideal selves of others), and embracing our (and their) lowliest selves.
The degree to which a facet of ourselves has been repressed and rejected, and to which its needs have been unmet throughout our lives
is the degree to which it will at first manifest in an ugly, distorted,
infantile, archaic, or seemingly crazy manner. As Beauty learned to
love the Beast, and through her love undid the charm that kept her
prince-to-be imprisoned in a bestial body, so we can only discover
the buried treasure within us by first being willing to embrace those
parts of ourselves which at first may threaten or repulse us.

If an important facet of our inner child was locked within a dark
closet many years ago, when we open the closet door we are not likely to at first encounter a laughing, loving part of ourselves. This frightened child is likely to be deprived, unresponsive, rageful, distrustful,
uncooperative. Like an autistic child who has retreated from the world,
she needs to be wooed back to life. We must learn to trust the beauty
that may be dormant within her, while tolerating the ugliness. This
process is not unlike unclogging a blocked drain, which may at first
involve pulling out the garbage which is blocking the pipes and
preventing the clean water from flowing.

As part of this process, those of us who have Mars or Pluto in or
ruling our twelfth house may encounter terrifying demonic energies
within ourselves. We may laugh perversely at the misfortunes of others;
we may gain considerable pleasure from hurting those who have hurt
us, in plotting their downfall, in getting revenge; we may even maso-
chistically crave experiences of emotional or physical self-abuse.
Discovering the inner Hitler within us is a terrible blow to our self-
image and self-esteem, and to the spiritual ideals we have embraced
all our lives. How can we live with ourselves, as we expand our consciousness of our own ugliness and potential for evil?

Our first experiences with our own demonic energies are almost
always the worst. The devil operates unseen; once out of the darkness,
he loses power. For some of us, the blustering displays of our demonic
energy are like the displays of Oz the Great and Terrible, who relies
upon clever showmanship to hide his own humbug smallness. Indeed, the most devilish and demonic facets of ourselves may at core

be the survival mechanisms of a terrified child, whose needs have been distorted for years by emotional abuse and neglect. To the extent to which we can make contact with that scared child, find out what she needs, begin to meet her needs and soothe her fears, we will create the nurturing conditions which allow her to transform.

John Beahrs, in his book on dissociated selves, *Unity and Multiplicity*, discusses the process of coming to terms with demonic subpersonalities. In summary, Beahrs advises us to establish communication with the demonic as object, as a force separate from our sense of self, and then, as our sense of safety increases (often with adequate therapeutic support), to identify with it or experience it as subject. His guidelines for dealing with demonic energies are:

1. Contact the demon, (as object), validate its own needs and make an ally or friend of it.
2. Re-own that which had been dissociated away, and experience it as subject (me).
3. Accept, use and direct that energy of Self which had formerly been defined as evil.
4. Be fully in control of this.[17]

One important discovery which we may make in regard to our demonic child self is that its energy is life-affirming rather than life-denying. Its intensity of expression often alerts us to the fact that it is a potent source of energy; the degree of delight which it experiences also indicates that unknown sources of delight and pleasure reside within us. Once we embrace rather than reject that demonic self, give it permission to be, and make friends with it, it will contribute to our well-being, rather than sabotage actions and behaviors which do not serve its needs.

Consider Mark, a young musician, who has Scorpio on his twelfth house cusp, Neptune in Scorpio late in his twelfth house conjunct his ascendant, and Pluto in Virgo in his tenth house. During the four years in which Pluto has been transiting Mark's twelfth house, Mark has been unable to do any original musical work. Most of the time, he feels uninspired, depressed, and listless. He is bored with the full-time job he has been compelled to take, as a result of failing to succeed in his musical ventures; he has also lost interest in sex.

When Mark talks about himself, he expresses little affect. But slowly, as he reveals his resentments in regard to his boss and his girlfriend, and shares the complaints they have about his behavior, his eyes gleam and he smiles perversely. Unable to draw upon his own resources to achieve his own aims, he has been unconsciously seeking satisfaction through frustrating others. Acknowledging the ploys of his inner demon is difficult for him; but as he does so and begins to let the demon out of hiding, he becomes expressive, energetic, playful. At first he delights in fantasies of the revenge which he concocts for his boss and girlfriend; then, as he feels more energized, he begins to want to direct his energy toward dealing with problems in his life in a more forthright manner.

As part of this process, Mark begins to honor his own mischievous, demonic self and the cleverness with which it has secretly controlled his life; he even becomes comfortable enough with this energy that he dresses up as a devil for Halloween, and allows himself to spend an entire evening being devilish. His spontaneity and playful childlike spirit emerge. Soon, his creativity returns, not in a manner that he has known, but in a new, more enlivening form. He loses interest in classical music; he develops his skill on the drums; eventually he joins a rock band, and finds weekend gigs which enable him to reduce his regular employment to only part-time. He also leaves his demanding girlfriend, who encouraged his passive-aggressive behavior, and develops a relationship with a young woman who is attracted to his mischievous, creative, and now sexually potent self.

In Greek mythology, the Furies are demonic women determined to seek revenge upon those who have done them and other women injustice. Feared by the Greeks rather than honored, they relentlessly pursue such evil-doers as Orestes, who killed his mother to avenge for her murder of Agamemnon, his father. When Orestes pleads to Athena, goddess of wisdom, for mercy, and the Furies refuse her request to leave Orestes alone, Athena intervenes. Rather than oppose the Furies, she honors their mission as protectors of women and the family; she validates their aims, and convinces them to cease tormenting Orestes by establishing a shrine for them in Athens, renaming them the Eumenides (the Compassionate Ones), and giving them a more socially respectable role. Rather than directly challenge their rage, she looks beneath it to the underlying needs, aims, and values; by affirming those values, and providing a more viable form of expression, she embraces the wounded feminine spirit of the Furies, and enables them to relinquish their rage at being neglected and violated.[18]

The rage and ugliness of the neglected and violated parts of ourselves are transformed through compassion. In the process of reowning our shadow selves, the first change that needs to occur is not a change in those selves, but a softening of our inner judge or persecutor—our superego. Through the encounter with our dark side, we are humbled. Our growth at this phase lies in our capacity to be with previously repressed parts of ourselves, and in the development of our compassion and trust. We need to learn to accept our limitations, our humanity, and our animality; we need to appreciate the ingenious survival mechanisms that parts of ourselves have developed in order to survive in a world in which they have not been welcomed.

We need to give ourselves credit for our courage in daring to enter these uncharted inner realms, in confronting and transmuting our own darkness, and also in attempting new behaviors which at first may not succeed. We are like sailors who cannot expect to sail into the wind that blows against us; rather, continually expecting to be blown off course, we must focus our attention not upon our failures, but upon the process of getting on course once again.

Commitment to our whole self, rather than our ideal self, means facing the despair of giving up the illusions which have sustained us. It means being willing to be nobody special, being able to accept our limitations, inadequacies, and failures. Rather than deem ourselves adequate only when we measure up to superhuman standards, and inadequate when we fail to do so, we need to affirm our adequacy when we are merely human, and affirm ourselves with additional support during those rare times when we do measure up to higher standards.

As we become capable of holding a mixed, good-and-bad, strong-and-weak image of ourselves, rather than alternating between a glorified self-image and a lowly self-image, we become more integrated. As our true, integrated self emerges and develops, we lose not only our grandiosity and ungrounded idealism, but also our self-denigration and self-defeating behavior. The self-esteem which results from encountering and accepting the whole self is grounded and substantial. Paradoxically, the erosion of our idealized self-image, occurring in relationship to the awakening of a more solid sense of self, leads to greater and more constructive power and accomplishment.

This process of integration does not mean that we relinquish our higher aims. Rather, we relinquish only our attachment to them as a means of preserving our sense of adequacy and sense of self. As our true self develops, as a result of encountering and integrating our previously rejected qualities, we have more self and less self-image. Only by having self can we hope to achieve the aims—the realistic aims—which we most value.

Embracing Our True Selves

As we become more integrated, we *discover, recover,* and also *develop* our true selves. We discover all the facets of ourselves which have contributed to our life satisfaction. We recover parts of ourselves which we have disowned—"dark shadow" selves which initially may appear unpleasant but which in time reveal their gifts, and "light shadow" selves which awaken sources of joy which we have lost or forgotten. As these selves emerge and evolve, we gain compassion and insight, as well as new behaviors and capacities. The more value we experience in our real and emerging selves, the more we will be able to let go of the false selves with which we have identified, and the more fulfillment we will experience in our lives.

Sometimes, as we shed our illusions and are forced by circumstances to let go of past relationships, roles, or identities, we face the inner vacuum of mourning what we have lost without yet knowing what we will gain. At other times, we are unable to let go of the ground upon which we stand until a few sprouts of the new seeds appear above the earth and promise us a new birthing. Frequently, when the old is crumbling around us, the new has already been fertilized; as it grows subliminally inside us, it may burst through the structures we have known and contribute to their dissolution.

How much more easily we can let go of the past when we have made contact with a newly discovered or recovered facet of ourselves, or a vision of future horizons. For this reason, we can benefit by learning to hear those subtle but unmistakable movements of the new seeds birthing within us, and by watering them with our attention, encouragement, and even reverence.

The myth of Iphigenia in Tauris, expressed in dramatic form by Euripides in *Iphigenia Among the Taurians*[19] portrays the process of recovering and rebirthing lost dimensions of the self. In the preceding play by Euripides, *Iphigenia at Aulis* (superbly dramatized in the Greek movie *Iphigenia*), the Greeks are unable to sail at the start of the Trojan War because there is no wind. When the oracle is consulted, the goddess Artemis, angry at the Greeks' violation of her sacred wood, declares that the wind will return only if Agamemnon, the Greek leader, sacrifices his eldest daughter Iphigenia at the altar of Aulis.

Agamemnon is tormented by this pronouncement; he does not wish to kill his daughter. But identified with his ambitious war aims, and responsible to his troops who are eager to sail, he lures her to Aulis by telling her that she will be wedded there to the noble young Greek Achilles. Iphigenia, devoted to her father, innocently prepares for her wedding. But when she arrives at Aulis and discovers the truth, she experiences rage, betrayal, and anguish. At first she entreats her father to change his mind and help her escape. But as her plight appears more hopeless, and she learns that the glory of Greece depends upon her sacrifice, she becomes a willing victim. Identified with patriarchal values which denigrate the feminine, she gives her life in order to glorify those values which seek to destroy her.

But Iphigenia is not sacrificed. At the last moment, Artemis spirits her away to the barbaric island of Tauris, where she assists the priests who sacrifice on their altars the male strangers who enter Tauris. Having been sacrificed, Iphigenia (identified with the aggressor) becomes the sacrificer, thereby enacting her rage at the male sex, which has betrayed her. Yet simultaneously, she struggles with a conscience which condemns human sacrifice. Through dreams and memories, she also begins to long for her beloved brother Orestes and the idyllic experiences of her pre-sacrificial childhood.

Through the inner recovery of positive images from the past, Iphigenia transcends her life as barbaric priestess, and plans a means of escape. The only means she has available is to secretly send a message to her brother Orestes, telling him that she is alive and asking him to come to take her home; the only way to send a message is to betray the priesthood, by freeing one of the sacrificial male victims, and helping him to flee from Tauris.

But the next stranger captured and prepared for sacrifice, unbeknownst to Iphigenia, is her brother Orestes, who has traveled to Tauris seeking an image of Artemis, which he hopes will redeem him from the pursuing Furies. When Iphigenia imparts her message to Orestes, he reveals his identity, and they embrace. At this point, Iphigenia demonstrates a remarkable degree of courage, ingenuity, and resourcefulness as she plots against the people of the island, who have for years been family to her, in order to escape and return to Greece, where she will begin a new life. The story of Iphigenia in Tauris is a superb portrayal of one aspect of the process of reowning twelfth house energies—that of recovering parts of the true self which we have lost while we have been re-enacting, often unconsciously, the parental/familial/karmic script which was passed on to us.[20]

Once we have discovered, regained, and developed the dimensions of ourselves which have been absent, neglected, or distorted, we need to bring these energies into dialogue with other facets of ourselves, and create a lifestyle which honors our multi-faceted personalities. The psychosynthesis work of Assagioli and his follower Ferrucci, as well as the study of psychological fragmentation and unity undertaken by Beahrs, the hypnotic work with part-selves described by Bandler and Grinder, and my own translation of these theories and techniques into astrological concepts in *The Astrology of Self-Discovery, Planetary Aspects,* and *The Square Aspect*[21] illuminate this process.

Our subpersonalities or planetary selves may engage in civil war or guerrilla warfare, battling against each other; they may, like East and West Germany, erect barriers of dissociation between themselves; they may fuse, blending their energies into new selves; they may create a means of peaceful coexistence, operating side by side and functioning cooperatively, often through a method of coordinated alternation; and finally, during peak times of our lives, they may blend their voices together, creating our own life symphony.

The more diverse, contradictory, and powerful each of our planetary personalities are, the more we need to develop a central self, both observer and source of will and action, which can coordinate our various energies. As a political system needs a central executive, and an orchestra requires a conductor, so we also must become our own executives and conductors, maintaining awareness of the needs and desires of each of our many selves, and directing their behaviors.

Our capacity to take charge of our lives begins with awareness, and with the intention to liberate ourselves from the self-defeating bonds of the past. Encountering, confronting, experiencing, and accepting our twelfth house energies are important steps in our process of integration.

Our Shadow Selves II

Hatred, cruelty, confusion, despair, and madness must be admitted into consciousness before they can be integrated. I have to reverence my anger and fear before they become civilized.
                    —Sam Keen

Confrontation with the shadow produces at first a dead balance, a standstill that hampers moral decisions and makes convictions ineffective or even impossible. Everything becomes doubtful, which is why the alchemists called this stage nigredo . . . chaos, melancholia.
                    —Carl Jung, *Mysterium Coniunctionis*

When consciousness draws near to the unconscious, not only does it receive a devastating shock but something of its light penetrates into the darkness of the unconscious. The result is that the unconscious is no longer so remote and strange and terrifying, and this paves the way for an eventual union. . . . What happens is that its contents cross over into consciousness more easily than before.
                    —Carl Jung, *Mysterium Coniunctionis*

I dreamed I had a child, and even in the dream I saw it was my life, and it was an idiot, and I ran away. But it always crept on to my lap again, clutched at my clothes. Until I thought, if I could kiss it, whatever in it is my own, perhaps I could sleep. And I bent to its broken face, and it was horrible . . . but I kissed it. I think one must finally take one's life in one's arms.
                    —Arthur Miller, *After the Fall*

PART IV

Self-Transformation through Dreamwork

Dreams, dreams that mock us with their flitting shadows,
They come not from temples of the gods,
They send them not, the powers of the air,
Each man makes his own dreams.[1]
                    —Petronius

A dream is a piece of reality . . . whose meaning is pregnant but uncer-
tain, and whose fate in the world of the waking-ego lies in our own
hands. If we treat it with respect, it serves us. There is never any doubt
as to its underlying concern for our ultimate welfare.[2]
                    —James Hall

Why Do Dreamwork?

During the past few years, I have become convinced that learning how to recall, reexperience, interpret, and work with our dreams is of inestimable value in regard to the process of self-integration and the channelling of twelfth house energies. Because many of the dynamics of our subconscious minds are inaccessible to our rational consciousness, as well as threatening, the internal imagery of dreams serves as a viable mediator between unconsciousness and consciousness. As Perseus of Greek mythology was only able to kill Medusa by encountering her image in a mirror (because looking at her directly was too potent an experience), so we may only be able to access and integrate the potent energy of our primitive *and* transpersonal selves through utilizing the metaphorical bridge of our inner imagery.

In our practical society, dreamwork has limited appeal for most people. "I don't remember my dreams," many people say, or, "They're so bizarre; I don't understand their connection to my life," or even,

"My dreams are so unpleasant and anxiety-provoking that I'd rather forget them." We can learn to remember our dreams; we can learn how to tolerate the anxiety which some dreams produce, and open ourselves to the awesome experience and delight of dreams which appear once we have faced our nightmares. We can learn how to interpret our dreams, and we can learn how to apply their insights to our daily life.

Why should we? Why should we invest the additional 5–30 minutes per day which dreamwork might require of us? How do we know, if we've never experienced profound insight and change as a result of our dreams, that such transformation is possible? What really is the value of dreamwork?

First, as we learn to recall and pay conscious attention to our dreams, we begin to create a bridge which allows more and more of our unconscious energy to flow into our waking life.

Second, our dreams reveal our psychodynamics, or what is actually going on beneath the surface of our consciousness. How do you really experience yourself, your world, other people? What assumptions and personal myths influence you? What repetitive tapes do you play and replay? What are the real psychic conflicts which underlie your struggles in the outer world? How do you attempt to resolve your problems? When and how are you resolving them? What fears underlie your impulse expression, particularly your anger and sexuality? What patterns or experiences from early childhood are influencing you now, and need to be accessed, so that by returning to the experience where certain behaviors were developed, you can reprogram them? What are your true desires and needs? How do you compensate when these desires and needs are not met? Your dreams can answer these questions.

You may answer: So can a therapist, or so can I, by reflecting upon my life or reading psychology books. True. But the advantage of dreams is that the images and insights which they provide arise from such a deep source within ourselves that they are indisputable. What we learn with our minds often remains within our minds, unintegrated on gut and heart levels. What other people tell us about ourselves may affect us, but usually does not penetrate deep enough to effect real change. Dreams, and the insights which dreams produce, do not have to work their way down to the deepest levels of our psyches in order to catalyze change; they emerge from those levels. One dream, fully experienced and at least partially understood, can have a deeper impact upon our psychological dynamics than most experiences in the outer world, because that dream connects us to the source of creative change within ourselves.

According to Carl Jung, "Innovations never come from above; they come invariably from below, just as trees never grow from the sky downward, but upward from the earth."[3] Indeed, dreams express the voice of the soul; they are our contact with our deepest self, our inner substance. The mere act of recalling, experiencing, and consciously honoring our dreams connects us with our real selves, and awakens previously unavailable levels of creativity and vitality *even without interpretation.*

Consider our unpleasant dreams, shadow dreams, or nightmares. These arouse uncomfortable degrees of anxiety. Yet they also discharge and release anxiety, enabling us to function more effectively. Through contact with often primitive terrors—fears of isolation, loss of self, our aggression and destructiveness, the aggression of others—we also regain contact with our source of power which resides beneath those primal fears.

"The shadow is 80% gold," wrote Max Zeller. "The wound itself contains the very raw material from which healing and a new orientation can arise."[4] Traumatic dreams, especially those with recurring themes, and dreams with unpleasant characters and events usually reveal pockets in our psyche where large amounts of creative energy are trapped and in need of transmutation. Simply increasing our capacity to remember and reexperience such dreams is valuable; learning to interpret them and apply the insights we gain to our daily lives is even more valuable. Such dreams may be one of the only keys we have to the release and integration of the repressed material which is keeping us stuck in debilitating patterns and preventing us from knowing the joys of being totally alive.

Change occurs when we fully allow ourselves to be where we are, to experience what is happening within ourselves. "You never overcome *anything* by resisting it," wrote gestalt therapist Fritz Perls, "You only can overcome *anything* by going deeply into it. If you go deeper into what you *are*, if you accept what is there, then a change automatically occurs by itself."[5] Likewise, Jack Downing, author of *Dreams and Nightmares,* emphasizes that change and self-fulfillment occur when we embrace the primitive, infantile self that our dreams often reveal, rather than reject that self in defense of our ego ideals or spiritual aims. "If I can't find love, compassion, acceptance, and understanding for that early self, then I sentence myself to. . . . loneliness," wrote Downing.[6] Dreams, he tells us, can help us to embrace our small selves, our faults, our limitations. Through compassion for ourselves, we catalyze the change process which enables us to evolve and become far greater beings than our faults alone might lead us to believe.

Yet working with dreams is not only an encounter with our small or shadow selves. Dreams also reflect new developments occurring or about to occur in waking life. For years, afraid of our anger, we dream of being pursued by a burly man with a knife; finally, after repeatedly confronting our therapist and becoming more comfortable with our aggression, we dream of facing that burly man, and even befriending him. Our dreams confirm the growth which we are experiencing, assuring us that real progress is occurring; they also reveal the changes that are happening inwardly, and will soon manifest outwardly. The birth of a child in a dream, the beginning of a new venture, the successful resolution of a dream struggle which has troubled us for years all foreshadow the changes we will experience in our outer selves, and provide confidence, hope, and trust in our inner capacities.

Occasionally, especially after we have experienced and confronted our shadow selves, we are rewarded with transpersonal dreams, which we know immediately have emerged from deep, archetypal levels of consciousness. We dream of a wise old woman or man who promises to protect us, of a quiet enchanted wood which provides refuge from our worries. We dream of Jesus embracing our child-self, or we have a fairy tale dream in which we encounter magical beings and awaken to sources of joy and delight within ourselves which were previously inaccessible. Sometimes, we remember only fragments of dreams, with little emotion; quickly, after waking, we forget them. But transpersonal or archetypal dreams may affect us so profoundly that they permeate our waking consciousness for days or months. Change begins with altered consciousness. Our entire sense of ourselves and the world in which we live may be transformed as a result of a guiding dream.

Yet ordinary dreams, as well as archetypal dreams, may provide significant guidance. We dream of nearly suffocating as we crawl through the narrow tunnels beneath a hill; we wake in terror, knowing on some level that we have just journeyed within our polluted lungs, and that we no longer have a choice—we are finally ready to stop smoking. We dream of our mother urging us to write her when we are at summer camp, and we wake, and feel the urge to write her—a loving letter which she receives the day before her unexpected death.

We dream of someone commenting upon a poem we wrote, and then we wake and spontaneously write a poem for the first time in years.

Or consider a middle-aged woman who has Venus in Scorpio in the twelfth house and a Mars/Neptune conjunction in Virgo. Years ago, the evening before her wedding, she was hesitant about her first sexual experience, since sexuality held little interest for her. That night, she dreamed of Jesus embracing her, telling her that she was his bride, and that she was not to worry about the sexual dimension of her life, because it would not be an issue for her. Indeed, her spiritual life always took precedence, and sexuality was not an important facet of her marriage, or of her subsequent relationships.

Dreamwork has undeniable personal value. It also has considerable collective and political value. Many of the conflicts between people and the wars between nations result from lack of personal integration, from tendencies to project the disowned facets of ourselves onto others and battle them externally, rather than come to terms with our inner demons—our helpers in disguise. To engage in the highly personal activity of dreamwork is to make a social and political contribution. Confronting, embracing, and integrating our rejected selves; facing the shadow which appears in our dreams; painfully relinquishing our grandiose self-image and ideals in order to make peace with our humanity; becoming larger in self because we have been willing to become smaller in self-image; learning the humility of encountering our primitive, infantile, distorted, wounded, destructive selves—these are political acts. Within ourselves, we begin to accomplish what couples, families, groups, and nations in conflict are failing to accomplish. Then, merely by *being*, without always *doing*, we become true contributors to humanity.

How to Recall Your Dreams

Until three years ago, I remembered and recorded approximately eight or ten dreams a year. Soon after I began consulting with a therapist who valued dreamwork, I was remembering several dreams a week. Now, I often recall three or four dreams a night. What made the difference? Certainly, being able to tell my dreams to an interested listener aided my recall ability. Discovering the immense power of sharing my dreams and beginning to understand them helped still further. Then, reading books on dreamwork and using a worksheet for recording dreams were additional aids. But most important of all was developing a clear intention and a focused dedication to the process of dreamwork.

My intention and dedication were fueled by the discovery that honoring my dreams through giving them conscious attention altered the kinds of dreams that I had. Fewer dreams were fragmentary, incongruous, indecipherable; more of my dreams emerged as coherent stories, clear, emotionally charged, insightful, illuminating, and often creatively inspiring.

What have I learned about recalling dreams during the past few years? First, that dream recall is aided by keeping a pen and dream journal by the side of the bed—and a lamp or nightlight pen (available at many stationery stores) within easy reach. Before going to sleep, I write in my journal the date and number of my next dream, and then give myself suggestions to remember and record dreams in the morning; sometimes I ask for dreams which illuminate certain issues in my life, or answer a question. This process of dream incubation can have significant results, especially if repeated for several nights. I also set my alarm clock for fifteen minutes before I need to get up and begin my day.

In the morning, when the alarm goes off (I always set the alarm so that it will ring every few minutes, to give myself time to "reel in" dream images on the periphery of my consciousness), I immediately turn inward to catch the emerging dream images. At this point I may do one of two activities. The first is to lie in bed and replay those dream images or fragments, so that the dream fully unfolds. Staying in the same position in which I was sleeping facilitates this process. The second activity is to write in my dream journal the key words or phrases which flood into my memory, so that I will have a record of the main points of the dream and can flesh out the details later. As I recall my dream, or as I lie in bed half-asleep, numerous thoughts scurry through my mind; these are often relevant to the meaning of the dream. Therefore, I record these associations, as well as my feelings upon awakening. (Some people prefer to speak into a tape recorder, rather than write down their dreams.)

Later, I frequently remember more details of the dream and gain insight into its meaning when I rewrite or type the dream, and when I share it with another person. Using a dream worksheet for dreams which feel especially important is helpful. Repeated experience recalling dreams has enabled me to differentiate dreams which emerge from various levels of consciousness, and which possess different kinds of emotional charge. Inevitably, I pay more attention to some dreams than to others.

Often, when I wake, I resist remembering and recording my dreams. When I have a sleeping companion, I may be distracted by the loving or disturbing presence of the other. Sometimes I feel too tired to open my eyes or reach for my journal, or I have an unpleasant reaction to a dream and want to push it out of my awareness. Such resistance is common, because dreams frequently reveal material which is anxiety-provoking, which threatens the ego or waking consciousness. The more disassociated our conscious mind is from our subconscious dynamics, the more inclined we will be to repress our dreams.

Another kind of resistance occurs when we are invested in having interesting, coherent, or extraordinary dreams, and are annoyed by dreams which are fragmentary, incoherent, or mundane. At such times, we tend to dismiss such dreams, refusing to take them seriously. Yet those fragments may be meaningful; the incongruities may reveal contradictions and transformations which are occurring within us; the most mundane dreams may elucidate our current patterns. Unless we honor our fragmentary, incoherent, and ordinary dreams, we are not likely to be rewarded with complete, coherent, clear, inspirational, or transpersonal dreams.

Finally, we may not be able to remember our dreams when our lives are particularly demanding, and we need to keep our attention focused on the outer world. Most people experience cycles in regard to dream recall—periods in which recall is easy, and periods in which their attention is focused on outer activities, and recall is difficult. Focus on dreamwork may be distracting during those high-pressured times when we must focus intensively on outer tasks. We also may need periods of release from dreamwork, so that the integration of our previous insights can occur. Sometimes, free associating to the statement, ''I don't want to remember my dreams because . . .'' may reveal the reasons why we are not accessing our dreams. We may not be ready to face what our dreams are telling us, or we may not be ready to take the action which our dreams might encourage us to take.

Hints for Dreamwork and Dream Interpretation

1. *The EXPERIENCE of the dream is important.*   Replay your dream several times. Say it aloud; share it with others. Recall each detail. The more deeply you experience the dream, the more fully you will open the channel between unconsciousness and consciousness.

2. *Look for the emotional charge in your dream.*   What part of the dream is the most vivid? Where does the most feeling occur? Which images are most haunting? In dreams, action often represents feelings; motion equals emotion. Speaking your dream aloud will release feelings and associations which you would not otherwise be able to access.

3. *Free associate to your dream symbols and characters. Discover your personal symbology.*   Although some dream symbols have universal meanings, most of the meanings of your dream characters and objects are likely to be personal. Past experiences, attitudes, and experiences of the preceding day, anticipatory experiences etc. all may be relevant to your dream. Ask yourself: what is the essence of this symbol or character? If you dream of a person in your life, do not immediately assume that your dream is about that person. Ask yourself: What qualities do you associate with that person? If, for example, you describe a character in your dream as "sly, manipulative, and untrustworthy," what is the dream revealing about your current behavior?

4. *Identify with everything in your dream.*   You are all parts of your dream. Characters separate from or in opposition to your dream ego (the character you identify with in the dream) are also a part of you, but a part which you may disown and project. You may also split a facet of your experience into two or more symbols. For example, your ambivalent feelings toward your kind but controlling husband may be reflected through your relationship in a dream to a kind man and a controlling man—who also represents the kind but controlling parts of you.

5. *Consider what your dream ego tells you about your self-identifications, attitudes, and behaviors.*   How active or passive is your dream ego? How confident, capable, or powerful? How insecure, fearful, or powerless? To what extent is he/she a victim? To what extent does he/she make wise choices? What age does he/she seem to be? (A younger self may reflect the self you were

when the conflict your dream ego is experiencing first developed.) Is your dream ego observing the main action of the dream, involved peripherally in the action, or center stage? What is his/her primary conflict? How does he/she contribute to resolution or lack of resolution? To what extent does your dream ego operate alone, in opposition to, or supported by other characters? What changes does he/she undergo? How is your dream ego similar to your waking self?

6. *Consider what your dream tells you about your emotional conflicts.* You create the obstacles and conflicts in your dreams. Your conscience may punish you for unacceptable feelings, attitudes, and behaviors by creating suffering or punishment. Your conflicts of ego vs. id (battle with desire and impulse), ego vs. superego (battle with conscience), and ego vs. world (battle with outer obstacles) are externalized through the plot of your dream. Parts of yourself which you reject may appear in your dream as adversaries which threaten your dream ego.

7. *Listen to your feelings as you associate to your dream and begin to interpret it. Aim for an "aha" experience.* You alone know the meaning of your dream. When you have a gut response to a particular association or meaning, trust it. Over time, you will fine-tune the inner resonance which enables you to discern the meaning your dream has for you.

8. *A dream is multi-dimensional; it has many meanings. When interpreting your dream, do not seek closure too soon. Stay open-minded.* Do not assume that you have exhausted the meaning of your dream when you have discovered one or two associations, or interpreted it in relation to a single event in your life. Dreams use condensation; one word or image can have multiple meanings. Puns are common.

Consider, for example, a dream character who is still *kneading* her clay in an art class, while a friend in class is completing her sculptures. This dreamer is lonely and *needing* companionship; she takes refuge from loneliness in her art studies, which are focused upon the work of *Klee*; she once was involved with a man named *Clay*. As a result of this dream, she becomes aware of competitive feelings in regard to her friend, and her own previously unrecognized sense of competition, which has its roots in her relationship to her mother, a professional artist. (This woman has a twelfth house Venus in Capricorn, squaring Saturn in Libra.)

Consider also a dream fragment from Karen, who is discussed later in this chapter. Karen had a dream in which a woman, presenting her with a loaf of freshly baked bread, said to her, "Only those who are ready to marry may eat of this bread." Karen, as dream ego, replied, "I can't eat bread. I have a yeast infection." Such a brief dream is likely to reveal numerous associations and meanings.

9. *Give your dream a title.* After you have re-experienced your dream and begun to interpret it, create a title which captures for you the essence of the dream. Titling your dream will help you sort out your diverse associations and discover your dream's most essential meaning.

10. *View your dream as a stage in your transformational process.* According to Ernest Rossi, dreams reflect the stage we are experiencing in our current process of transformation. Frequently, dreams can be classified as: a) portraying blockages to growth; b) indicating the emergence of a new energy; c) revealing the conflict between the old and the new; d) demonstrating and affirming the integration we are experiencing between the old and the new.[7] I also find this process related to the progressed lunation cycle and the cycles of each planet in relation to itself: the new birth of the conjunction, conflict in action at the first square, expansion of consciousness at the opposition, and the struggle for conscious integration at the last square.

Dreams reveal our attempts to find our own equilibrium in regard to the polarities in our life. How do we forge a self that honors both our true self *and* our persona? How do we satisfy needs for independence *and* dependence, for freedom *and* security, for assertion/individuality *and* relatedness, for being who we are *and* doing or becoming? Dreams chronicle our process of shifting back and forth between these polarities as we seek to integrate them. Dreams also indicate our process of separation from our parents and the values/attitudes/behaviors which we have introjected from them and have attempted to make our own. Anger, and even hatred, are necessary parts of the separation process. The aggression and fear which appear in our dreams may reflect both the fear of separating from the old parent-related sources of security, as well as the destruction of the old which must necessarily occur in order for us to embrace and develop our true selves.

As you recall and record your dreams over time, you will also become aware of the evolution of your dream ego, dream characters, and dream action. Conflicts of previous dreams will recur until they resolve themselves; new healing images or characters will appear; an equilibrium will be reached; then another conflict will occupy center stage. The more you honor your dreams and work with them, the more clearly they will reflect your transformational process, and provide insights and guidance which can benefit you in your daily life.

Dream Symbology

Although dream symbols abound with personal meanings based upon our past experiences, many symbols have universal meanings. Becoming familiar with the common, universal symbolism found in dreams can help us begin to interpret dream language.

Our bodies, for example, are frequently symbolized by houses, vehicles, machines, and animals. The rooms of a house usually represent facets of ourselves—the attic, our minds or spirits; the basement, our "id" or primal energies; the kitchen, our gut feelings, our need for nourishment. Windows symbolize our openness and receptivity to the outside world; doors, passageways between different facets of ourselves; walls, our personal boundaries, and the psychic barriers which both protect and limit us.

Animals usually symbolize both higher and lower instincts. Birds frequently relate to the soul, imagination, or spirit; fish, to our spiritual nature, our capacities for devotion, the potential for rebirth. Cats in a dream may refer to the female genitals ("pussy"), or to tendencies toward "cattiness" or gossip; peacocks, another feminine symbol, often represent beauty, vanity, and the sense of unlimited possibilities suggested by all the colors of the peacock's tail.

Snakes, commonly associated with the phallus, may also refer to the awakening of the primal kundalini energy, or the quality of sneakiness; wolves—ravenous, devouring instincts, distorted by past traumas, and inclined to fierce and destructive expression. Lions, on the other hand, can represent such noble qualities as strength, courage, and power, as well as the untamed, devouring, aggressive instincts; the appearance of a lion in a dream may also be a pun for "lying." A bear may refer to the "baring" of the body or the soul, as well as the potent male force, or the need for hibernation. Bulls may signify "bullshit" or "bullheaded" stubbornness, as well as brute force and power.

Rodents and insects appearing in dreams often indicate parts of ourselves which we regard as dirty, ugly, or bothersome. When our conscience is plagued with guilt or shame in regard to our sexuality, anger, or lower motivations which color our relationships, we may dream of bugs and rats gnawing, stinging, or otherwise pestering us. Recently, a student in my dream group missed a class after refusing to give a voice to the hornet in a dream which was attempting to sting her; she was not ready to own her "stinging qualities," or learn how to effectively express her anger. When I called her to find out if she had missed class because she had been threatened by her work on the hornet dream, she said no, that she had the flu. "It has nothing to do with the hornet," she told me, "I just had the bug."

Sometimes in dreams, body parts may appear directly and symbolize different facets of ourselves. Arms may refer to reaching out to people, experiencing our strength, or "bearing arms"; legs and feet, to our sense of support in the world, our grounding and mobility. Eyes (and lenses) can symbolize spiritual and mental perception or omniscience, as well as the lens through which we view reality. Teeth frequently represent aggression, our urge to bite or cut through an obstacle; teeth falling out or being extracted may show fears of impotence or castration.

Common male sexual symbols include: guns, poles, knives, swords, snakes, rats, bananas, noses, pens, teeth, balls, and keys. Common female sexual symbols include: purse, container, cave, ring, lake, boat, peach, flower, box, vault, garden, gate, oven, oyster, ship, and well. Sometimes, puns and plays in language may reveal otherwise unnoticed sexual meanings. For example, a woman in my dream group who shared a dream about foreigners and mail delivery mentioned that a man friend of hers had recently moved back to his native India. Her dream ended with her disappointment at not having received any letters. "I don't understand what this is about," she told the group. "Why should I be so upset that there's no mail in my box?" "M-A-L-E?" we asked her. "In your BOX?"

Actual sexual experiences occurring in dreams between ourselves or dream egos and another person may suggest sexual interest in that person, or simply a desire for greater closeness. Such dreams may also be completely symbolic; we may be internalizing or taking into ourselves the qualities that we associate with that person, or fusing with them psychically rather than physically.

Images of nature also reveal significant messages in regard to inner experience. Cosmic dreams may appear when we are experiencing major changes in our views of reality. Earthquakes herald the crumbling of old foundations; tidal waves, the building up of uncontrolled, overwhelming feelings (usually fear or anger) which threaten our consciousness. Earth symbolism usually refers to the body, grounding, practical reality, and the mother principle. Water symbolism, also related to the mother principle, represents the emotional body, the unconscious, the life-giving source, and the desire to return to the womb; water can also indicate primal chaos, hidden mysteries, and the process of purification. Sometimes, dreams of water simply indicate the urge to urinate. Fire symbolism, on the other hand, is more suggestive of the primal energy of anger, desire, and sexuality as well as the transformative influences of creative and spiritual power.

What about natural locations? Climbing mountains obviously refers to the pursuit of worldly and spiritual apsirations; descending or falling into a valley suggests descent to a lower part of ourselves or return to the womb. The ocean, of course, is the womb, the mother, the unconscious; forests, too, carry the symbolism of the unconscious and spirit realms, as well as threshold experiences, seclusion, and the female pubic area. An island is suggestive of isolation, but also of a safe refuge from the waters of chaos; a desert may likewise signify emotional isolation as well as barrenness, the experience of being abandoned or separated from God. Yet in Biblical symbolism, the desert was a place where God frequently revealed himself. When interpreting our dreams, we must not be too quick to apply the most obvious universal interpretations. If you have lived on a desert, then the symbolism of the desert will have different meanings for you than it would for someone who associates deserts with the plight of the Israelites or the movie "Dune."

Likewise, such natural symbols as trees, suns, and stones may have both universal and personal meanings. Trees dig their roots deep into the soil while stretching their limbs toward heaven. Symbols of renewal, they suggest the unity of body and spirit, of self and nature. Phallic in appearance and yet growing like breasts upon the body of mother earth, trees integrate both male and female qualities. Stones are another expression of mother earth, but tend to represent parts of ourselves which are cold, hard, solid, enduring, or which have quiet concentrated power. The sun, a symbol of renewal, may indicate our relationship to God, the father, the warm life-giving energy of the heart, or our fiery passions. Astrologically, the sun also symbolizes enlightenment or the light of consciousness.

Sometimes, characters in dreams do not represent themselves but are archetypes, or universal psychic representations of our inner reality. The wise old man, the wise woman, the hero, the villain, the princess, the seductress, the terrible mother, the terrible father, the anima, the animus, and the trickster are common archetypes which appear in dreams. Also significant are archetypes of the child, and the related symbols of seeds and eggs, indicating new growth occurring within the psyche. The appearance of a child within a dream may indicate the awakening of new possibilities within ourselves, or regression to a part of ourselves that is fixated in early trauma. The birth of a child or animal is also related to the birth of a new facet of ourselves, often an impulse toward creative expression.

Likewise, mother images (earth, water, cows, milk, hills, nests) and father images (authorities such as policemen, God, government officials, kings) may refer to mother or father archetypes, to our expression of the mother and father principle in our current lives, or to our personal mothers and fathers, and the unfinished business that we have with them. Primitive scenes from early in life carry the remnants of early nonverbal experiences which still influence us today. For example, I once dreamt of looking up at the sky, hoping for rain, and seeing, instead of clouds, two enormous buttocks in the heaven, dropping turds down upon me. Such dreams may appear when we are working through a view of reality which originated in early emotional and bodily experiences of which we are no longer conscious.

The death of a character in a dream may represent an actual death wish in regard to a particular person, or an attempt to come to terms with a past or current death or loss. Frequently, death dreams indicate that the qualities/experiences which we associate with the dream character who is dying are passing away; we may be ending one phase in our lives, shedding an old self, and preparing for the new.

Frequent Dream Themes & Their Symbolic Meanings

The following themes commonly occur in dreams:

1) *traveling on a journey, burdened with luggage*—experiencing difficulty in the journey of life because of the burdens of the past which we carry with us.

2) *missing a train or plane, or being late for an important event*—feeling unprepared or being developmentally delayed in regard to tasks before us; fearing the event or journey and secretly wishing to avoid or miss it; sexually, the fear of not being able to come, of being too late in our timing.

3) *falling*—fearing loss of control, of consciousness, or of grounding in reality; the experience of regressing or going backward.

4) *flying*—the release of our spirit from its earthly bondage; the urge to escape or emancipate ourselves.

5) *deliberating over what clothes to wear, changing clothes, dressing inappropriately*—confusion in regard to our persona, how we wish to show ourselves to the world.

6) *sense of inadequacy in regard to a public performance in a con-cert, play etc.*—insecurity concerning roles we must play; not feeling prepared; fear of public humiliation.

7) *watching a movie within a dream*—observing ourselves playing a role in our life scripts, usually one which is canned or melodramatic and not expressive of our true selves.

8) *being naked, without clothes, exposed*—desire to expose oneself physically or emotionally; shame and vulnerability in regard to exposure or exhibitionism.

9) *anxiety, lack of preparation, or failure in regard to an examination*—feeling tested by life; fear of failing to perform adequately in a task before us.

10) *tidal wave, flood, and fear of drowning*—fear of losing ourselves or our consciousness; being overwhelmed by feelings or forces of chaos; sometimes a warning of a cold or illness which may occur if feelings are not experienced.

11) *being blind, unable to see, impaired vision*—the unwillingness to be conscious of some facet of our lives which is too threaten-ing to face; fear of the darkness or the light.

12) *being pursued, invaded, raped, or robbed by an intruder or vio-lator*—usually, the projection of some denied part of ourselves which is threatening to us, and which is attempting to get our attention; may warn us of a real person in our lives who may be dangerous to our well-being.

13) *experiencing damage to our automobiles or houses (e.g., brakes are inadequate, pipes leak)*—feeling deficient in regard to our impulse control or our emotional capacities; the need for psychic repair.

14) *being convicted of a crime for which we are or are not guilty*—the need to punish ourselves to atone for our guilt in regard to aggression, wrongdoing, etc.

Many other dream stories and symbols become easier to understand once we are familiar with our common dream themes and images. Bridges in dreams reveal transitions and connections between polarities—self vs. other, spirit vs. body, heaven vs. earth. Ladders or stairs suggest ascent into our mind/spirit or into future developments, or descent into our bodies/primal energies or back down into the past. Keys may represent capacities we have which can open new doors of opportunity.

However obvious the symbolism of such images may appear, we need to remember that our personal associations may have more meaning than the common or universal associations. Were you grounded the night of the senior prom because you stole the keys to your parents' car? Did your ex-husband just return to you the keys to the house you lived in together for fifteen years? Did your daughter and her boyfriend disappear behind the locked door of her room when you were going to bed last night? Do you suspect that he was putting his "key" into her "lock," while you were sleeping alone? Any of these experiences reveal deep emotional charges associated with the image of key.

Finally, we want to pay attention to colors in dreams. Black usually represents death, mourning, emptiness; blue—spirituality, serenity, sadness; green—newness, fertility, abundance, renewal, envy, money, prosperity; red—desire, anger, energy, vitality. Reading a book on the psychology of color can help you learn more about color symbolism, but you will benefit more from exploring your own personal associations to the colors which appear in your dreams. The "key" to dream interpretation is in your hands, not in a symbol dictionary.

The Dream Questionnaire

The dream questionnaire on the following pages is a useful tool for beginning (and advanced) dreamwork. You may copy it and use it repeatedly.[8] Once you have developed some facility in working with your dreams, you may want to dispense with the worksheet and follow your intuitive promptings. Learning a new skill at first involves conscious attention to detail and technique; once we have absorbed and integrated these learnings, we can forget them, and develop our own approach and methods.

Dream Questionnaire
(© 1986 by Tracy Marks)

INITIAL RESPONSE

Immediate feelings upon awakening:

The emotional charge in the dream:

Immediate associations:

THE DREAM ITSELF

Time/location and associations:

Key symbols/images and associations:
1)

2)

3)

Key characters and associations:

1)

2)

3)

Key words/phrases/puns and associations:

1)

2)

Feelings present within the dream:

Antagonistic forces:

Healing/helping forces:

Archetypes:

THE CONTEXT

Previous day (and before-sleep) experiences and concerns:

Following day anticipations and concerns:

Associations to other dreams and experiences:

When you felt a similar way:

How dream reflects your life situation:

THE DREAM ITSELF

Do one or more of the following exercises:

1) Describe yourself as a character or symbol: "I am . . ."
2) Dialogue with one of the characters or symbols.
3) Retell your dream from another point of view.
4) Rewrite dream on the left side of a page, leaving space for associations on the right side.

ANALYSIS

Describe the dream ego in terms of:

  involved/uninvolved in action:

  active/passive:

  behaviors and actions:

  attitudes/beliefs:

  apparent age/emotional age:

Describe the problem/conflict:

Describe the resolution/lack of resolution:

Describe incongruities/transformations/new developments:

What's missing in the dream?

What are the unanswered questions?

What are the messages of the dream?

Why do you need this dream now?

What does the dream want from you?

What action will you choose to take?

EXPANDING THE DREAM

Do one or more of the following exercises:

1. What happened before and after? Expand and continue the dream.
2. Rewrite the dream creating a more viable resolution. (What might this have required of the dream characters?)
3. Enact the dream with one or more people. Create a psychodrama.
4. Give creative expression to the dream—a collage, drawing, painting, poem, story, dance, etc.

Before you try the questionnaire with your own dream, you may wish to become more familiar with its use by studying a dream which has been amplified and interpreted with the help of the questionnaire. As an example, I include my work with "The Water Giver Dream." Although this is an especially clear archetypal dream, I do not by any means wish to suggest that the questionnaire can only be used with dreams of this nature. (I am guilty of the cardinal dream sin of being overly attached to extraordinary dreams. But I confess here, and only here, that most of my dreams are quite ordinary. Many of them are fragmentary. And some of them I will probably never understand.) Even the smallest and most incoherent fragments can be amplified, associated to, analyzed, interpreted, and expressed in creative form. Often, they will reveal rich and diverse meanings.

*   *   *   *   *   *   *   *   *   *   *

The Water Giver Dream

(Transiting Saturn in the 12th sextile 9th house Libran Sun; t-square formed to transiting Uranus in Sagittarius in the 12th by transiting Jupiter in Pisces and 9th house natal Mercury in Virgo; transiting Venus sextile 12th house Sagittarian Mars; transiting Neptune square natal Sun.)

> The land in which I live is dry, and turning into desert. Because I can find no water to fill my cup, I decide to make the long journey to the lake (originally written "lack") at the center of my community in order to procure water from the Water Giver there. As I journey, I intercept a messenger who is bringing me a message. For the next year, I am told, I am to be the Giver of Water; I must now report to the central Lake. My first response is anxiety and hesitation—I do not have the water to give. I tell the messenger that I would prefer to return to my barren land, at the far edge of our world, than be the Giver of Water. The messenger points out that I have traveled too far from my home to turn back now, and that my home is too far out on the edge of our world for the lake to reach it—far from center, as our solar system is far from the center of our galaxy.

"THE WATER GIVER DREAM" WORKSHEET
INITIAL RESPONSE

Immediate feelings upon awakening: pleasure, sense of awe in regard to task as Water Giver, contact with deeper realms

The emotional charge in the dream: being told I am to be the Giver of Water

Immediate associations: lack of water in my chart, feeling lonely and deprived, friends out of town, many work commitments

THE DREAM ITSELF

Time/location and associations: archetypal/fantasy world; lake at summer camp; Lake Tahoe (dream workshop); Negev desert

Key symbols/images and associations:

1) the lake—when I first recorded the dream, I wrote "lack"; central to community, clear, serene, receptive, sacred; the lake in sandplay therapy; safe, enclosed, unlike the ocean
2) Water (Giver of)—feeling, unconscious, baptism, giving life, spirit or nourishment, purifying, cleansing, renewing
3) cup—containing, holding, receptive vehicle, feminine, "my cup is full"; "is your cup half-empty or half-full?"
4) far edge of community/far-out arm of galaxy—being off-center, too far out, away from source of nourishment, out of contact, my ascendant at the Galactic Center (transiting Neptune near it)

Key characters and associations:

1) Me—wanting, out of water, alone, far away, journeying, seeking to receive from another, feeling honored but hesitant to take on giving role, not trusting what I have to give
2) the messenger—faceless, intermediary, dutiful, seeks to help
3) the Water Giver—God?, whoever gives nourishment, the Mother, the feminine principle, the spiritual source, therapist

Key words/phrases/puns and associations:

1) lake/lack—dried up, one must go into the lack in order to find the lake of inner nourishment, natal Saturn conjunct Venus, loneliness, lack of serenity/containment, nostalgia for the community of childhood summer camp—spiritual singing around the lake; dreamwork community at Lake Tahoe

Feelings present within the dream: wanting, needing; desire to meet needs; anticipation of journey; anxiety/disappointment at having to be the Water Giver; sense of awe and honor

Antagonistic forces: desert, no water; at first, the messenger

Healing/helping forces: the messenger, who also honors me and gives guidance; the Water Giver; the lake

Archetypes: lake, water, Water Giver

THE CONTEXT

Previous day experiences and concerns: friends leaving town for vacation, wanting time at the beach, creating sandplay scene with central lake surrounded by musicians

Following day anticipations and concerns: clients, dream group

Associations to other dreams and experiences: lake in previous dreams—on boat, looking for inlet, presence of female spirit; dreams of searching for summer camp; Lake Tahoe dreamwork training, community and communion of the spirit

When have you felt a similar way?: when needing to give out energy/inspire others; when I wish to retreat or am in need of replenishment; satisfaction in giving nourishment
How dream reflects your life situation: when my "outer lake" runs dry, my "inner lake" runs dry—difficult to give

THE DREAM ITSELF

Do one or more of the following exercises:

1) Describe yourself as a character or symbol: "I am . . ."
2) Dialogue with one of the characters or symbols.
3) Retell your dream from another point of view.
4) Rewrite dream on the left side of a page, leaving space for associations on the right side.

EXERCISE: BEING A SYMBOL—THE LAKE

I am the lake where the Giver of Water gives water to those seeking replenishment. I am at the center of community, yet I am serene, contained, enclosed by the mothering earth. At my bottom, I am the sand of the earth, solid and enduring. My soft blue waters, rippling with gentle waves, reach down into my placid depths. I am flowing, fluid; my waters renew themselves by evaporating, and then returning again as rain. Small fish play and thrive within me; I nourish the life which feeds from me. I nourish those who swim in my waters and drink of my waters, as I myself am nourished. Although I am the water that sustains life, I too am sustained by larger waters, by a larger source, of which I am a part and from which I give and receive.

EXERCISE: DIALOGUE

Messenger: Greetings, traveler. I am a messenger from the sacred Lake, delivering to you a message concerning your sacred task. What leads you to be travelling toward Center?

Me: I am so pleased to encounter you on my way to the Lake! As you can see, my cup is empty. The waters of the Lake are not reaching into my land. I must fill my cup before I return to my people. I seek the Giver of Water, so that I may be nourished and replenished by the waters She gives me.

Messenger: You seek in the right place, for as I find you whom I seek, you find She whom you seek. I come to bestow an honor upon you, a sacred task. You are the new Giver of Water.

Me: I, the Giver of Water? But my own cup is empty. I am thirsty; I wish to be nourished and fed. What have I to give others? I will not journey to the sacred Lake, if in doing so I am required to give from an empty cup, rather than fill my own. I seek the Giver of Water; I am not the Giver of water. I would rather return home to my desolate land, parched with thirst, than take on such an impossible task.

Messenger: You must not return now, so long into your journey. Your land is desolate; the waters of the Lake have not reached you because you have built your home too far from community. You live too far from the common spring, the sacred Lake, where all are replenished. As our solar system has expanded ever outward, moving far from the center of our galaxy, so you too have been ever-expanding, losing touch with the central pulse of the Lake as you journey further and further from its source.

Me: And so I seek to return to the Lake, but in order to receive, not to give from waters I do not have.

Messenger: You have been away so long you do not remember. As Giver of Water, you yourself will be immersed in water. Giving and receiving are not separate acts when one is immersed in the sacred source. As Giver of Water, you live and breathe the water that you give. What greater gift of receiving can there be, what greater promise of cups ever-filled than to embrace your task as Giver of Water? Do not fear it. It is not you who must give from your own empty cup, but the Lake which will give to you and through you. Will you choose to honor She who honors you?

ANALYSIS

Describe the dream ego in terms of:

> involved/uninvolved in action: involved, central
> active/passive: active, traveling on quest
> behaviors and actions: seeking to meet needs
> attitudes/beliefs: that another has what I need; that I must fill
> my cup before I can fill the cups of others
> apparent age/emotional age: young adult

Describe the problem/conflict: I am in need, and seek another to meet my needs. But I am told that I have to take on the role of that other. The way I am seeking to meet needs is frustrated but another way is given me. Will it satisfy?

Describe the resolution/lack of resolution: I am given a task which may or may not be a resolution. Will my cup be filled through the process of being the Giver of Water?

Describe incongruities/transformations/new developments: I am given something other than I seek. I intercept someone on my journey. I have contact with a messenger, not the Giver of Water. There is no Water Giver available but me.

What's missing? The original Water Giver. Arrival at the lake.

What are the unanswered questions? How did my cup get empty? Why is there desert at home? Who is the messenger? What happened to the first Water Giver? Why do I live so far out? Why am I to be the Water Giver? What happens when I reach the lake? Do I fill my cup by filling the cups of others?

What are the messages of the dream? By choosing to give, I may receive more than by seeking to receive. But first I need contact with the lake of spiritual/emotional sustenance.

Why do you need this dream now? So that I can consider that giving/working now may not drain me, but replenish me; so that I find fulfillment in the tasks before me.

What does the dream want from you? To embrace my role as giver, to allow myself contact with the greater source (the lake) so that I may be given from it; to create more community.

What action will you choose to take? To attune more to my inner source; to be more open in my counseling/teaching; to seek out more healing contact and sense of community.

EXPANDING THE DREAM

Do one or more of the following exercises:

1. What happened before and after? Expand and continue the dream.
2. Rewrite the dream creating a more viable resolution. (What might this have required of the dream characters?)
3. Enact the dream with one or more people. Create a psychodrama.
4. Give creative expression to the dream—a collage, drawing, painting, poem, story, dance, etc.

EXERCISE: A PROSE-POEM

(A journey into the Lack, before returning to the Lake, written over a year later, with transiting Saturn in the twelfth house squaring natal Venus conjunct Saturn in the ninth house, and the New Moon conjunct natal twelfth house Mars in Sagittarius)

Desert, Where Is Your Water?

Desert, where is your water? In what cactus flower may I sip your wine? Yet you, my barren home, have fed me with your heated heart and howling sands strewn by windstorms. How am I to abandon you—your wild wastes, your desolate dunes which leave me parched and yearning? How desperately I hoard each sunburnt drop of water you sparingly serve me; how painfully I uncover and relive my past in each excavation, digging into your subterranean depths, questing for your secret nourishment.

You, my savage land, far from the Lake, far from the Water Mother—what Earth Mother are you, so infertile, so bleak in face, so thin and hard your wasted body? Has no one held you, soothed you, plucked you with warm watery limbs from those scorching tendrils of fire which brand your soul? Have you only promising mirages which tempt and tease? How can you, who have not fed, feed those who beseech you, those who seek moisture from your familiar stones?

They turn to you repeatedly, the pilgrims, like me, seeking lands far from home—pilgrims who love only that which eludes them, that which burns them, that which punishes their hunger with thirst, their thirst with sun-blistered visions of tomorrow's wombs, or past oases which never sustained them. They turn to you rather than risk drowning in the waters, rather than risk the quenching of the fire, rather than risk the soft soothing embracing unfamiliar arms of your Sister, the Lake.

*   *   *   *   *   *   *   *   *   *

Soon after dreaming "The Water Giver," I dreamt "The Pond Fills With Water." Transiting Uranus in my twelfth house was now squaring my Venus, which transiting Jupiter in Pisces was also opposing. Transiting Saturn in my twelfth was sextile my natal Sun, while Neptune was stationary squaring my Sun. This dream clearly reveals that I was becoming the Giver of Water, and that the giving required little effort on my part, only the ability to create a channel through which the water could flow, and the willingness to enter the water.

The Pond Fills With Water

I dig a pond for swimming. It is shallow, but swimmable, and the water feels calm and soothing. I am surprised that I only had to dig a few inches for a large swimming area several feet deep to fill up with water. I swim for awhile, put up a sign by the pond, and then walk back (wearing only one shoe) to the house where I live.

Later in the day, I tell others about the pond, and return to it early in the evening with several friends. The pond is nearly dried up now—it has become three or four very shallow areas of water which are quickly evaporating. Nevertheless, when I enter the first of the shallow ponds, it immediately fills up again, merging and cohering with the waters of the other ponds, forming one large swimming area. My friends are impressed that this pond fills up with water as soon as it is entered; they say that I should write on the sign that I created and discovered it. Refusing to take credit for the pond, I tell them that all I did originally was to dig a few inches into the water, and that the pond then filled up by itself.

Cosmic Dreams

In *The Night Sky: The Science and Anthropology of the Stars and Planets*, and other books, Richard Grossinger records some of his inspirational planetary dreams. Grossinger has Uranus in Gemini in the twelfth house opposing Venus in Sagittarius, both forming a t-square to Jupiter in Virgo. Early in 1981, as the Jupiter/Saturn conjunction stationed near his natal Neptune, Grossinger had the following dream:

> I return to the village in Vermont where I once lived and am walking by the river at night. I understand that I am in the Solar System and begin looking for the planets. I see the moon Ganymede of Jupiter, radiant, enormous, and intricately engraved. It is sitting in someone's front yard. I begin to look for Jupiter itself. I suspect it must be over the large bell in the center of town. The forest is so dense that I cannot work my way through. I am very careful, for at any misstep I could stumble and fall into the largeness of Jupiter.
>
> On the way up the hill, I turn to see a tiny moon spinning rapidly in a bush in front of a house, and I think, "How cute. That's the fifteenth moon." I realize that dozens of these fiery radiant moons may be hidden in the bushes all around here, but the heaviness is pulling me up the hill to where I suddenly see through the utter black to an enormous limb of brilliance, so overwhelming it seems literally to force me back. I see the broad bands of the planet and I feel I cannot help but fall into it.
>
> It is too late. A voice is suddenly telling me that I don't understand gravitation at all. "These are not the real planets," it says. "They are painted balls." I understand that it is speaking about actual planets in space; it is saying that they themselves are only painted balls and that these replicas of them are mere symbols of the internal planets. There is another gravity, inside gravity, which is the real core of substance. I feel a wholeness and a bigness as if all that cannot be connected or realized in a lifetime is joined in a unity of self for this one moment.[8]

When cosmic or transpersonal dreams occur, they often have an enduring effect upon our consciousness. We are changed, as if we have encountered a god within ourselves. The messages which these and other dreams reveal are sacred truths which none can take from us, for they are the truths of our inner being, our channel to the source within us, the pathway to our soul.

Many poets have written of the magical nature of the dream world, and its capacity to frustrate and fulfill our desires. In "The Shadowy Waters," W. B. Yeats wrote:

> *. . . All would be well*
> *Could we but give us wholly to the dreams,*
> *And get into their world that to the sense*
> *Is shadow, and not linger wretchedly*
> *Among substantial things; for it is dreams*
> *That lift us to the flowing, changing world*
> *That the heart longs for.*[9]

Yet because we are physical beings living on the earth plane, we cannot expect to find fulfillment in our dream world alone; indeed, the greatest value of our dreaming is its ability to enrich our waking life—to discharge troublesome emotions, to evoke inspirational feelings, to provide insight and illumination in regard to our attitudes, behaviors, conflicts, vulnerabilities, talents, gains, and growth process.

> *Dreams—are well—but Waking's better,*
> *If One wake at Morn—*
> *If One wake at Midnight—better—*
> *Dreaming—of the Dawn—*
> —Emily Dickinson[10]

The Dream Experience:
Twelfth House Case Studies

During the past few years, I have been leading weekly dream groups in which students share, explore, interpret, and creatively express their dreams. This year, every one of my dream group participants has one or more twelfth house planets. Six have agreed to reveal their dreams and current issues, in order to demonstrate the value of dreamwork, and the relationship between dreams and the twelfth house.

Karen: Twelfth House Saturn in Capricorn & Jupiter in Aquarius

Karen, an art education student in her mid-twenties, lives with her boyfriend, an instructor at her school, who is often preoccupied with his work. Currently undertaking a demanding school and internship schedule, she also has little time for relationship, for her own creative expression, and for spiritual pursuits which she values. Several years earlier, Karen had been a devotee of a well-known guru. Many of her dreams reflect her yearning for a guru or spiritual leader and show the conflicts she has experienced as a result of giving up her power to men (often father figures) whom she idealizes.

Karen's twelfth house contains Saturn in late Capricorn conjunct Jupiter in early Aquarius. Jupiter rules her tenth and eleventh house; Saturn rules her twelfth house. Together, these planets express her desire for social and spiritual transformation through group experience. Because twelfth house energies are often projected, and because this conjunction sextiles her first house Sun in Pisces, Karen is likely to be seeking a spiritual hero who embodies a new social order. Both planets also inconjunct her seventh house Pluto, semisextile Mercury, and square her second house Venus in Aries, which is represented in her life by her art work and by her attachment to aesthetic objects, such as crystals, which have transcendent meaning for her.

In many of Karen's dreams, she is working through her experience of living at the guru's commune. In one dream, members of the commune walk on her drawings and dirty them. This dream raises the issue of whether she can create for herself an environment or community which supports her personal expression. During the dream group, she shared the following dream:

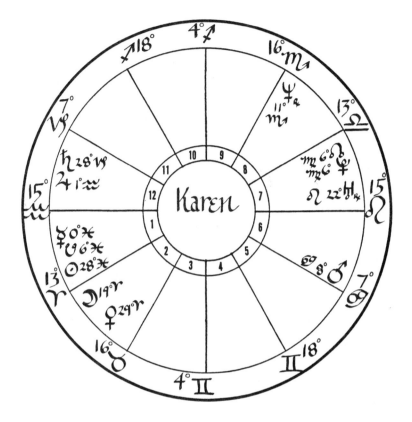

I'm at the commune, near a large building. The guru is speaking on the roof. I go outside into a crowd of thousands of people to listen to him. At first, it's raining lightly; then it begins to pour. Because everyone wants to hear him, we continue to stand in the rain. But a fatherly older man puts his arms around me, and guides me inside, out of the rain.

In discussing this dream, Karen expressed her objections to the guru—his use of power, his willfulness, his lack of responsiveness to his disciples' feelings and needs. She also shared the guilt she feels in having left him, a guilt which may be an extension of her guilt in separating from her parents (especially from her father) and in beginning to express and trust her own power. The Capricornian twelfth house suggests Karen's tendency to deprive herself for the sake of authority figures whom she idealizes, as well as her search for a father figure. In this dream, the fatherly man is an alternative to the guru, but without the charisma, glamour, and power that he offers.

Another dream expresses some of the conflicts with authority which Karen experienced in her graduate school courses:

> My brother and I are climbing a hill through the woods, on our way to a communications workshop; I'm wearing sandals which are inadequate for climbing. When we get there I feel arrogant about the material and don't pay attention. I get up and put my crystals up on the bulletin board—large crystals, which I place in a semi-circular design.
>
> During the break, the leader tells me that I have energy like my crystals. At first, I feel complimented, but then I realize that he does not like crystals, and that he is insulting me. I joke with him.
>
> Later I notice that he has taken all of my crystals down, and is selling his own. When I ask for mine back, he won't return them. I am so angry that I spit in his face and in the face of a woman he sends to talk with me. He then gives me all of mine but the two which are the most valuable. When I describe them to him and demand them back, he points to two large broken crystals on the floor, as if these are my crystals. He then brings me ones he's found in the swimming pool filter. I insist that these are not my crystals, and that I want mine back. He doesn't give them back.
>
> Afterwards, I'm with my grandmother, cleaning the toilet and sink with the toilet brush, removing layers and layers of dirt.

Here Karen is struggling with issues in regard to giving her power away to others, and reclaiming it. This dream occurred after a class at school in which she had harshly judged another student's work. Karen initially felt pleased that she had expressed her opinion, but was upset by the negative reaction of the class. In her dream, the only way she knew how to assert her power when it was taken from her was to spit in the leader's face. But metaphorically, the spit came back to her—not only did she fail to get her crystals back, but she soon was cleaning up the dirt in her grandmother's bathroom. This dream raises issues of whom Karen trusts with her personal resources (the loss of the crystals representing the square to second house Venus), and her process of reclaiming the power of her twelfth house Saturn/Jupiter, without resorting to the potential viciousness of a Mercury/Pluto opposition.

Debby: Twelfth House Saturn
conjunct Pluto in Leo

Debby is a hard-working professional who operates her own home-based advertising business; she has developed professional and sports-related friendships with men, but shies away from romantic and sexual involvements. Although heterosexual, she acknowledges that she is too afraid of physical intimacy with men to allow them to get very close to her. The youngest and only daughter in a family with three sons, Debby was actively coached by her father to excel in sports and in her studies. When her father died of cancer when Debby was only fifteen, she was devastated, and unable to redirect her interest to boys. She still idealizes her father.

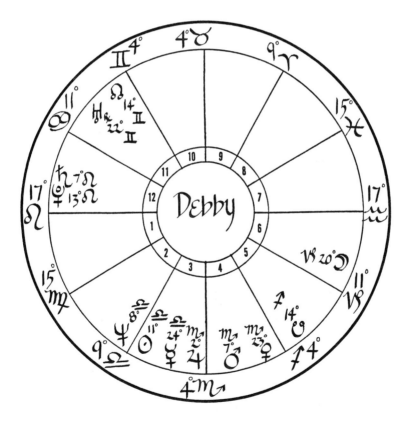

Debby has a twelfth house Saturn/Pluto conjunction in Leo, squaring a Mars/Jupiter conjunction in Scorpio, and sextiling a Sun/Neptune conjunction in Libra on the second/third house cusp. Her sixth house Moon is in Capricorn, sextiling Venus in Scorpio. Transiting Pluto was approaching Debby's Mars/Saturn square when she had the following dreams:

1) I am outside near a large baseball field in a walled-in structure with an open roof but a locked gate. Two of my friends are talking to me through the gate, planning to help me get out. Later they return with a key and unlock the gate, so that I can leave. After they have left, I walk out into the open field, but feel so exposed that I return to the enclosure, not through the gate but by climbing over the walls which suddenly appear to be only a few feet high. Then, a number of rough-housing young guys run onto the field, see me, and begin making obscene comments. One walks right up to the enclosure, and starts to climb over the walls. I am afraid that he is going to sexually threaten me.

2) A friend of mine, Jim, is visiting. He is tired, and falls asleep on the couch. Because my roommate Andrea and her boyfriend Tom are due home, I suggest that we go upstairs to my bedroom. But then Tom and Andrea arrive. Jim gets up and opens a closet door, which reveals a secret stairway. He wonders if there is a room at the bottom. I climb down the dark stairway, which now has become a rope ladder; after a few rungs, the ladder ends, and I step down into nothingness. I am holding on by my arms, afraid to fall into the blackness below. I know that Jim is at the top of the stairway and can reach down to pull me up, but I call out to Tom for help, hoping that he will rescue me.

3) I am in high school. Today we choose partners for the "Vault," the vehicles we will journey in after death. During this journey, we will be in complete communion with our partners, physically and spiritually. Our teacher tells us that we may not choose a current friend or boyfriend, but that we must choose someone with whom we are not in relationship in this life. I want to be with Sam, a very popular boy who has never talked to me. A very brainy unpopular woman asks Sam to be her partner; he turns her down and then chooses me. I am thrilled.

4) I am at a beach where huge waves crash against the beach wall. A man is with me who is tanned, has long grey hair, and is muscular and strong. I say that the waves aren't very big, but then a huge wave breaks against the sea wall, and I realize that they are larger than I thought. We both have to go somewhere along the wall, and the only way to get there is by swimming through the waves crashing against the wall. He tells me that I shouldn't worry, that he is a powerful swimmer, and that I should let him hold me against his chest, while he puts one arm around me, and swims; one of my arms will be against him,

and the other will be free. I feel a sense of trust and safety, knowing that he can protect me from the waves.

In the first dream of this series, Debby is afraid of letting down her walls and exposing herself to males, who are too sexually threatening. She feels safer locking the gate of her feminine sexuality, but still cannot keep out the male intruders—her inner male energies climb over the walls and threaten her. In the second dream, she is considering sexual contact with a male friend (who, like her sexuality, is asleep), but the prospect of inviting him into her bedroom awakens fears of descent into her own dark bottomless fears. Seeking to be rescued from these fears, she calls out to her roommate's boyfriend, who is not a potential lover. These dreams clearly express her fear of sexual involvement, expressed by her twelfth house Saturn/Pluto in square to Mars/Jupiter in Scorpio.

The third dream becomes particularly revealing when we realize that Debby's father's middle name was Samuel, and that he was called Sam during his school days. This dream raises the question: Is Debby wedded to her father's spirit? Can she only allow herself full communion with a man through death? Debby may be the brainy unpopular girl in the dream, but she is also Sam's chosen one. This dream portrays the depth of her psychic, sexualized bond with her dead father.

In the fourth dream, another shift occurs. Debby's trust in men is increasing; she can allow physical contact, if only to protectively shield her against the turbulent waters of her unconscious. The man is greyhaired, older; he is strong, powerful, and nurturing. At the time of this dream, although Debby does not have a lover, she has been exchanging friendly massages with her friend Jim, and experiencing a greater trust with him. Slowly, she is working through some of the barriers which she has developed against intimacy.

One significant feature of all four dreams is that they portray situations in which Debby is looking to others (mostly men) to reach out to her or rescue her. Unable to fully own the power of her Saturn/Pluto conjunction in square to Mars/Jupiter, she experiences it outside herself as threatening or protective males. As Debby begins to come to terms with her father's death and confront her terror of intimacy, she is likely to awaken to her emotional/sexual energy and power, which until now she has channeled into a driven, obsessive focus upon her business.

Christian: Twelfth House Neptune in Scorpio

Christian is a young South American completing a bachelors degree in philosophy in Boston while simultaneously opening to new spiritual horizons by attending New Age community workshops. A Sagittarian with a t-square to a first house Sun/Mercury conjunction, Christian has a twelfth house Neptune in Scorpio, which sextiles his third house Venus in Capricorn, his second house Mars in Capricorn, and also sextiles an eleventh house Uranus/Pluto conjunction. Uranus and Pluto also oppose his Piscean Moon, ruler of his ninth house.

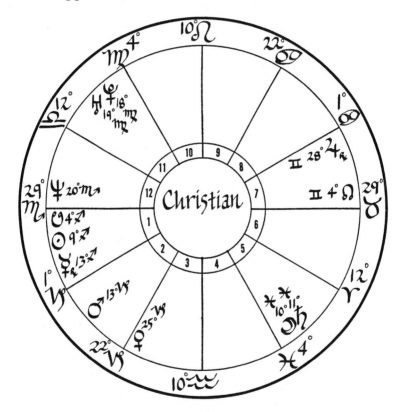

While participating in the dream group, Christian is wrestling with his discontent in regard to his studies, which do not feel relevant to his spiritual quest. The specter of "society's" requirements menaces him. Because of the power of the culture and establishment in his native country, because of his perceptions of requirements for success in U.S. society, and because of the values of his father which he has internalized, completing a college degree is important to him. Yet because he is finding fulfillment in his personal quest, and feeling powerless in regard to society and its educational institutions, Christian is considering dropping out of school. During the dream group, he shares the following dreams:

1) I am with friends, passing by a Boston University administration building. My friends start throwing tennis balls, breaking the very high windows of the building. Because I am afraid of being caught or of harming someone, I don't throw any balls at the windows. Instead, I walk back to see if anyone in the building is looking at us. As a result, I am in the angle of vision of the people inside; I hear them describing me as a "dark long-haired guy," obviously considering me to be guilty of breaking the windows.

2) I am observing a black knight, with four other knights. One is the father of a young knight who is soon to be leaving. They have all arrived in town, after taking part in an honorable venture or battle. Several of the knights, speaking to the father, praise the son for his good qualities. The father disagrees, insisting that his son is not good or noble, that he only wants to do what he wants to do, and declares "He is not my son." The other knights try to convince him of his son's virtues.

3) Don Quixote is trying to tame an old horse. Finally, the horse surrenders, falling down in the hay, as a crowd of people watch and laugh. He and the horse appear to be putting on a show for the audience. Don Quixote is really not attempting to tame the horse, which is only going through the motions of pretending that he is being tamed.

These dreams reflect the dilemmas of Christian's dedication to his noble Neptunian ideals, his sense of victimization in regard to adapting to society's requirements, his difficulty owning and expressing his anger (and wilder instincts) at the expense of being civilized and chivalrous, and his experience of going through the motions of adaptation while simultaneously refusing to allow his free spirit to be tamed. Christian's spiritual quest may be motivated by the willful rebellion against society expressed by his eleventh house Uranus/Pluto conjunction as well as the call of his Neptunian soul and his Venusian hunger for connection with kindred spirits. He is also influenced by Spanish ideals of chivalrous male behavior, at odds with the ideals of the questing inner knight of New Age America.

Some part of Christian wants the respect of his father and the respect of society. Yet the pursuit of Capricornian values starves rather than feeds his soul. The outer world appears to require a sacrifice of his vital Sagittarian horse spirit; yet he refuses to make such a sacrifice. In the administration building dream, the only expression of power appears to be reactive—a destructive aggression against the power source. Unable to rebel outwardly, Christian allows his friends to express his aggression for him; yet he is even more victimized as a result. Discussing this dream, the group explored alternatives besides destructive power and victimization. How could Christian fulfill some of his ideals through and within his school program? Could he do independent studies or gain credit from some of his workshop experiences? Another important question was raised by the sharing of these dreams. To what extent is Christian attached to the idea of being a victim, defending his ideals against a powerful enemy, and to what extent is he committed to bringing those ideals out of his twelfth house, empowering himself to live them within the institutions and structures of society?

These dreams emerged soon after Christian's progressed New Moon occurred at one degree Capricorn. According to Dane Rudhyar, the Sabian Symbol for this degree is: "An Indian chief claims power from the assembled tribe." Rudhyar's interpretation refers to "the religious ideal materialized or crystallized into sheer power . . . the capacity latent in every individual to claim and assume authority in a vital group situation . . . Energies released through group cooperation, deepened and emotionally experienced as forces of great potency, and given meaning and conscious purpose, are now stabilized and hierarchized."[11] This symbol is likely to guide the integration process of Christian's twelfth house Neptune throughout his new lunation cycle.

Ann: Twelfth House Sun/Mercury in Aquarius, Moon/Venus in Pisces

Ann is an electronics engineer in her late twenties, a pilot, a dedicated runner, a closet poet, and an active participant in the feminist spirituality movement. As one of three daughters of an often unemployed machinist who had no sympathy for his wife or children, she spent her early years doing household and yard chores, car repairs, and secretly writing poetry about nature. She never felt allowed to be a child, to have nice clothes, or to exist at all as an individual.

Terrified of her father, who physically abused her mother and verbally abused his daughters, Ann is seeking to overthrow her negative conditioning in regard to men, and eventually to marry. Recently, she experienced the painful end of a live-in relationship with a man who

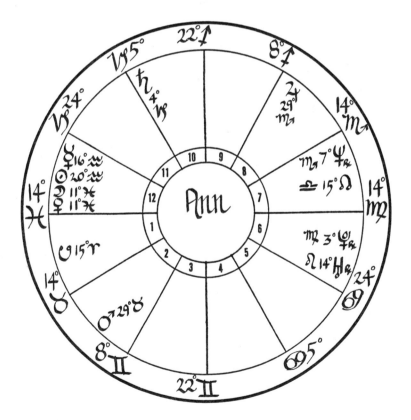

"blew hot and cold," who frequently rejected her, and was unreliable in regard to commitment. Ann has a twelfth house Sun/Mercury conjunction in Aquarius opposing Uranus, and a twelfth house Moon/Venus conjunction which opposes Pluto and trines her Neptune.

Soon after her boyfriend left her, Ann dreamt that she could escape from threatening men by flying:

> My father and I are walking through a large field with flowers and vegetables when we meet a scrungy drunken man and see the shack where he lives. He warns us to stay away from his rows of plants. Later, when we are walking again, he unexpectedly appears, harasses me, and pushes me around. Then he yells at me, "Nyahh, nyahh, you need your father, little girl," and I scream. My father and I walk away.
>
> On the way home, we see a strange airplane, long with wide wings and a young pilot in the cockpit. On the tail, a man is getting ready to parachute. My father tells me what kind of plane it is. When it lands, the pilot gets out and helps the parachutist. My father goes home, but I stay.
>
> Then the man appears again, taunts me and grabs me. "Don't touch my garden," he tells me. I run as fast as I can through a field of tall grass as he pursues me. When he gets close, I lift off the ground and am flying above the earth in a horizontal position. I am actually flying! I kick my legs for leverage.
>
> Later, I am running down a street lined by fruit trees which are touching each other. I see the man again, running down a dirt path away from me, in the opposite direction. I watch to make sure he is not going to follow me.

In this dream, the male image is split into two—the father/companion (Sun/Mercury in Aquarius) and the unpredictable harrassing man (Uranus, Pluto). This scoundrel's concern with protecting his plants and gardens (Moon/Venus in Pisces) may symbolize the need of the unintegrated male force to protect its feminine nature or sensitivity from exposure, as Ann's father may have done by aggressively striking out at the feminine outside himself, and as Ann may do by maintaining her treasured Moon/Venus in Pisces garden of poetry and feminist spirituality.

When Ann had this dream, she was not only mourning the end of a relationship, but also feeling burdened by family responsibility; her father, who has a deteriorative illness, is now unable to walk. When asked about needing her father, she said, "No. My father needs me now." Yet she also admitted that she was feeling badly about her potential for marriage, and struggling against her need for a man. Her yearning may also be related to half-forgotten walks with her father during childhood.

Ann was inspired by the exhilaration of flying in her dream and by her capacity to lift off as a means of getting away from a threatening male. What does flying mean to her? "Being aware," she says, "using my mind, understanding the situation, weighing the positives and negatives, rising above it."

Her Sun/Mercury conjunction in Aquarius reveals itself not only in her dream, but also in a poem she wrote afterwards. Here too is her Moon/Venus awareness of a female spiritual force:

> *Looking down from my mile-high perch,*
> *Twisting, turning, through each cloud I pass,*
> *Viewing the world from another dimension . . .*
>
> *Take off becomes a quick escape*
> *Leaving confusion and worry behind.*
> *Now my focus is one, the challenge before me.*
> *With each foot of altitude, my wings keep expanding;*
> *New eyes are projecting through smog and despair.*
> *This slithered shell sheds away from me, falling,*
> *Exposing soft weakness of belly beneath.*
> *Cold sting of waking wind slaps at my face,*
> *Reminding me that I'm on my own.*
>
> *Like the crown of a prince,*
> *Power is bestowed upon me*
> *By Mother Nature whose daughter is Air,*
> *She thrusts out her hand and I take it.*
> *Oh, how wondrous and magical a time.*
> *Like a child in awe, my eyes swell with tears.*
> *I worship her lovingly, as my plane banks and rolls,*
> *Never leave me! This floating fantasy . . .*
> *The lure of air, the breath of life . . .*
>
> *Three hundred sixty degrees of horizon,*
> *The focal point of infinity is me.*

Another dream which Ann shared with the dream group occurred the night after a Halloween celebration of death, which involved facing one's fear of dying (symbolized by the death of the Sun), purging oneself of negative emotions, and awakening to spiritual energies:

> I am walking, crossing a street marked by a sign which reads, "Entering small and large intestine." I know that I'm inside myself. I encounter

a man pointing to a blinding white light in the sky, who says that those who look at the light must wear protective dark glasses.

Then I'm observing people on stage. A friend puts on dark glasses, and a black-robed magician turns on the light. When a woman in the group looks at the light without glasses, she is told to put on dark glasses; she doesn't listen, and becomes dizzy and collapses. I wake to the lines from a song, "walking this land, walking this wasteland."

The small and large intestine in this dream reflect Ann's absorption/assimilation of her Halloween experience, and her letting go of emotional waste products. The contrast between light and dark forces (Moon/Venus in Pisces in the twelfth house opposing Pluto, ruler of her eighth house) is expressed by the black-robed magician and the power of the light. One interpretation of this dream is that it suggests fear of the sublime, fear of the process of opening to higher energies, which inevitably releases dark energies which have blocked the light; it also expresses the awesome power of the spirit, which may feel like annihilation of the ego and bodily self.

When we have a history of childhood abuse or deprivation, the experience of letting go of familiar past patterns or opening oneself to loving, affirming energies is more terrifying than maintaining past patterns. What we know as our self is threatened; our boundaries dissolve, and we may fear internal collapse. We are torn between deep unsatisfied yearnings to open to greater fulfillment, and the terror of loss of self, along with the release of past fear, anger, and pain that such opening catalyzes. Such openings may occur through spiritual or creative experience, and through allowing ourselves to feel and receive love and to relax into the warm bonds of community.

For Ann, as for many of us, the fear of the light is not only fear of the spirit, but also fear of awakening to love. At the time of the dream, she had been avoiding contact with a former partner, afraid to experience love and the yearning for closeness. With her Moon/Venus opposing Pluto, and with a mother who cowered in fear of beatings by her father, Ann had no role model for a woman who maintains power and strength with men. To be receptive to intimate relationship would be to open to the light of love (as well as desire and emotional need) and feel overpowered and weakened in relation to a threatening male.

Soon after this dream, when Ann was feeling powerless in a difficult work situation, as well as struggling with fears and yearnings in regard to relationship, she had a compensatory dream. For years, Ann had admired Lucille Ball, about whom she says, "She's spontaneous, funny, imaginative, a sweetheart to millions of people. She's successful; she has her life in her own hands. And she doesn't let her husband push her around. When he tries to, she always schemes behind his back, so that she can do what she really wants anyway." For Ann, Lucille expresses the integration of her Moon/Venus in Pisces femininity and sensitivity, as well as the inventiveness and independence of her twelfth house Aquarius Sun/Mercury opposing Uranus (which happens to conjunct Lucille Ball's natal Sun!). In her dream, a friend was taking pictures of Lucille, with Ann in the background; afterwards Lucille assured Ann that she would marry during the next year. Ann found this dream reassuring and encouraging, not only because of the marriage prediction, but also because it revitalized for her the identification with Lucille Ball, a constructive female role model for Ann in her attempt to forge an independent, self-affirming, and integrated identity.

Jennifer: Twelfth House Jupiter
& South Node in Scorpio

Jennifer is a forty-year-old woman with a Ph.D. in French literature. Several years ago, when her mother died and Jennifer received an inheritance, she left academia and devoted herself to her own personal growth; she has since been experiencing "a spiritual revolution," during which her beliefs about herself and reality are dramatically changing. During this time, she has met a number of men, struggled with issues in regard to trust (related to her new financial status), and encountered hostility from men who reject her spiritual beliefs.

Although Jennifer has scored high on vocational tests related to her professional interests, she has avoided taking action in regard to pursuing a new career. She seems to be facing discrepancies in regard

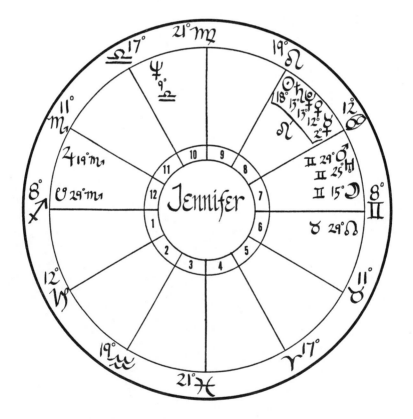

to the smallness and largeness of her self-image—she has a Ph.D., wealth, and leisure, but she has lost both her parents, is developing a new sense of identity, and is anxious about entering a new professional field.

Jennifer has Jupiter and the South Node in Scorpio in her twelfth house. Jupiter squares her ninth house cusp Leo Sun, which conjuncts eighth house Saturn, Pluto, and Venus in Leo. The dreams she shares in the group reflect her current process of transformation, particularly in regard to issues of smallness/largeness of self, and learning to trust a new reality which honors her relationship to spiritual forces:

> I am standing at the check-out counter of a plant store. A lady who knows the clerk pays for an item and gives the clerk a piece of Swedish ivy as a gift. Then someone else hands him a worm, which resembles the ivy stem; it is light green, with a faint red line.
>
> Next, the clerk and I are sitting at a white filigree garden table; the cutting and worm are on top of the table. As we talk, the worm begins to do antics, taking on various amoeba-like shapes. We watch in fascination and amusement. Finally, it turns into a small crustacean, a nautilus, and then turns on its back, like a dog or cat, as if inviting us to scratch its tummy. We find the creature very endearing, and feel drawn to adopt it or take care of it.
>
> Then, my friend Marianne appears. We are both in a musical group, preparing to take a show on the road. When she sees the creature, she says that we must not leave it behind; she insists that we delay our trip in order to give it the care that it needs. We deliberate what we will do.

In the dream group, Jennifer contacted deep realms of sadness as she identified with the worm. Speaking as the worm, she described herself as small, soft on the inside, trapped deep beneath the earth, and feeling alien, as if from another world. Crying, she embraced her small vulnerable self, relinquishing the confident persona of her Leo Sun and Sagittarian ascendant. Yet as she allowed herself to be the worm, and to be appreciated by a responsive audience, she felt herself changing into a nautilus and then moving up the scale of evolution to become higher forms of animals, and eventually human. This dream reflects the subliminal growth process of Jennifer's twelfth house Jupiter in Scorpio, which, in its square to her Leo stellium, seeks largeness of self, but can only attain that largeness by first encountering her small, rejected Scorpionic worm-self, and embracing it.

A few weeks later, Jennifer had the following dream, just before an important romantic relationship developed with a man who shares her belief system:

I am Shirley MacLaine and have a husband; we are dining with another couple. I feel bonded to them, because we are believers in and promoters of New Age thought. However, because my husband retains some skepticism, my man friend challenges me to influence him. He says, "by Sunday morning" and I respond with "Oh, Sunday morning," making a clown face, smiling and winking, accepting the challenge. As Shirley MacLaine, I am devilish, humorous, and audacious, much more so than I am in my daily life.

Sunday morning my husband and I drive up to a hill of rocks, next to a broken, rusty metal fence. Climbing the rocks, we see the sun rising over the boiling ocean. The scene is peaceful, beautiful. Then, suddenly, a huge wave rises up above the rocks and above our heads, and crashes down, terrifying us. The wave's enormity and power are so awesome that my husband instantly becomes a believer, convinced in the reality of spiritual forces greater than ourselves. Although I am clever and cunning, I had not arranged for this to happen; the wave was unexpected, undeniable in its power, convincing to both of us.

In discussing this dream, Jennifer acknowledged the skeptical part of herself that only slowly has been able to embrace a new sense of reality. She also revelled in the playfulness of what she identified as herself as Shirley MacLaine, which clearly reflected her twelfth house Jupiter in square to a Leo stellium. Enacting the tidal wave of the dream, Jennifer breathed deeply, and spoke of her experience as a large, awesome force of nature. In connection with the tidal wave, she felt calm, centered, large enough to encounter and contain the insecurities of her human/worm/nautilus self. A few months later, Jennifer mentioned, "I do this breathing and remember the dream, particularly the wave, whenever I feel stress, need strength, or need to 'come into myself.'" For the last dream group, a creative dream ceremony, she arrived dressed as Shirley MacLaine, completely at ease expressing this facet of herself. She also revealed plans to marry the man she met after having the dream.

Laura: Twelfth House Sun
& Venus in Virgo, Neptune in Libra

Laura is a divorced mother in her mid-forties who recently moved across the U.S. with her youngest son in order to live with her lover, a sensitive Cancerian psychotherapist. Previously a practitioner in the holistic health field, she is now taking time off from work to be with her partner, to develop massage skills which focus upon mind/body integration, to pursue her talent in sculpture, and to come to terms with the inner conflicts which have troubled her most of her life. Laura experienced considerable emotional and physical abuse as a child, and is deeply ashamed of her limitations. Because her father could not tolerate expressions of love or happiness, and because her mother was plagued by her own emotional problems and could not

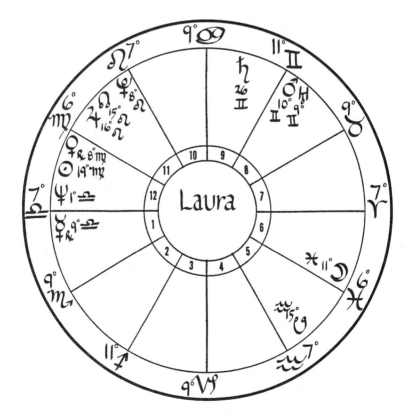

respond to her daughter, Laura learned to devalue even her most positive attributes. She is currently attempting to heal the wounded child
within herself.

Laura has three planets in her twelfth house. Sun and Venus in
Virgo oppose her Piscean Moon in the sixth house and square her
eighth house Mars/Uranus conjunction, the focal point of her t-square.
Both her Virgo Sun and her Libran Neptune square her ninth house
Saturn in Gemini. Laura has eight squares and oppositions to twelfth
house planets, but no sextiles or trines.

Because she has had many recurring dreams since childhood, Laura
decided to focus upon these dreams. One, which stopped occurring
soon after she divorced and began to abandon self-sacrificial relationship patterns, first occurred when she was ten years old and had a
crush on a boy:

> I am going with my father to see the boy whom I like, and his father.
> All four of us are driving in the car, when we pass through a large
> gathering of people, and my father decides to stop and find out what's
> going on. I am surprised that he stops, because the gathering appears
> to be a religious ceremony, and he is not religiously inclined. When
> we get out of the car, we see three black mountains. On top of the moun-
> tains, priests in white robes are conducting sacrifices, throwing their
> victims off the mountains. My father decides to participate in the
> ceremony by sacrificing me. I feel betrayed, and am terrified. I wake
> up in horror as the priests lift me up in order to throw me off the
> mountain.

This dream clearly expresses the dilemma of Laura's twelfth house
Sun and Neptune square her ninth house Saturn, and the violent
squares to her eighth house Mars/Uranus. Reminiscent of the Iphigenia
myth, in which Agamemnon sacrificed his daughter Iphigenia to the
gods, it portrays the anguish and betrayal of growing up in a family
in which the father's belief system and personality cannot support
or tolerate the true self of his daughter; he must destroy her. The
daughter, as a result, feels that in order to maintain her bond with
the father, or with a man that she loves, she must also sacrifice herself.

Fortunately, through psychotherapy and spiritual development,
Laura has been working through this pattern. One series of recurring
dreams, also beginning in childhood, reflects her discovery of her
inner light. The first dream occurred repeatedly when she was a child:

> I am walking in a garden, a maze of hedges, desperately looking for something which is in the center of the garden. But I can't find what I am looking for, and I can't find my way to the center. I wake up in a state of intolerable yearning for something which is out of reach.

Years later, married and with young children, and only beginning to awaken to her true self, Laura experienced a significant change in her dreams. Transiting Pluto and progressed Mercury were conjunct her Neptune when she dreamed:

> I am now in the center of the garden. My view is hampered by a fog which obscures everything. Yet through the fog I have a dim view of a nativity scene. I am close to it, but unable to see it clearly, or get any nearer.

These dreams reflect the yearning which Laura must have experienced for love and acceptance, and for the recovery of her inner self, which is linked to her innate spiritual sensibility. Her twelfth house Venus, in close opposition to a Pisces Moon, reflects her unsatisfied yearning, symbolized by the quest in the garden. Likewise, Sun and Neptune in square to ninth house Saturn suggest the obstacles which she experiences in her search.

Early in the 1980s, when Jupiter and Saturn conjuncted her Sun and Neptune, Laura turned away from traditional religion, devoted herself to her spiritual awakening, had an out-of-body experience at the birth of her youngest child, and separated from her husband. At this time, she had the following dream, which has unfolded still further in subsequent dreams and meditations:

> I am in the middle of the garden, with my son, Tim. Walking into the Zen temple there, we see on the wall a large picture of Christ, who has an expression of ecstasy upon his face as the light shines through him. I say to my son, "This is the *Ecce Homo*," although I know it isn't, because in the *Ecce Homo* Christ is suffering, bleeding, pierced by thorns. I point again to the picture, and say, "Tim, the important thing is to look at the light." I wake feeling ecstatic, bathed with light, totally at peace.

In a more recent dream, Buddha in the Zen temple beckoned to her to enter, saying "What are you doing sitting outside? Come into the light!" In both these dreams, Laura is contacting her spiritual source, beginning to heal herself. Yet the task remains to integrate her spirituality into daily life, so that she does not alternate between being the unloved, shamed, suffering daughter, worthy only of her father's betrayal, and the woman attuned to her divine source, bathed in light, and capable of loving and healing others.

A Twelfth House Dream Journey

For most of my life, I have lived in my twelfth house. Although I have only one twelfth house planet, Mars in Sagittarius, Mars rules my nadir, home of my Arian Moon. Outer planet transits passing through my twelfth house—Neptune, Uranus, Jupiter, and Saturn—have also sensitized me to its psychological and spiritual meanings. As a dedicated journal writer, I have recorded not only the experiences of my conscious self, but also the journeys of my subconscious self through dreams.

Most of the dreams I have recorded during the past twelve years directly reflect my twelfth house issues. Certain themes repeat themselves; all are related to Mars square a second house Aquarian Jupiter, semi-square Neptune, and sextile a ninth house Libran Sun. My most frequent dream stories are:

1) *missing a long-distance plane flight because I spend too much time packing, and because I am overburdened with luggage;*

2) *traveling in a foreign country, struggling to make connections with planes and buses, in search of a secret, mystical lake and the familiar woods which surround it;*

3) *standing on the beach of a foreign island, witnessing a tidal wave approaching, while deciding whether to run or protect my body with a covering of air mattresses and soft objects;*

4) *arriving in school to discover that I have been scheduled to take auto mechanics, science and physical education instead of the creative writing and poetry classes I had chosen.*

What do my dreams reveal about my Mars and its aspects, and my twelfth house transits? Many dreams reflect my Mars/Jupiter square, involving not only Jupiter's second house placement, but also its rulership of my ascendant—issues concerning my relationship to my body and the outer world. Repeatedly, I have dreamt of physical, emotional, and financial violation, of aggression, of attachment to possessions, and of having inadequate or adequate resources. I have dreamt of disowning and reowning my body, and of the experience of the inner male—rejected, projected, and overpowering or protecting my female self. Finally, my commitment to a life of inner expansion and the issue of whether to expose myself or to remain in hiding are prevalent themes.

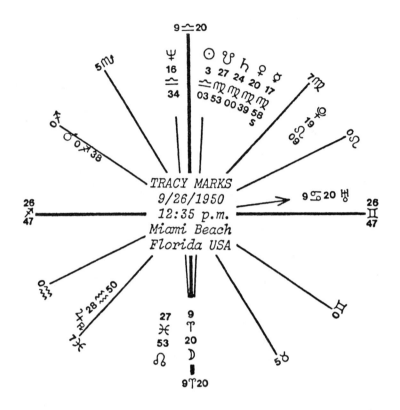

Over the past twelve years, I have witnessed my progress in these areas as reflected in the development of each theme, and in my increasing capacity to have and recall dreams which portray my rejected shadow. Whenever another unpleasant shadow dream bursts into consciousness, it is often followed by dreams of birthing, resolution, and breakthrough, which eventually manifest as new and rewarding growth experiences in my outer life. A traumatic dream or nightmare often signifies the release of a past psychological pattern which has been obstructing me. Sometimes, a dream will repeat itself—variations on a theme—until I have confronted and made peace with the issues which are symbolized.

In this chapter, I am presenting dreams and dream interpretations which reveal my twelfth house dynamics for a number of reasons: 1) as an example of an in-depth exploration of twelfth house issues;

2) as a catalyst for helping you to access your issues and clarify your process of integration, which may be both similar to and different from my own; 3) as a means of encouraging you to learn to recall, record, and interpret your dreams, so that you may discover the treasures that lie buried within your twelfth house.

Many of my dreams—and most likely, many of your dreams—are unpleasant. But contrary to common expectation, the experience of the ugliest, most fearful dreams allows us to reown and integrate our rejected selves. Having and understanding a disturbing dream usually transforms the energy which the dream reveals. It also enables us to receive dreams of new birthings, of growth, of guidance, and of transcendence, as we become capable of expressing these new attitudes and behaviors within our lives.

Here are some of my most significant dreams which portray my successful and unsuccessful attempts to confront and resolve twelfth house conflicts!

Trusting Inner Guidance

The Ring Dream

I am on a cruise ship traveling from America to Europe. One day, as I am leaning over the railing looking down into the water, my treasured amethyst ring slips off my finger, and disappears beneath the ocean. When I ask the captain to stop the boat so that I can recover my ring, he laughs at me. Not only is the ring at the bottom of the ocean by now, he tells me, but we don't even know where, since we have passed the place where it fell. He believes that I should accept that my ring is lost, and I will never recover it.

But I refuse to believe him. When I arrive in Europe, I take the next ship back to the U.S.; there I attempt to hire a boat and a skindiver to recover my ring. Everyone laughs at me for attempting an impossible task. I can't even describe precisely where my ring fell; by now it could be almost anywhere in a huge expanse of ocean.

Finally, I give up seeking help, and rent a small boat by myself. For days I paddle out into the ocean, until intuitively I know that I am in the vicinity of my ring. Then I dive into the water, and pick up my ring from the bottom of the ocean. In spite of what everyone said, I KNEW that I would recover my ring again, and was able to do so by trusting and following my inner guidance.

"The Ring Dream," one of my earliest recorded dreams, occurred in 1975 when the transiting North Node was conjunct my twelfth house

Mars. The amethyst ring is an actual ring I wear, which my mother bought for me in a region of Tuscany, Italy where I had had a deja vu experience when I was a child. The ring has always symbolized to me my connection to my deepest self, the internal experience of "coming home," and my own spiritual purpose.

For me, "The Ring Dream" was a message to trust my inner guidance. Having recently been laid off from my first teaching job, I was hoping to earn a living independently, write a book, teach astrology and creative writing, and do astrological consultations. No one who knew me believed I would be able to do so. But I was determined to follow the call of my inspiration. During a year of public school teaching, I had nearly lost my connection to my soul; now I was regaining it.

Only years later did I become aware of another message implicit in "The Ring Dream," one which states a problem rather than indicates resolution. In this dream, my inner life and the response of the outer world are at odds with each other. As my twelfth house Mars in Sagittarius square my Ascendant ruler Jupiter suggests, the outer world laughed at my inner quest; to pursue it was to pursue it completely alone, without support or guidance. Within this dream was the deep-rooted assumption that asserting my inner guidance would put me at odds with the outer world, and that following it meant turning away from the world and drawing all sustenance from within. In my experience, the inner and outer were split off from each other, rather than harmoniously operating together.

In "The Book of the Future," one of my most profound, philosophical dreams, the inner vs. outer theme is expressed in a different way. Here, the question is: to what extent should I trust the guidance I have received, and to what extent follow it, when following it may have detrimental consequences in regard to my outer life? This dream occurred over ten years later, when transiting Saturn in my twelfth house sextiled my Sun, transiting Uranus in the twelfth squared Mercury, and several inner planets aspected my Mars.

The Book of the Future

I observe a man looking up a book title in a giant card catalog; then I seem to become that man. My company will be entertaining foreign ambassadors on Monday; over the weekend I need to read a specific book about entertaining and negotiating with foreign ambassadors. Although I don't find the book I'm looking for, I do find a book with the identical call number, but with a different title. This book, entitled

How To Prevent Nuclear Disaster, provides guidance in regard to anti-nuclear issues—how to handle waste products, deal with nuclear debris, and build new, safer, and more effective generators.

I leaf through the book cursorily, intrigued by the title, and discover references to learnings resulting from the nuclear crisis of the year 2020. I am more intrigued. I wonder if this is a science fiction book. I read further. The book refers frequently to the history of the early 21st century, and focuses upon lessons mankind has learned during this time period, particularly in regard to anti-nuclear issues. The material is profound. I check the copyright date. It is in the 2020s. I have the gut feeling that the book is actually a transmission from the future, but I don't completely trust my instincts, and am afraid that people will think I'm crazy if I tell them what I believe.

A week later, I am feeding my boss lines of inspiration from the book, without telling him the source. He's impressed, but he trivializes the material by saying, "I've often thought of designing stationery with quotes making a frame around the center." Soon, he puts me to work designing stationery for the company, using a few significant quotes from the book. The lines I have chosen to use are too long—they require two rows on the left and right sides of the page. Yet because they are important, I want to include them all on the stationery.

Meanwhile, I am studying the book, and don't know what to do. I believe that I have discovered important political information, but am afraid to trust that it is really guidance from the future. Another problem is that the company for which I've worked all my life is not only apolitical; it is also operating in a manner which is at odds with my learnings from the book. If I continue to express the insights I am gaining from the book, I will be at odds with company policy. I could lose my job. This is a big risk, because there are no other jobs for which I feel qualified, and because I don't even know if the book is true.

On the other hand, how can I continue working here knowing what I know now? This book contains important guidance for myself and perhaps all of humanity. I feel a responsibility to live by its teaching, and to share the knowledge contained within it.

When I had this dream, I was attending a Jungian-Senoi dream-work training. I had recently completed the first year of a graduate degree in clinical social work, which required me to put my inner quest on hold and turn my attention toward "political" matters. Although I was seeking further training in psychotherapy, a major portion of my coursework was political; also, the process of adapting to the demands of the degree program required me to conceal many facets of myself, and to learn to negotiate effectively with an institutional process I did not value.

After years of following my inner guidance in regard to work, and failing to earn an adequate living, I had decided to learn how to adapt to the outer world; but such adaptation was a high price to pay. Not only was I increasingly out of touch with my inner wisdom, but also, because I was operating in an environment which did not value it, I could no longer trust it myself. Simultaneously, I was doubting the usefulness of much of the guidance I had given in my books and workshops, because it had not helped me to resolve the issues in my life which still troubled me.

"The Book of the Future" is a multi-dimensional dream, addressing many areas of my life. At this time, I had also discovered that my inner/outer conflict had its origins in my alientation from my outer vehicle—my body—and I had been receiving guidance and dreams in regard to ways of reowning my body which I was not always able to follow. I did not know how to find the time and energy for exercise and physical caretaking when I was working full-time, attending school, and struggling with an incapacitating physical illness; I also was afraid that full commitment to the life of the body would interfere with the expression of my intellectual, spiritual, and emotional selves, and my own somewhat-disembodied but familiar sense of identity.

The company in the dream refers to the psychological structure and lifestyle I had known all my life. An assumption implied by the dream is that following my current path of growth could not occur within the strictures/structures of this "company." Could my inner self exist within the outer structures I had chosen? Or must a transformation occur within my inner self, a change in inner structure, so that I could more effectively live within my body and the world? Clearly, a crisis was approaching, a crisis of faith and of commitment to both inner and outer worlds. (A year later, I took a leave of absence from school, embraced the inner world again, and began to write this book.)

Dreams of Violation

The alienation I have experienced in regard to my physical being and the outer world may have its origin in early physical traumas which led me to turn away from the life of the body and the physical world, and to espouse the life of the spirit. Some of these traumas are reflected in dreams of violation and rape. As I own and learn to constructively express my Martian anger, assertiveness, physical energy, and sexuality, dreams of violation burst into consciousness, followed by dreams of increasing physical competence, self-confidence, and sexual satisfaction.

Fire in the Jungle

I live in a small clearing in the jungle with my tribe, surrounded by six levels of jungle full of wild animals, but we only venture into the first level for game because of the danger. On the outskirts of the clearing is a tall savage black man from the jungle, who guards us from the jungle creatures; darkness is in his blood, and he has left his tribe in order to be redeemed. He is a raw savage, yet deep within he possesses a quiet power. At the center of the clearing is a fire which warms us and feeds us.

We are in crisis now because the fire is dying; it has almost gone out. Two people, male and female, are needed to venture through all six levels of jungle to the other side to bring back more fire. It is a very dangerous journey because of the wild animals. The male will be the black guard/protector, but a woman must also be chosen. She must be someone who is his counterpart—light where he is dark, spirit where he is animal, gentle where he is fierce.

I am the chosen woman, and must go through an initiation rite of six weeks. The black man tells me that as I am now, I could barely survive the first level of the jungle, much less all six levels. I must receive training that will enable me to gain the power I will need to survive; I must experience my aggression and my rage in order to be able to make the journey without being destroyed. Then he rapes me repeatedly seven days and nights a week for six weeks, until I am ready to make the journey.

At this time, the transiting Sun, Mercury, Venus, and Uranus were all conjunct my natal Mars; progressed Mars in the twelfth house was square natal Saturn. The transiting South Node, Mercury, Jupiter and Uranus were also in my twelfth house.

"Fire in the Jungle" vividly portrayed for me the connection I experience between the spiritual and animal facets of myself (reflected also in the placement of my Moon and Midheaven at my Mars/Pluto and Sun/Neptune midpoints), as well as the relationship between my spiritual/creative expression and physical/emotional pain, or bodily abuse. Most of all, it revealed to me a lifetime pattern of using, and sometimes subconsciously inviting, experiences of violation as a means of experiencing my rage and regaining my power. As I became aware of this pattern, I was able to ask myself: What are the origins of this pattern in my past? Are there less destructive methods of self-empowerment available to me? Must discovering my spiritual force occur simultaneously with damage to my physical being? Asking the right questions is always the first step in discovering the right answer.

Yet there is another way of viewing this dream, a way which portrays the violation experience not as a debility, but as a sign of growth. In order for the human spirit to fully manifest itself on the earth plane, it must be penetrated by earthly reality. In order for the pure, innocent girl-child to mature and become adult, she must awaken to her sexuality, and allow herself to be penetrated by the male. In order for the female-identified woman to discover her androgynous power, she must take within herself the power of the male, as a necessary preliminary to integrating and expressing both female and male energies.

But must this experience be a rape? Must a woman, like Persephone, be abducted by Pluto into the underworld, separated from the easy, familiar world of motherly love, and forced against her will to confront the power of sexual instinct? Not if she is capable of choosing the next step in her development, of choosing to abandon her innocence, of embracing a new dimension of earthy, instinctual reality, of willingly letting go of the self she has known.

Much of our lives, we live in a closed room and hear knocks on the door, the knocking of our future selves seeking attention, wanting to be invited into our current reality. But because we do not listen to the sounds of growth, because we are afraid, and because in our fear we turn up the volume of the old voices rather than open ourselves to the new, we do not respond. The knocks grow louder; then suddenly, the door bursts open, and an intruder in a black cloak picks us up and carries us off into his dark room. The cloak is not really black, nor is the room really dark, but our fears create the dreaded scene. We are convinced that underneath the cloak is a monster who will destroy us rather than a helping spirit who has come to carry us into those new realms of growth which we have refused to willingly enter.

In "Sleeping Beauty," the fairy who was not invited to the birth ceremony cursed the newborn child; if she had been invited, she might have brought valuable gifts. Likewise, those energies which we do not invite, those planetary gods which we do not honor, will curse us, rape us, violate us, threaten us, chase us, compel us against our will, kicking and screaming, into the next stage of growth. What if we invited them? What if we could differentiate realistic fears from unrealistic fears, and dissolve the phantoms which needlessly frighten us? Perhaps we do not need the trauma of rape and violation, but could benefit more from developing our capacity to hear the emerging voices, to soothe our fears, and to trust our own growth process.

Dreams of Incapacity & Capacity

Mars symbolizes the capacity to say "I can" and "I will"; Jupiter and Sagittarius reflect our belief systems; the second house concerns personal and material resources—the "I have" house of the zodiac. My Sagittarian Mars squaring a second house Jupiter clearly indicates deep-seated beliefs about my inability to use my physical energy constructively and to receive adequate financial remuneration. These beliefs had their roots in early experiences. Bringing home a report card with 11 "A's" in academic subjects and a "D" in physical education may have fueled my intellectual confidence, but it also convinced me that I was physically uncoordinated and incompetent.

I dreamt "The Softball Game" when transiting Venus conjuncted my Mars, transiting Uranus in my twelfth house squared Saturn, and transiting Saturn in the twelfth squared Mercury. The transiting South Node was conjunct Neptune, semisquaring Mars. At this time, I had temporarily suspended a daily practice of exercise and dance, and was absorbed with playing the piano.

The Softball Game

I am standing in line practicing the softball throw. Each time I throw the ball, it goes straight up in the air and falls to the ground. I am unable to throw it the required ten yards in order to pass the physical fitness test. Then, when I am up to bat during the softball game, I only hit the ball as far as the pitcher; as a result, I am tagged out at first base. The next time it is my turn to bat, I decide to challenge the pitcher to a test of intelligence rather than attempt to hit the ball. When I tell the girl next to me the question I will ask, "Name the flats in the key of B minor," she says that the question is too easy, and that besides, I can't get out of taking a turn at bat by playing question-and-answer. I decide to leave the team, rather than participate in the game.

Fortunately, not all my dreams express a sense of inadequate resources; nor do all reflect a split between inner and outer. At various times, when I have been able to surmount these problems, my dreams registered my growth. One such time was when I returned to graduate school. I was not sure that with my increased workload, I would have leisure time to myself or time for friends. When Jupiter sextiled my Mars, and transiting Uranus in the twelfth squared my Mercury, I dreamt "The Leap of Faith."

The Leap of Faith

I am trying to board a train, carrying a large suitcase. A friend on the train is saving a seat for me. However, I arrive at the train station as the train is departing; the passenger cars have already passed, and the boxcars are now passing me while the train is gaining speed. The only chance I have of getting on the train is if I run toward the last of the boxcars and jump onto the stairway. Carrying my bag in one hand, I run and jump, barely landing on the steps leading up to the boxcar. The car is a solid wall on the outside, with steps leading to the open top. I climb up the steps and jump down into the boxcar.

Three people are already in the car—one in each corner. The other corner is empty, and I take it. I sit there, relieved, at rest, content in my own space, experiencing the open expanse of blue sky and the streaming sunlight. I am also proud of myself for having caught the train, and having been able to run and leap onto the stairway without falling or mangling my legs. Although I miss being with my friend, I am pleased to be where I am.

Soon, the train stops, and from a doorway which appears at the other end of the boxcar, my friend enters and welcomes me. I am pleased by her visit and surprised to find a direct connection between the boxcar and the passenger cars. She tells me that whenever I wish, I can join her in the seat she has saved for me.

Here, I experience my physical capacity to run and jump to safety in a potentially dangerous situation. My successful Sagittarian leap onto a moving train resulted in a sense of pride, enjoyable leisure, and the option of meaningful social contact. Soon after I had this dream, I gave up my own apartment and rented a house with a friend. During this first year at school, I handled a demanding work schedule, while replenishing myself emotionally and socially during my leisure time.

The Inner Male

"The Leap of Faith" is one of a number of dreams which reflect my increasing ownership of my inner male in terms of physical capacity. Yet for many years, this inner male was locked up within me, subliminally running me, but threatening my self-image and the unconscious ideals of femininity I had learned as a child. Being physically active, asserting oneself, and expressing anger were taboo behaviors in my family. I remember being told that only boys get angry, and being ashamed of my awful secret that inside I was really a boy. The extent of this fear was not revealed to me until I saw the movie

"Tootsie," and had an anxiety attack of such proportions that I had to leave the theater; I was terrified that people would find out that Dustin Hoffman, masquerading as a female, was really a male.

One of my earliest recorded dreams, "Mirror Image," reveals the horror I used to experience at confronting my inner male, and the fear that this disowned part of me would lead to social rejection. This dream occurred when transiting Mars conjuncted my Ascendant, and the transiting Moon opposed my twelfth house Mars. At the time, I had just experienced unsuccessful surgery for endometriosis, and my doctor was recommending that I try danazol, a male hormone with emasculating side effects.

Mirror Image

Having been asked out to dinner by a man who attracts me, I put on a lacy feminine dress. We are joining an older couple at their house; I feel awkward when I meet them, because of their sophisticated dress and demeanor. When we arrive, the woman is cooking a gourmet meal. I ask if I can help, and awkwardly make a simple dessert which apparently is inappropriate. Everyone is silent when I serve it.

When we consider going out after dinner, I suggest the movie, "Small Change." Everyone looks at me disapprovingly; the men decide to go instead to a bar/club in a dangerous part of town. As we walk there, my date walks ahead of me, talking with the other couple; I feel ignored. At the club, he invites another woman to join us at our table, flirts with her, and then asks her to dance. I tell the older man beside me that I am angry at being mistreated. He then points to the dress that I am wearing and says, "Just look at you! What do you expect?" When his wife laughs, I tell them both off and then take a taxi home.

At home, I look in the mirror, and am horrified to discover that I have a man's hairy chest. The thick dark hair from my chest is protruding through the delicate lace.

During the '70s and early '80s, I often dreamt of being scheduled for high school courses commonly taken by males. In most of these dreams, I am enraged at being deprived of the creative writing courses which interest me and at being assigned to courses which threaten my sense of identity. When I dreamt "Auto Mechanics," my progressed Mars was squaring my Saturn and progressed Moon opposing my Mars. Transiting Neptune in the twelfth house was also squaring Venus.

Auto Mechanics

On the first day of school, I drive in the wrong direction down Biscayne Boulevard, and arrive late—too late to get the best seats in class, or to sit near the boys who interest me. Because the seating schedule is determined the first day, I already feel isolated. Then when I receive my schedule, I discover that I have been scheduled for machine shop and auto mechanics rather than mythology and creative writing. I am so upset that I spend the entire day in the principal's office, trying to get the courses I want. Because of my first name, the school had mistakenly assumed that I was male. I keep telling the principal, "I'm a girl, not a boy."

As I became comfortable with my "male energy," this dream series changed, and then ceased altogether. In the last dream I had about being scheduled in traditionally male courses, I was assigned to a biology field expedition. I and a group of handsome young men were to spend our days on a tropical beach, studying the mating habits of lobsters! Needless to say, I no longer objected to missing out on creative writing.

In 1983, when the "male energy" theme in my dreams was in the process of transformation, my father died. For six weeks I was ill, and devoid of energy. I experienced a hole at the center of my being so vast that I could not pull myself together. As I was recuperating from illness, and painting watercolors of "cosmic eggs," I dreamt "The Boy Force." Transiting Venus was conjuncting my Mars, as was the transiting Pluto/Neptune midpoint. Transiting Jupiter, emerging from my twelfth house, was now conjunct my ascendant. Although I was involved then with a man who embodied puer—the archetype of the boyish free spirit—"The Boy Force" has less to do with him than with the birth of my inner male.

The Boy Force

I have two lovers. One has gone away, and left me with one whose name seems to be Vava—at least that's the only word he can say. He's from another planet, and has the body of a child. Not only is he uncomfortable having an earthly body, but he's also unable to maintain an erection. I must help him come to terms with his male body, and be like a mother to him. Although I am fond of Vava, I feel resentful because my real lover has left me, and Vava is a boy, not a man. I am told that the boy-force must be raised, and that Vava must discover and express his maleness before my true lover will return to me.

Usually, when a facet of ourselves is rejected, it appears in dreams in a distorted, alien form—often as an intruder or antagonist. Sometimes we begin to own and integrate a facet of ourselves, and then slip back for awhile into old patterns. Such was the case when for six months, in 1986, I began a daily routine of dance and exercise, and then abandoned it to float in Neptunian realms of piano and mythology. When transiting Venus conjuncted my Mars, and both Saturn and Uranus squared ninth house planets, I dreamt "The Devil's Circle." At the time, I had been celibate for a year, and was ambivalent about fully owning my physical body. The more I lived within my body, the more I experienced sexual and emotional desire which I was not always able to satisfy.

The Devil's Circle

I am being pursued by a frightening, sleazy looking man with long black hair who is following me home through city streets. Whenever I turn a corner, he appears unexpectedly. At one point, he grabs me, and I break free, but he lets me know, "You aren't going to escape from me." Finally, a kindly older man chases him away, then returns to tell me, "It's your own unowned dark energy pursuing you. It's your own unowned desire for your father."

Then I'm in a group with friends and relatives. We are captive, sitting around a huge fire. The Devil is in charge. He says to my brother, "I'm tempted to let you go, because I know I'm not going to lose you." He tells me that I have 1400 miles to go before my current dilemma will be resolved.

We are terrified, but my friend Ilana and I joke about our situation. Ilana says that she wants to remember everything that happens, so that we can tell people about it later. I tell her and others that they know only one part of the story. "Before the Devil brought us here," I say, "something terrible happened to me. I was walking out of the city on a concrete road, and a man was chasing me."

While we sit feeling helpless and afraid, in the Devil's power, I suddenly realize that I can call out to protective forces. I start chanting, "Healing Guides, come to me," and Ilana chants with me. As we chant, our fear diminishes, and I feel suffused with healing energy. In front of us, the Devil begins to dematerialize, changing his form. He turns into a dark witch-like mother, and then vanishes altogether.

This dream has many interpretations, beginning with the oedipal issue of my desire for my father, who was both seductive and rejecting. The conflicts I experienced as an adolescent in relation to my father led me to struggle with considerable guilt and anxiety in regard to my own desires and sexuality.

Another interpretation of this dream relates to my mother, who lives 1400 miles from me, and whom I was soon to visit. Because she was seriously ill when I was growing up, and I was led to believe that my assertion, aggression, and natural spontaneity could kill her, I had learned early to keep my anger and resentment inside, and never express my feelings. Naturally, intense feelings which are buried for a long time tend to become distorted and destructive. During my next visit to my mother, after months of dancing and physical exercise, I could no longer repress those buried feelings. For the first time, the unexpressed resentment and hatred which had contaminated our family relationships burst forth and were expressed.

According to developmental psychology, young children learn to transmute and channel their aggression when they have "good enough" mothering. If the parents allow expression of feeling, and are more often loving and accepting of their children than they are rejecting, the children begin to internalize that love and acceptance, and develop the internal resources capable of handling and moderating their aggressive feelings. When such loving acceptance of the child's real self does not occur, or when parents are incapable of constructively responding to their child's anger, the child is not able to come to terms with his/her anger, and splits it off from consciousness. As a result, he/she is alienated from a vital energy source, and frequently feels powerless, as if pursued by inner and outer demons.

Until the necessary transmutation of aggression occurs, a child, and later the adult, perceives people in terms of black and white or good and bad—the good mother who is nurturing and responsive, and the bad mother who is rejecting. The inner image of the good mother must be solid enough and large enough in order for the bad mother image to be integrated into a larger image of mother (and of human relationships) which contains ambivalence.

In "The Devil's Circle," although the aggressive male force is perceived as alien and threatening, my capacity to call upon healing guides at the end of the dream suggests that a process of transmutation is occurring. As the healing forces of inner sustenance increase in power, the devil disappears; eventually, the new, integrated male forces of vitality and assertion begin to actively express themselves in life.

Dreams of Aggression

Aggression which is not integrated expresses itself subliminally and indirectly. In my own life, with Mars in Sagittarius square Jupiter, I have always had a sense of humor and a mischievous, playful spirit which frequently provides a harmless outlet for aggressive energy. Nevertheless, my playful teasing behaviors have sometimes hurt others, and occasionally had the boomerang effect of hurting myself. That untamed, unintegrated Martian energy may also assert itself without control or reality-testing, leading to poor judgment and unwise risk taking. "The Mermaid and the Shark" is a delightful dream which expresses these dilemmas. It emerged many years ago at my Mars return, when transiting Uranus also conjuncted my Mars, and a twelfth house transiting Neptune squared natal Saturn.

The Mermaid and the Shark

I am a mermaid with long slender legs, with which I do the sidestroke. I and other merfish live in a roped-off, protected area of water close to shore, where we play daily. Sometimes, we venture into rougher waters past our protected home. The only dangers we face are that the rough waters may exhaust us, so that we are unable to swim home, and that occasionally—once in many years—we may encounter sharks.

One day, for fun, I convince a renegade fish to start a rumor that he sighted a shark in the rough waters where we go for adventure. Warnings are posted. No one dares to leave our sanctuary. However, I, knowing that the danger isn't real, show off my daring. I race joyfully and carelessly into rough waters, feeling great pleasure and pride in my reckless spirit, and in the impression I am making upon all the merfish who don't have the courage to join me. I am so caught up in my own delight that I don't look around me. Then, suddenly, I discover that I am swimming into the gaping jaws of a giant shark.

Here, my playful aggressiveness is evident. But in other dreams, aggression reveals itself in a terrifying manner. "Agent of Destruction" is a nightmare I had after a close friend moved across country; at the time, I had been unable to acknowledge and express feelings of hurt, anger, and abandonment. This dream occurred when the transiting Sun was opposing my Jupiter, forming a t-square to Mars. Transiting Mars was conjuncting Pluto.

Agent of Destruction

I have been captured and made an agent of war. Other captives and I are herded onto a bus, and only allowed to carry a few belongings. Books are outlawed. Because I have a book with me, I hide it in the back of my pants. The woman sitting next to me sees it, and confides that she also has a book with her; she suggests that we share our books later.

We are told by the authorities that we are to be infiltrated with an animal which will grow within our spinal cords and take control of our bodies. Although we will develop immunity and survive, anyone who comes into contact with us will become ill and die. Basically, we will be used as weapons of biological warfare. During the next few weeks, we will be trained to live with selected families, whom we will infect, before moving on to our next victims.

Now, in the future, the animal virus has been effective. Hardly any of our people are alive. We are released from our mission. I wish to return to normal life now and form caring relationships once again, but the animal virus has taken over my nervous system. The only people I can risk being near are those who have been infiltrated by the same animal virus. But those people are few; they, like me, are ashamed to reveal their secret destructiveness; and they are scattered across the remains of what once was our land.

This dream profoundly disturbed me. Yet its emergence indicated that I was now capable of dealing with the buried aggression I had carried for many years, and with the barriers to intimacy which I created because of my fear of destroying those I loved.

Once my dream series of "male classes" began to transform and then end, several new dream series began—dreams of Nazi Germany and Holocaust survival, as well as shooting guns. (As a child I had spent summers at a girls' camp which had a riflery range. Having the last name of Marks earned me the title of Marksman first class, for I excelled in riflery. My aim was careful and deliberate. Riflery allowed Mars in Sagittarius square Jupiter to demonstrate its excellent aim and channel aggression into socially acceptable outlets.)

Yet in real life, I did not know yet how to adequately handle and aim my aggressive energy. I was too afraid of its destructive potential, and too inexperienced in directing it constructively. Dreams about guns began when I began to live with a close male friend, whose own twelfth house Mars in Cancer conjuncted my Uranus, squaring my Sun and Moon. Within a few months, I was raging about his passive-aggressive behavior—leaving the burners turned on, the doors unlocked, and threatening the security of our home. But at first, I was unable to express my anger. I dreamt "Front Line" when Saturn conjuncted my Mars, and Uranus in the twelfth house squared Mercury.

Front Line

I am in the front portion of a room with a group of women. Because I had been away, I had missed a preliminary meeting about our current activities. Now, I learn that we are at war, and we are shooting men. I don't even know who the enemy is, or how to load and shoot the guns which are available to us.

Then I am near the end of the front line, and the shooting is beginning. I notice that those ahead of me in the line are in a position of power. They are wearing fine clothes, and are obviously being rewarded for their willingness to face grave danger. Those in the back line are poorly dressed, have little power, and are in little danger.

Suddenly I realize that I don't want to be here. I don't want to risk either killing or being killed. Nor do I see any reason to wage a war against men. The rewards of power and richness are not worth the cost. I turn around, and make my way to the back line.

A year later, I am willing to "shoot," but am needing to learn more about how to make my "gun" work effectively. Daily, I assert myself now, but not always appropriately. Frequently, I explode in temper tantrums, which fail to meet my aims, and which are often reactive and defensive. When transiting Saturn squared Mercury, transiting Uranus squared Saturn, and the transiting Moon squared Mars, I dreamt "Marksmanship."

Marksmanship

I am in a riflery class, being instructed in marksmanship. However, I have arrived late for class, and step one has just been completed. I begin with step two, learn step three, and then attempt to shoot, but my gun backfires and will not shoot properly.

Because I missed step one, I stay for the second class, but now there are more students then there are guns, and I miss step one again. When I ask for help, the other girls treat me as if I am a stupid child, because I don't know the first step. I am angry at their arrogance and tempted to turn my gun on them once I learn to shoot it.

During the year in which I was learning to assert myself and express anger, I was also opening to deeper levels of love and tenderness in all my relationships. Because neither my housemate nor I were in intimate relationships, we satisfied many of each other's needs for closeness and contact. Inevitably, the tenderness and caring we expressed toward each other became intricately interwoven with anger and sexuality. Because we had chosen not to be lovers, we often engineered conflicts as a way to keep our sexual desires under control and to maintain greater distance. "Fear of Tenderness" emerged early in our live-in relationship, and warned of the anger that we would soon be experiencing toward each other. Transiting Venus was opposing my Mars, Saturn was trining my Moon, and Uranus was squaring Venus. In our composite chart, transiting Jupiter was conjunct our twelfth house Mars.

Fear of Tenderness

Jake and I are gently and tenderly caressing each other. I feel myself melting into loving desire. Both of us are wondering whether we should surrender to our feelings, and become more actively sexual. Then the doorbell rings, and unexpected guests arrive for a visit.

Suddenly, I am an Indian woman, and a group of gentle, friendly Indians of another tribe are visiting our tribe. They, the Crow's Feet, are currently being pursued by an aggressive, violent tribe called the Black Paw, who have sworn to hunt them down and murder them. We welcome our guests, whom we love dearly, but then debate about whether we should allow them to stay. We are afraid that their presence will lure the dangerous Black Paw to our door.

I had at this time quit smoking, a habit which had enabled me to handle my excessive pent-up energy and to compensate for inadequate grounding. Without this safety mechanism, my aggressive and sexual energies were running rampant. Could I trust my ability to handle them without exploding and unduly alienating the people around me? The dream "Capable of Withstanding Fire," recorded two days after "Fear of Tenderness," gave me faith in my growing capacities to contain and channel my increasingly conscious Martian energy. At this time, my progressed Mars was at twenty-six degrees Sagittarius, ready to cross the Ascendant.

Capable of Withstanding Fire

I live in a wood frame house near a neighbor with whom I'm in conflict. Inflamed with anger toward me, my neighbor carries large fiery poles to my house with the intention of setting it on fire. Apparently, he has decided to stage a major drama in order to impress the wealthy landowners of the town, who now arrive to observe the event.

Meanwhile, I panic at the prospect of my house and belongings burning. Although the house is insured, I know that the insurance will not compensate for the loss of my books and unfinished manuscripts. I watch, unable to stop him, as he sets the fire. Flames appear along the top of the house, and then go out immediately; the house will not burn. It appears as if the house has been soaked in some fire-resistant substance. Again, the outside wood frame flares up slightly, then the flame dies. No fire or smoke damage occurs inside or outside the house.

I, and the wealthy landowners, watch in amazement. Before they depart, they compliment me on my house, and ask if I am willing to sell it; they make a very high offer. Apparently, its property value has gone up considerably as a result of its proving to be fire-resistant and smoke-resistant.

In another dream occurring that same week, I witness the end of a pattern of internal escalation. For many years, I had lived a life of melodrama; the excessive internal energy of Mars in Sagittarius square Jupiter, locked within the twelfth house, and within a body lacking a grounding connection to the earth, would escalate and generate excessive emotion. Now that I was learning to handle that energy, and to transmute it through new internalizations gained in therapeutic and personal relationships (as well as through physical activity), I was no longer at the mercy of many fears from the past. Frequently, dreams within dreams, or movies within dreams reveal the new attitudes and behaviors we adopt as we observe the scripts of the past.

Plane Crash

I am on a plane, flying in rough weather. The movie being shown on board is about a plane ride and ends with passengers panicking as the plane crashes. As we watch, the passengers on my plane begin to panic, although our plane isn't crashing. I know that we are safe, so I am able to keep calm. However, I'm angry that the airline is irresponsibly showing this movie during a plane flight and generating so much fear; I also feel responsible for calming the other passengers.

Increasingly, my dreams reflect my growing capacity to confront and express anger, and to quiet the fears of devastation which I experience when I encounter my aggressive energy.

Beyond the Body: Dreams of Expansion

Why should I live in my body when, unencumbered by its demands and restless energy, I can soar in my mind? Mars in Sagittarius sextiling a ninth house Sun, semisquaring Neptune, and squaring Jupiter yearns for the heights of experience. Yet most of my life, I have lived the myth of Icarus, have flown on wings far above the earth and been burned by the Sun. Aflame with visions, I have suffered the burning sensations of internal bleeding within my body (chronic endometriosis), and inhaled smoke from the fires of ecstatic experience. The heights still call me, and still reward me. But slowly I learn also to love, and to embrace the earth, and the earthly vehicle within which I live.

Dreams of expansion occur, sometimes as illuminations, sometimes as warnings. Taking off on a Sagittarian flight of expansion, as I wrote a lengthy paper on gifted children and neglected other dimensions of my life, I dreamt "Go No Further." Transiting Uranus was squaring Venus (ruler of the fifth), Mercury was conjuncting Mars, and Saturn was trining the Moon.

Go No Further

I am in a small cell-like room, with one large window. Every night, I journey out that window, by stretching my body as far as I can, attempting to reach the end of the known world. Finally, one night I reach a semi-open area in a forest, with many logs and fallen trees in the center, and a sign which reads, "Danger. No Trespassing. Go no further." I am afraid, and yet I feel like Columbus, burning with the desire to go further, to discover what land lies ahead of me. Yet, like Columbus, I also fear that if I continue further, I might fall off the edge.

Suddenly, I realize that I have been holding my breath for many minutes, and that here at land's end, the air is too thin in oxygen for me to breathe. If I truly wish to breathe again, I must return to my room.

Back in my room, I discover that I have been gone five entire days, and that my cats have been alone, without food or care. Neighbors have left notes on my door, complaining about the whining of the cats, which I had so unknowingly neglected.

The cats, for me, symbolize my animal bodily self with its instinctive needs, as well as my female self. The more I am absorbed in my mental flights, the more I neglect the cats of my physical and emotional needs.

An earlier dream, "Kaleidoscope," occurred when transiting Uranus in my twelfth house approached a square to natal Mercury, and the transiting Moon opposing natal Jupiter was making a t-square to Mars. The transiting Sun was also conjunct my Neptune, while Mars and Venus conjuncted natal Venus.

Kaleidoscope

I'm attending an exhibit on the development of the human potential, where I'm told that I'll be given glimpses of my own and others' potential for expanded consciousness. In the exhibit are ten levels, each more dazzling than the last. I've just viewed level #8, an enormous aquarium of diverse, unusually colored fish. Half an hour before closing time, I'm told that I can only briefly glimpse the two highest exhibits not only because of time, but also because viewing them directly is like gazing at the sun or the face of God—we can be burnt by the intensity of opening to a level of future consciousness which requires opening too wide and stretching too far beyond our current capacities. Exhibit #9 is a surreal participatory experience in which I am suspended over brilliant mountain foliage vivid with moisture.

I walk up to level #10. Ascending the stairs, I hear the laughter of children. I am told that this exhibit, still unfinished, is staggering in its vision of human potential and can only be glimpsed by adults who can access the consciousness of a child. Because I am almost ready to see it fully, it will be soon be revealed to me. Now I am only allowed a glimpse from the top of the stairs—dozens of children, building and operating a giant KALEIDOSCOPE which fills the room and points toward their future.

Leaving the exhibit, I discover that I am in a car on a car trailer. All other cars are driving off the trailer at the base of the exhibit. I am told that I am to remain in my car on the trailer, and that soon I will be transported.

This transcendent dream elicited many associations. In high school, I had edited an award-winning literary magazine entitled *Kaleidoscope*. The day of the dream, I had had a delightful experience with a kaleidoscope. The dream also triggered my interest in gifted children. A week later, I learned about a program for gifted children called Kaleidoscope, to which I applied as a mentor.

Encounter With the Shadow

Although "Kaleidoscope" was a transcendent dream, it did not have the impact on me that a later dream, "Daphne," was to have. Yet before I was to experience "Daphne," I needed to encounter my shadow self in its current form. First, I had an ugly, incestuous shadow dream about my brother. Then, my shadow appeared to me not as an aggressive male, but as a female who manifested qualities abhorrent to my Sagittarian ideals—qualities which expressed the dark, unredeemed facets of my Sagittarian twelfth house.

When we identify with an ideal or self-image, we constellate a shadow self which expresses its opposite, and which threatens our sense of identity. The memory and experience of Carolyn in "No Exit" was repugnant to me; yet within her I encountered the dumb, large, fat, gross, scared, helpless, and overgrown child within me that I had been defending myself against all my life. Facing her was more disturbing than facing the inner Devil; it was also more liberating.

The night before my "Daphne" dream, I dreamt "No Exit." Transiting Jupiter was squaring Mars, Uranus was stationary squaring Venus, Saturn (now in the twelfth) was stationary trining Moon, the Moon was opposing Mars, and Mars, emerging from my twelfth house, was conjunct my ascendant.

No Exit: Nuclear War With My Shadow

I know that a nuclear war is about to start, but no one believes me. Only Carolyn, who looks like Baby Huey, and is fat, dumb, and helpless, believes also in the impending catastrophe. I choose to take shelter in a large laundry room underground, where I cover myself with layers of clothes as a protection against the radiation. Everyone else is wandering around outside, except for Carolyn who, cowering with fear and jabbering incoherently, hides away with me. I realize with horror that if a nuclear bomb drops and everyone above ground is killed, I may be trapped for the rest of my life with Carolyn, whom I find intolerable. Then I experience a blinding flash of light as the bomb drops, and I cover my eyes to block out the burning glare.

Owning the Body: Increasing Capacity

The night after "No Exit," I had two dreams. The first, "Loss of Innocence," was an actual memory of my thirteenth year, when my parents left me for an evening with the children of wealthy friends—

two crude fourteen-year-old girls who had secretly invited boys over for a beer-and-sex party. I was appalled by their behavior, and fled the scene of the impending crime. The second dream was "Daphne."

Daphne

I live in the Black Forest of Germany and am five years old. My best friend is a young tree, a sapling, named Daphne, who is a nymph with long flowing hair and is also a tree spirit. Young, lithesome, playful, and innocent, she also dances.

Daphne dances with total delight and freedom; her joy in her being-ness and in nature is unlimited. She speaks the language of the leaves and blossoms, of the rain, sun, sky, and wind. When I visit the forest every day, she invites me to enter her consciousness. Doing so, I experience what it feels like to know the wind rustling her leaves, the rain pelting her branches, the sun warming her bark, and her foliage changing color. Daphne, who is completely open to the sensory world of her tree essence, enables me to experience the world through her eyes. She seems to be pure and untouched, yet earthy, untamed, and alive.

My family is soon to move from the Black Forest to America, where I am to start school, to learn to read and write. I can't bear leaving Daphne. But then I am told that I can turn her into a human being, a little girl, so that I can take her with me. I'm not sure if I will tell Daphne about this transformation. If I do tell her, she doesn't understand, because she can't perceive anything alien to her tree consciousness. For her, a change in being is a change in the caress of the wind, rain or sun, or a change in the seasons. If I choose not to tell her, I am trying to protect her from knowing that she won't be a tree anymore, able to commune with the sun, wind, and rain in the way she has known and loved. Instead, as a child, she'll learn to read and write, to live in the human world and to conform to the ways of adults, with other children.

Then I am outside in the trees behind my parents' North Carolina house, reading a book about Daphne, the tree spirit. By reading, I discover the next chapter of her story. I feel the intense, endless, agonizing pain she experiences as she discovers that her tree body is gone, and that she is in human form, which feels awkward and alien; as she realizes that she won't be able to experience the natural, free, innocent, and sensory delight of her essential treeness. I see her stretched on the ground of the forest, sobbing from the depths of her heart, feeling that she has lost everything that she has known and valued—the beauty, delight, joy, and innocence of her magical world.

I feel also her dawning awareness and anger that I, her dearest friend, betrayed her. I compelled her to give up her tree-body, to lose the self she had treasured. Reading her story, I feel racked by her pain and by her longing for all that she has lost.

"Daphne" was a magical dream which permeated my waking life for months afterwards. I woke with the experience of Daphne's consciousness as tree and human ever-present within me. Even now, almost two years later, I can contact within myself my Daphne spirit, in all its purity and sensory delight.

This dream reawakened my creativity. I wrote over one hundred Daphne poems (many haiku poems—three lines of 5 syllables, 7 syllables, 5 syllables); I painted Daphne paintings, discovered and adapted a Daphne song for the piano, studied tree spirits and trees. Several months later, I began to dance as Daphne danced. I also wrote a paper—a psychotherapeutic study of the myth of Daphne, which I discovered was integrally related to my dream.

According to myth, Daphne was a forest nymph dedicated to Artemis and her ideals of freedom and purity. When Apollo fell in love with her, pursued her and threatened to rape her, she appealed to her father, the river god, who saved her by transforming her into a laurel tree. Having identified with her free spirit and denying her Martian energy, Daphne was pursued by her shadow in the form of Apollo. But rather than embrace him, she died to her human form and became immobilized as a tree—an experience of outer rigidity but inner aliveness, and a symbiotic regression to oneness with mother nature.

The Daphne of the dream is delightfully alive as a tree spirit. Because the tree form is the only form she knows or remembers, she identifies her essence with her form. In her reality, she is a tree—not a spirit within the body of a tree, or a spirit soon to live within the body of a human being. Her dilemma raises profound questions about the relationship between spirit and body, and between essence and form. To the extent that Daphne can allow her identity as spirit to extend into and through her human body, she can remain Daphne and can express her pure sensory delight through a new form. But when the dream ends, she is in anguish—experiencing betrayal, mourning the loss of her symbiotic bliss as a tree spirit, angry at possessing an awkward and alien human body.

One of the most transformative repercussions of my Daphne dream, which occurred near the spring equinox, was to experience spring while possessing the consciousness of Daphne. Trees bursting into

Dialogue with Daphne
by Tracy Marks

Who put this cloak of
Human skin upon me? I
Am Daphne, a tree.

This flesh does not fit.
This garment is misshapen.
Give me back my bark.

Is this life, this grief,
This yearning to be turning
Over a new leaf?

When was I Daphne?
When the rain caressed my
        limbs —
Leaves, bark, not skin.

Sunlight, warm my limbs,
Breeze, caress me. Rain,
        leave me
Shimmering with silver.

Daphne, did you know
Rain pelting silver on your
Bark? Remember rain.

Daphne, did you wave
Your limbs in the summer
        breeze
As a young sapling?

Daphne, did you dance,
Flapping your bark, boughing
        your
Crimson autumn head?

In fall, you dazzled
Us with color. You, Daphne,
Blushed scarlet and gold.

And did you flower,
Daphne? Did you burst into
Blossoms in the spring?

I know bark, not flesh.
Only the wind touches me.
My name is Daphne.

In spring I flower.
I shake loose my hair, my
        curls,
Pale golden blossoms.

My nectar is sweet.
With tremulous desire,
I spread my petals.

I flirt and flounce, toss
My blossoms, pale crown of
        curls,
Feverish with spring.

Daphne, you tremble
With desire. Your petals
Quiver with longing.

Daphne, your spring glow
Allures me. You tantalize
All the honeybees.

How does a tree dance,
Daphne? How does a tree wave
Its limbs, shake its roots?

My dance is the dance
Of time, says Daphne. My dance
Is my unfolding.

flower were overwhelmingly beautiful, sensual, orgiastic, and cele-
bratory for me. I rejoiced in their fertility, reveled in the bursting forth
of each blossom, in the frenzy of color, in the lush verdant growth
of leaves upon their outstretching branches. For a month or more, I
was Daphne, the tree spirit—fully sensory and alive, yet pure and
innocent, *within a human body.* Several months later, I was to reclaim
that body even further and to discover my own delight in dance.

Soon after ''Daphne,'' while attending the Jungian–Senoi Dreamwork training, I had another significant dream which expressed the
changing relationship between my body and mind/spirit. Uranus in
the twelfth house was squaring Venus, Saturn in the twelfth sextiling Sun, and Mercury trining Mars.

Throwing Out the Flying Machines

My people and I are attempting to decide whether to throw out our
flying machines. Those of us who are ahead of the others in rank use
them and discover that they are dangerous and unpredictable. We don't
know when or for how long we will be aloft once we start flying, or
what damage we will experience in flight. So we throw them into the
sea.

Then, returning to the Yews, our rulers, without the machines, we
realize that they, the Yews, who have their own impeccable flying
machines, now have much greater power than we do. The Yews can
use their flying machines against the serfs, the lower classes, to
discipline and punish them. Flying close above the fields where the
serfs labor, they can harass them into obeying their will. Since we've
now given up our only source of power, we can do little to stop their
maltreatment of the serfs.

As we return from the Yews, we confer about our loss of our previous
means of power and our role as protector of the serfs. We plan to
establish a task force in order to determine how we can maintain greater
power with the Yews.

This dream is rich in meaning. The ruling class, the Yews, suggest
the power of the ''Yous''—of other people; these Yews mistreat people who are beneath them and ''use'' them to meet their needs. The
Yews also symbolize the soaring intellect, which lacks compassion
for the sensitive middle class (feeling) and the lowly serfs (body). I,
as the dream ego, identify myself with the middle group, as a mediary
between mind and body. Our group or class has not been able to soar
effectively; we choose to give up the ecstasies of flying high in an
unstable vehicle rather than endanger ourselves and others. Yet our

flying machines have helped us to function as near-equals to the Yews and to help compensate for their hatred of the serfs. In deciding to give up an unreliable and dangerous source of power, we choose to humble ourselves, to function with little sense of our power, while we attempt to uncover other sources of power within ourselves.

Here, graphically portrayed, is the relationship between my body, feelings, and mind at this stage of my life, as well as my changing relationship with the outer world. No longer am I alone; I belong to my people. No longer am I high-flying Icarus, relying upon the power of my intellect, detached from and antagonistic toward my body; my role is as a protector of the body and of my earthly labor. No longer do I conceal my smallness by soaring dangerously into the heights; I choose to own it and to seek real sources of power within it. I don't know yet how to find my power while grounded, living close to the earth; but with my people, I take action—I become "political," in order to more effectively negotiate my role on earth.

During the training I was attending, I participated in a psychodrama enacting this dream. At first, being the sole representative of my group, surrounded by soaring Yews towering above me and struggling serfs working the earth below me, I felt helpless. My attempts to convince the Yews to leave the serfs alone fell on deaf ears; they only harrassed me as well. The only means of power seemed to be to join the serfs, to unite my people with them in order to discover the power we might have together. With considerable inner resistance, I allowed the serfs to surround me as they worked; I felt their body heat and helped them in their labor. In doing so, I was amazed to discover the warmth and safety I experienced, and the power that seemed to exist within them and within the earth upon which they lived. I knew then that the path to personal power is a path through the body/earth, not apart from it.

Several nights later, I dreamt "The Book of the Future" (described earlier in this chapter). The next day, I, who hadn't danced more than a few times in twenty years, spontaneously created a dance for Daphne, and danced until I fell on the ground, sobbing with Daphne's pain, letting go of her grief. Daily then, and now, I celebrate my soul within my body; I dance.

Then, when Saturn stationed sextile my Sun and near Mars, and a new moon conjuncted my Mars/Jupiter midpoint, I dreamt "Snowclimb."

Snowclimb

I am climbing up a mountain in a light snowstorm, after having camped at the base of the mountain. I have a home on the top and at the bottom. Slowly and deliberately, crawling up a sheer cliff, I look for footholds and toeholds; I place one foot where my hand has been, carving out deep niches in the packed snow. At some point, my foothold gives way, and I am swept down to a rock beneath me. But I am un- harmed. Finding a niche for climbing again, I start over, holding my body tight against the rockface, feeling comforted by my contact with the solid surface. Over and over again, I reach up and pull myself up- ward, until I'm approaching the top of the mountain. Then instead of stopping, I continue to climb up the side of the house at the moun- tain's top, until I reach an open window. Before my friends, standing in the window, can warmly welcome me and pull me inside, my lips meet my lover's lips, as he greets my arrival with a loving kiss.

"Snowclimb" is a dream about depths and heights, about body con- sciousness, and about moving upward as a result of using rather than disassociating from the body. It is a dream about personal resources and capabilities, and about love which welcomes and rewards the constructive use of one's powers. I, who had never climbed a moun- tain, but had instead soared over them, was now climbing a moun- tain. At last, I was coming home to myself. I was coming home.

Letting It Out & Letting Go

The path of growth is a painful path and a joyful path. Sometimes, the self must be ripped apart, the wounded heart exposed, the terror of annihilation confronted. I could not have dreamed or lived "Snowclimb" five years earlier, when I dreamed the following dream, "The Open Heart." The split between my body and mind could not heal until my heart opened and began to create a passageway of love and compassion between my two estranged selves, and between myself and the world. Heart surgery, which my mother had experienced re- peatedly while I was growing up (she had indeed died and returned to life), had significant emotional meaning for me. In 1981, when Jupiter and Saturn conjuncted my Sun, I recalled how I had prayed to God when she was in the operating room, promising Him that I would give Him my heart if He saved hers. I remembered the ripping apart I experienced then, and the subsequent flight from turbulent emotions into my mind.

My mother's eighth house Jupiter, Sun, and Saturn conjunct my South Node; my Neptune is on her North Node. When Jupiter and Saturn conjuncted my Sun, I began to redeem my heart. Through a relationship with a spiritual teacher and psychotherapist, I opened in ways I had never thought possible. The following year, at my Mars return, when transiting Uranus conjuncted Mars, and twelfth house Neptune squared Saturn, I had the following dream:

The Open Heart

I decide to have an operation in order to remove the pain in my heart. My doctor advises against surgery, because the risk of death is great, but I take the risk. When I'm on the operating table, he begins to cut out my heart and prepares to transplant a new one. During the twelve minutes in which the transfer of hearts will occur, I may die. Even if I don't die, I will experience the death of twelve minutes without a heart.

As soon as the surgeon cuts me open and begins to separate my old heart from my body, I feel exposed and terrified. Panicking, I jump off the operating table and run out of the hospital. My old heart is hanging out of my open chest. I no longer feel willing to go through the moments of death that will exist between hearts.

Later, I am in my parents' home; Mom and Dad are criticizing me. They tell me that if I walk around with my chest cut open, I'll be locked up. Their criticism cuts me further; I hide in my room, where, listening to the radio, I learn that a warrant has been issued for my arrest. Anyone who finds me must drive me back to the hospital so that the operation can be completed.

My panic increases. I feel too vulnerable to stay with my parents. I can't run around the streets with my heart hanging out, exposing myself to anyone who is out to get me. I can't go back to the hospital, because I'm not willing to experience twelve minutes of being kept alive by machines, in total blackness, without any heart. I feel trapped. As I attempt to calm my panic and plan a course of action, I realize that my heart is bleeding excessively now, and that the life juices are slowly beginning to flow out of my body.

At the time of this dream, I was unable to make the leap of faith necessary to complete my "heart surgery." Trust in the surgeon was required, but I did not trust the "Yews" of the outside world. Yet I made the initial leap of my Sagittarian Mars square Jupiter, sextile the heart planet, the Sun, and semi-square the faith planet, Neptune; I chose to begin the operation.

How dangerous vulnerability and exposure seemed, in a hostile world. How could I risk wearing my heart on my sleeve, revealing need and expressing love? How could I overcome the terror of entering the deathspace without a heart to sustain me? In order to risk the minutes between hearts, I would have to trust, in my most vulnerable moments, in the hearts of others. During the five years following this dream, through therapy, friendship, and loving intimate relationships, I began to develop that trust.

Now, with transiting Uranus and Saturn, as well as progressed Mars, crossing my ascendant, I begin anew. I dream of loved ones dying, of saying goodbye, of starting new unknown ventures. Some dreams are painful; others are humorous. As Saturn squares Venus, and the Moon opposes Mars, I dream "Outreaching Arms." A new cycle begins, a new letting go, a new reaching out, a new Sagittarian journey.

Outreaching Arms

I am packing for a trip. I begin to put my clothes in my suitcase and have the space to pack all but two long-sleeve sweaters. The sleeves of the sweaters seem to be inordinately long. Suddenly, I realize that they are the lengthy arms of a tall, gangly, long-limbed man. He climbs inside my suitcase, leaving the zipper partly open, and dangles both long arms outside. Then he tells me, "I learned from my previous experience of being locked in your suitcase that it's quite uncomfortable there. This time, I must have room to stretch while I'm in the baggage room. I need to reach out my arms."

Letting go of the past may not be possible until seeds of growth are planted and begin to root. How can we let go of the ground upon which we stand? The tremors of new movement must be sensed within the soil; the baby must kick within the womb. Meanwhile, our consciousness may be unaware of the impending birth. For a while, we are confused, listless, impotent, ineffective. A part of us sleeps, lending its energy to the subconscious, so that it may nurture the newborn self.

We need to trust. Most of all, we need to trust that the self we are now is passing through us, moving up to the surface, and that we will shed it as we make the leap into the new self that is forming. The old self is afraid of that leap; from its perspective, the transfer of consciousness to the new self is death. It will muster every weapon in its arsenal to avoid experiencing that death, and to hold onto the reality that it knows. How important then, that we learn to listen to the signals of the new self within its womb, to feed it, and to celebrate its growth. The time will come when we will become that new self, when we will burst free of the bonds of the past, and let go.

Several years ago, on a houseboat in Sausalito, I had an active imagination session in which I journeyed into my womb, to the source of my uterine pain and the source of my creative spirit. There, I found a large egg, and I entered into its consciousness. Recently, I relived that session in a dream. In "The Hatching," I tell students in a lecture hall about my experience as a baby bird bursting out of my shell.

The Hatching

I am a baby bird, not yet born, too large for the shell that encloses me. In fact, experiencing its pressure crushing against me, I feel suffocated, constrained, trapped by a barrier which once warmly protected me. It is time to be born, to burst through, to enter the world. But I am unable to stretch, to expand, to exert the energy necessary to break through the shell. I am too afraid of the pain of bursting open, afraid of the shell fragmenting as it breaks apart.

My guide gently encourages me to breathe deeply, to feel my body pushing against the shell. Slowly, I draw my consciousness within my body and experience its warmth and expanding power. I stretch. I become larger. I stretch again. Then, as sunlight emerging from behind a cloud streams through the windows of the houseboat and floods the room with golden light, I burst through into life, and open my eyes.

My response to the world is sheer delight. I laugh golden, sunlit laughter. I shake my arms and legs, and peer in awe at the new world around me. I feel so alive.

"Where's the pain?" my guide asks me. I look at her in amazement. "There isn't any pain," I say. I laugh again, understanding now the fear that had constrained me. "I thought I was the shell."

From the point of view of the shell, breaking free of past patterns is indeed a death, annihilation of the old self. From the point of view of the baby bird, it is a birthing into an enchantingly new universe.

In the twelfth house, we internally live out the past; time and time again, we play for ourselves the old dramas, rehearse the old scripts. Yet here the new is born; we are fertilized, grow new bodies, gestate, mature within the dark safety of our underwater sanctuary. Then, when planets emerge from our twelfth house and cross our Ascendant, we leap forth from our shell and embrace our new lives.

I have experienced the inner richness of my twelfth house. Here, even my shadow self, my rejected being, and the dark pain and rage of past wounds that festered without healing have revealed their hidden treasures. Each tremor within the twelfth house is a new life waiting to be born. Each encounter with a repressed energy is initially a threat to the old self which denies it; it is cloaked at first in the darkness of our fear; the distorted shapes it takes are the shapes of our fear.

Yet as we trust the new birthings within us, as we fill ourselves with the breath of new life, fear dissipates. We open to, and are healed by, the light of consciousness and of compassion. We feel ourselves, we know ourselves, we own ourselves—our true selves—and not merely the images which have sustained us while our true selves lived in hiding, awaiting birth.

I have experienced, and still experience, the richness of the twelfth house. So can you.

Footnotes

The Twelfth House: Your Hidden Wisdom

(1) Greene, Liz and Howard Sasportas, *The Development of the Personality*, Samuel Weiser, York Beach, Maine, 1987, Chapter One.

(2) Jung, Carl, *Psychological Reflections*, Bollingen Foundation, New York, 1953, p. 219. Originally published in AION, 1951. Also quoted in *The Portable Jung*, "Aion: Phenomenology of the Self," Viking Press, New York, 1971, p. 145.

Planets and Signs in the Twelfth House

(1) Williams, Strephon Kaplan, *The Practice of Personal Transformation*, Journey Press, Berkeley, California, 1984, 1985, page 60.

(2) An inspiring story relevant to people who have twelfth house Moons is "The Buried Moon" in *The Buried Moon and Other Stories* by Molly Bang, Charles Scribner's Sons, New York, New York, 1977.

(3) For more information on reowning the lunar energy, see the chapter on the Moon in *The Astrology of Self-Discovery*, by Tracy Marks, CRCS Publications, Sebastopol, California, 1985.

(4) Williams, Strephon Kaplan, page 55.

(5) For more information on reowning and constructively channelling Neptunian energy, see the chapter on Neptune in *The Astrology of Self-Discovery*, by Tracy Marks.

(6) Williams, Strephon Kaplan, page 120.

(7) For more information on the demonic, see *Unity and Multiplicity*, by John Beahrs, *Voice Therapy: A Psychotherapeutic Approach to Self-Destructive Behavior*, by Robert W. Firestone, and *Love and Will* by Rollo May. The neurolinguistic programming books of John Grinder and Richard Bandler also discuss the reowning of disassociated subpersonalities.

(8) For more information on how we keep ourselves powerless, and the process of regaining Plutonian power, see the chapter on Pluto in *The Astrology of Self-Discovery* by Tracy Marks.

(9) Greene, Liz, "Myth and the Zodiac," in *The Astrology of Fate*, Samuel Weiser, Inc., York Beach, Maine, 1984.

(10) For more information on the nodes of the Moon, see the chapter on the lunar nodes in *The Astrology of Self-Discovery*.

Additional Note: The quotations included in this chapter to illuminate the meanings of twelfth house planets are compiled from over a hundred quotation anthologies (secondary sources) as well as dozens of personal journals. The original sources of most of these quotations are not known. Because of copyright law, I have limited the number of quotations I have used by the same author and by contemporary authors, omitting many pertinent quotations which might require further documentation.

The Psychodynamics of the Twelfth House

(1) Fossum, Merle A. and Marilyn J. Mason, *Facing Shame: Families in Recovery*, W. W. Norton and Company, New York, 1986.

(2) Fossum and Mason, p. 86.

(3) Firestone, Robert W., *Voice Therapy: A Psychotherapeutic Approach to Self-Destructive Behavior*, Human Sciences Press, New York, 1988, p. 110.

(4) For more information on ways in which we give up our power and choose to remain victims, see the Neptune and Pluto chapters of *The Astrology of Self-Discovery* by Tracy Marks.

The Process of Integration

(1) Bugental, James, *The Search for Authenticity*, Irvington Publishers, New York, 1965, 1981. Highly recommended.

(2) Williams, Strephon Kaplan, *The Practice of Personal Transformation*, Journey Press, Berkeley, California, 1984, p. 56.

(3) Source of Coleridge quotation unknown.

(4) I highly recommend Erich Neumann's retelling and psychological study of the Cupid and Psyche myth, *Amor and Psyche: The Psychic Development of the Feminine*, Bollingen Foundation, Inc., New York, and Princeton University Press, 1956.

(5) Williams, p. 55.

(6) Greene, Liz and Howard Sasportas, *The Development of the Personality*, Samuel Weiser, Inc., York Beach, Maine, 1987.

(7) Johnson, Stephen M., *Characterological Transformation*, W. W. Norton and Company, New York, 1985, p. 111. For further information, see Richard Bandler and John Grinder's *Frogs Into Princes* and *Reframing*, Real People Press, Moab, Utah.

(8) Segal, Jeanne, *Living Beyond Fear*, Newcastle Publishing Co., N. Hollywood, California, 1984, pp. 58, 74.

(9) Quoted by an EST participant.

(10) See Lowen, Alexander, *Fear of Life*, MacMillan Inc., New York, 1980, and *Bioenergetics*, Penguin Books, New York, 1976. An excellent summary and adaptation of Lowen's work is also contained in Johnson, Stephen M., *Characterological Transformation*, W. W. Norton and Co., New York, 1985.

(11) Ibsen, Henrik, *Peer Gynt*, Methuen, Inc., New York, 1981.

(12) LeGuin, Ursula, *A Wizard of Earthsea*, Parnassus Press, Emeryville, California, 1968, pp. 179–80.

(13) Neumann, Erich, *Depth Psychology and the New Ethic*, Harper and Row, New York, 1969, 1973.

(14) Firestone, Robert W., *Voice Therapy: A Psychotherapeutic Approach to Self-Destructive Behavior*, Human Sciences Press, New York, 1988.

(15) Butler, Pamela, *Talking To Yourself: Learning the Language of Self-Support*, Harper and Row, New York, 1981.

(16) Van Scyoc, Sydney, *Darkchild*, Berkley, Madison, New York, 1982, pp. 169–70.

(17) Beahrs, John, *Unity and Multiplicity: Multilevel Consciousness of Self*, Brunner/Mazel Inc., New York, 1982, p. 150.

(18) For more information, see Euripides' play, *The Eumenides*.

(19) Euripides, *Iphigenia Among the Taurians*, in *Ten Plays*, translated by Moses Hadas, Bantam Books, New York, 1960.

(20) The story of Iphigenia is the basis of a future book I hope to write, *Becoming Your Own Heroine*.

(21) See bibliography for complete citations.

Self-Transformation through Dreamwork

(1) Arbiter, Petronius, "Somnia," quoted in Brook, Stephen, *Oxford Book of Dreams*, Oxford University Press, Oxford, New York, 1983, p. 255.

(2) Assumed to be from Hall, James, *Jungian Dream Interpretation*, Inner City Books, Toronto, 1983. Found in personal journal.

(3) Jung, Carl, quoted in the documentary, *Matters of the Heart*.

(4) From Zeller, Max, *The Dream—Vision of the Night*, Analytical Psychology Club of Los Angeles, 1975.

(5) Assumed to be from Perls, Fritz, *Gestalt Therapy Verbatim*, Real People Press, Lafayette, California, 1969.

(6) From Downing and Marmorstein, *Dreams and Nightmares*, Perennial Library (Harper and Row), New York, 1973. Quoted in an unknown secondary source.

(7) Rossi, Ernest, *Dreams and the Growth of Personality*, Brunnel/Mazel, New York, 1972, 1985, Part One.

(8) No portion of this book may be reproduced in any form except for the dream questionnaire, which may be duplicated for personal use.

(9) Grossinger, Richard, *Dreams Are Wiser than Men*, edited by Richard Russo, North Atlantic Books, Berkeley, California, 1987, p. 242. Originally published in *The Night Sky* by Richard Grossinger, Sierra Club Books, 1981.

(10) Yeats, William Butler, "The Shadowy Waters," quoted in Brook, Stephen, *Oxford Book of Dreams*, Oxford University Press, Oxford, New York, 1983, pp. 252–53.

(11) Dickinson, Emily, quoted in *Oxford Book of Dreams*, p. 244.

The Dream Experience: Twelfth House Case Studies

(1) Rudhyar, Dane, *An Astrological Mandala*, Random House, New York, 1973, pp. 229–30.

Bibliography

Astrology

Bacher, Elman, *Studies in Astrology: Vol. II*, chap. 6, "Neptune Patterns-The Twelfth House," Rosicrucian Fellowship, 1962.

Greene, Liz and Howard Sasportas, *The Development of the Personality*, Samuel Weiser, Inc., York Beach, Maine, 1987.

Greene, Liz, *The Astrology of Fate*, Samuel Weiser, Inc., York Beach, Maine, 1984.

Halevi, Hai and Halevi, Zahava, *Astrology and Psychoanalysis*, S. Y. S. Publications, Jerusalem, Israel, 1987.

March, Marion and Joan McEvers, *The Only Way to . . . Learn Astrology: Volume III*, Astro-Computing Services, San Diego, California, 1982, pp. 105–113.

Marks, Tracy, *The Astrology of Self-Discovery*, CRCS Publications, Sebastopol, California, 1985.

Marks, Tracy, *Planetary Aspects* (originally entitled *How To Handle Your T-Square*), CRCS Publications, Sebastopol California, 1979, 1987.

Marks, Tracy, *The Square Aspect*, Sagittarius Rising, Arlington, Mass., 1982.

Marks, Tracy, *The Twelfth House*, Sagittarius Rising, Arlington, Mass., 1978. [Most of this material is included in this book.]

Rudhyar, Dane, *The Astrological Houses*, "The Twelfth House," CRCS Publications, Sebastopol, California, 1972.

Rudhyar, Dane, *An Astrological Mandala*, Random House, New York, 1973.

Psychology Books

Bandler, Richard and John Grinder, *Frogs Into Princes*, Real People Press, Moab, Utah, 1979.

Bandler, Richard and John Grinder, *Reframing*, Real People Press, Moab, Utah, 1982.

Beahrs, John, *Unity and Multiplicity: Multilevel Consciousness of Self*, Brunner/Mazel Inc., New York, 1982.

Branden, Nathaniel, *The Disowned Self*, Bantam Books, New York, 1971.

Bugental, James, *The Search for Authenticity*, Irvington Publishers, New York, 1965, 1981.

Butler, Pamela, *Talking to Yourself: Learning the Language of Self-Support*, Harper and Row, New York, 1981.

Fensterheim, Herbert & Jean Baer, *Stop Running Scared!*, New York, 1977.

Ferrucci, Piero, *What We May Be: Techniques for Psychological and Spiritual Growth*, J. P. Tarcher, Los Angeles, 1982.

Firestone, Robert W., *Voice Therapy: A Psychotherapeutic Approach to Self-Destructive Behavior*, Human Sciences Press, New York, 1988.

Fossum, Merle A. and Marilyn J. Mason, *Facing Shame: Families in Recovery*, W. W. Norton and Co., New York, 1986.

Freud, Anna, *The Ego and the Mechanisms of Defense*, International Universities Press, Inc., New York, 1966.

Jeffers, Susan, *Feel the Fear and Do It Anyway*, Harcourt Brace Jovanovich, New York, 1987.

Johnson, Strephen M., *Characterological Transformation*, W. W. Norton and Co., New York, 1985.

Jung, Carl, "Commentary" in *Secret of the Golden Flower* by Richard Wilhelm, Harcourt, Brace and World, New York, 1931.

Jung, Carl, "Aion: Phenomenology of the Self," in *The Portable Jung*, ed. by Joseph Campbell, Viking Press, New York, 1971.

Jung, Carl, "The Development of the Personality," and "Problems of Self-Realization," in *Psychological Reflections*, edited by Jolande Jacobi, Princeton University Press, 1953.

Klein, Melanie and Joan Riviere, *Love, Hate and Reparation*, W. W. Norton and Company, New York, 1964.

Lowen, Alexander, *Fear of Life*, MacMillan Inc., New York, 1980.

May, Rollo, *The Meaning of Anxiety*, Simon and Schuster, New York, 1950, 1977.

Miller, Alice, *The Drama of the Gifted Child: The Search for the True Self* (originally entitled *Prisoners of Childhood*), Basic Books, Inc., New York, 1981.

Miller, Susan, *The Shame Experience*, The Analytic Press, Hillsdale, New Jersey, 1985.

Miller, Julian, *Breaking Through: Freeing Yourself from Fear, Helplessness and Depression*, Thomas Y. Crowell, New York, 1979.

Neumann, Erich, *Amor and Psyche: The Psychic Development of the Feminine*, Bollingen Foundation, Inc., New York, and Princeton University Press, 1956.

Neumann, Erich, *Depth Psychology and A New Ethic*, Harper and Row, New York, 1969, 1973.

O'Connor, Elizabeth, *Our Many Selves*, Harper and Row, New York, 1971.

Peele, Stanton, *How Much Is Too Much?: Healthy Habits or Destructive Addictions*, Prentice-Hall, Inc., Englewood Cliffs, New Jersey, 1981.

Rubin, Theodore Isaac, *Compassion and Self-Hate: An Alternative To Despair*, Ballantine Books, New York, 1975.

Sanford, John, *Evil: The Shadow Side of Reality*, Crossroad Publishing Company, New York, 1981.

Segal, Jeanne, *Living Beyond Fear*, Newcastle Publishing Co., N. Hollywood, California, 1984.

Von Franz, Marie-Louise, *Shadow and Evil in Fairy Tales*, Spring Publications, New York, 1974.

Warner, Samuel, *Self-Realization and Self-Defeat: Freeing Your Creative Potential*, Grove Press, Inc., New York, 1966.

Williams, Strephon Kaplan, *The Practice of Personal Transformation*, Journey Press, Berkeley, California, 1984, 1985.

Dreamwork

Brook, Steven, *Oxford Book of Dreams*, Oxford University Press, Oxford, New York, 1983.

Faraday, Ann, *The Dream Game*, Harper and Row, New York, 1974.

Hall, Calvin, *The Meaning of Dreams*, McGraw-Hill, New York, 1953, 1966.

Hall, James, *Jungian Dream Interpretation*, Inner City Books, Toronto, 1983.

Mattoon, Mary Ann, *Understanding Dreams*, Spring Publications, Dallas, Texas, 1984.

McDonald, Phoebe, *Dreams: Night Language of the Soul*, Continuum Publishing, New York, 1987.

Morris, Jill, *The Dream Workbook*, Little, Brown and Company, Boston, Massachusetts, 1985.

Reed, Henry, *Getting Help From Your Dreams*, Inner Vision Publishing Company, Virginia Beach, Virginia, 1985.

Rossi, Ernest, *Dreams and the Growth of Personality*, Brunner/Mazel, New York, 1972, 1985.

Taylor, Jeremy, *Dreamwork*, Paulist Press, New York, 1983.

Williams, Strephon Kaplan, *The Jungian-Senoi Dreamwork Manual*, Journey Press, Berkeley, California, 1980.

Fiction

Bryant, Dorothy, *The Kin of ATA Are Waiting for You*, Moon Books/Random House, New York, 1971.

Euripides, *Iphigenia Among the Taurians* (sequel to *Iphigenia at Aulis*), included in *Ten Plays By Euripides*, translated by Moses Hadas, Bantam Books, New York, 1960, 1981.

LeGuin, Ursula, *A Wizard of Earthsea*, Bantam Books, New York, 1968.

Neumann, Erich, *Amor and Psyche*, Bollingen Foundation, Inc., New York, and Princeton University Press, 1956.

Van Scyoc, Sidney, *Darkchild*, Berkley Books, New York, 1982.

Wilson, Colin, *The Mind Parasites*, Oneiric Press, Berkeley, California, 1967.

BOOKS BY TRACY MARKS

THE ASTROLOGY OF SELF-DISCOVERY: An In-depth Exploration of the Potentials Revealed in Your Birth Chart . . . 288-page paperback, packed with information! **$9.95**
A guide to utilizing astrology to aid self-development and self-knowledge, to resolve inner conflicts, discover and fulfill one's life purpose, and to realize one's potential. Emphasizes the Moon and its nodes, Neptune, Pluto, and the outer planets' transits. An important and original work!

THE ART OF CHART INTERPRETATION: A Step-by-Step Method of Analyzing, Synthesizing & Understanding the Birth Chart . . . 180-page paperback . . . a must for students! **$7.95**
A great value and a great book, this is a revised, expanded version of the author's book on Chart Synthesis. It is a guide for determining the most important features of any birth chart; there is no book like it! Includes worksheets that allow the reader to systematically evaluate the patterns and themes of any chart.

PLANETARY ASPECTS—FROM CONFLICT TO COOPERATION: How to Make Your Stressful Aspects Work for You . . . 228-page paperback . . . a best-selling classic! **$11.95**
This new edition of *How to Handle Your T-Square* focuses on the creative understanding and use of the stressful aspects and emphasizes the T-Square Configuration both in natal charts and as formed by transits and progressions. The most thorough treatment of these subjects in print! Includes techniques for handling these challenges.

YOUR SECRET SELF: Illuminating the Mysteries of the Twelfth House . . . 264 pages **$12.95**
The most comprehensive treatment of the 12th House and its subtleties ever published. The importance of the 12th House for self-knowledge and the dimensions of psychological and spiritual potential that it symbolizes are emphasized. It also demonstrates in a fascinating way how the themes of a birth chart emerge in one's dreams and how working with dreams is one of the most effective gateways into the hidden meanings of the 12th House.

OTHER IMPORTANT CRCS TITLES

THE ASTROLOGER'S MANUAL: Modern Insights Into an Ancient Art by Landis Knight Green **$10.95**
One of the rare books on the subject that can accurately be called original, this in-depth text is intended for those who want a fresh, modern perspective on astrology. Includes extensive sections on relationships and aspects.

THE PRACTICE AND PROFESSION OF ASTROLOGY: Rebuilding Our Lost Connections with the Cosmos by Stephen Arroyo **$7.95**
A challenging, often controversial treatment of astrology's place in modern society and of astrological counseling as both a legitimate profession and a healing process.

THE JUPITER/SATURN CONFERENCE LECTURES: New Insights in Modern Astrology by Stephen Arroyo & Liz Greene **$8.95**
Deals with myth, chart synthesis, relationships, & Jungian psychology as it relates to astrology. An original & important work.

THE LITERARY ZODIAC by Paul Wright **$14.95**
A pioneering work, based on extensive research, exploring the connection between astrology and literary creativity. A one-of-a-kind approach to the astrology of great literature, based on 3,000 writers' charts.

ASTROLOGY IN ACTION: How Astrology works in Practice, Demonstrated by Transits, Progressions & Major Chart Themes in Famous People's Lives by Paul Wright **$12.95**
Presents 70 astrological/biographical profiles, which demonstrate that an in-depth, clear and precise picture of an individual can be obtained by blending only a few major factors.

ASTROLOGY IN MODERN LANGUAGE by Richard Vaughan **$12.95**
An in-depth interpretation of the birth chart focusing on the houses and their ruling planets—including the Ascendant and its ruler. A unique, strikingly original work.

THE OUTER PLANETS & THEIR CYCLES: The Astrology of the Collective by Liz Greene **$7.95**
Deals with the individual's attunement to the outer planets as well as with significant historical and generational trends that correlate to these planetary cycles.

A JOURNEY THROUGH THE BIRTH CHART: Using Astrology on Your Life Path by Joanne Wickenburg **$7.95**
Puts the pieces of the birth chart together for self-understanding and encourages creative interpretation of charts by helping the reader to think through the endless combinations of astrological symbols.

THE SPIRAL OF LIFE: Unlocking Your Potential with Astrology by Joanne Wickenburg & Virginia Meyer **$7.95**
Covering all astrological factors, this book shows how understanding the birth pattern is an exciting path toward increased self-awareness and purposeful living.

(These titles can be ordered from your local bookstore or direct from the publisher. See address on title page.)

CRCS Books

THE ANCIENT SCIENCE OF GEOMANCY:Living in Harmony with the Earth by Nigel Pennick $12.95. The best and most accessible survey of this ancient wholistic art/science, superbly illustrated with 120 photos.

AN ASTROLOGICAL GUIDE TO SELF-AWARENESS by Donna Cunningham, M.S.W. $7.95. Written in a lively style, this book includes chapters on transits, houses, interpreting aspects, etc. A popular book translated into 5 languages.

THE ART OF CHART INTERPRETATION: A Step-by-Step Method of Analyzing,Synthesizing & Understanding the Birth Chart by Tracy Marks $7.95. A guide to determining the most important features of a birth chart. A must for students!

THE ASTROLOGER'S GUIDE TO COUNSELING: Astrology's Role in the Helping Professions by Bernard Rosenblum, M.D. $7.95. Establishes astrological counseling as a valid and legitimate helping profession. A break-through book!

THE ASTROLOGER'S MANUAL: Modern Insights into an Ancient Art by Landis Knight Green $10.95, 240 pages. A strikingly original work that includes extensive sections on relationships, aspects, and all the fundamentals in a lively new way.

THE ASTROLOGICAL HOUSES: The Spectrum of Individual Experience by Dane Rudhyar $8.95. A recognized classic of modern astrology that has sold over 100,000 copies, this book is required reading for every student of astrology seeking to understand the deeper meanings of the houses.

ASTROLOGY: The Classic Guide to Understanding Your Horoscope by Ronald C. Davison $7.95. The most popular book on astrology during the 1960's & 1970's is now back in print in a new edition, with an instructive new foreword that explains how the author's remarkable keyword system can be used by even the novice student of astrology.

ASTROLOGY FOR THE NEW AGE: An Intuitive Approach by Marcus Allen $7.95. Emphasizes self-acceptance and tuning in to your chart with a positive openness. Helps one create his or her own interpretation.

ASTROLOGY IN MODERN LANGUAGE by Richard Vaughan $12.95, 336 pages. An in-depth interpretation of the birth chart focusing on the houses and their ruling planets-- including the Ascendant and its ruler. A unique, strikingly original work.

ASTROLOGY, KARMA & TRANSFORMATION: The Inner Dimensions of the Birth Chart by Stephen Arroyo $10.95. An insightful book on the use of astrology for persoal growth, seen in the light of the theory of karma and the urge toward self-transformation. International best-seller!

THE ASTROLOGY OF SELF-DISCOVERY: An In-Depth Exploration of the Potentials Revealed in Your Birth Chart by Tracy Marks $9.95, 288 pages. Emphasizes the Moon and its nodes, Neptune, Pluto, & the outer planet transits. An important and brilliantly original work!

ASTROLOGY, PSYCHOLOGY AND THE FOUR ELEMENTS: An Energy Approach to Astrology & Its Use in the Counseling Arts by Stephen Arroyo $9.95. An international best-seller, this book deals with the use of astrology as a practical method of understanding one's attunement to universal forces. Clearly shows how to approach astrology with a real understanding of the energies involved. Awarded the British Astrological Assn's Astrology Prize. A classic translated into 8 languages!

CYCLES OF BECOMING: The Planetary Pattern of Growth by Alexander Ruperti $12.95, 274 pages. The first complete treatment of transits from a humanistic and holistic perspective. All important planetary cycles are correlated with the essential phases of personal development. A pioneering work!

DYNAMICS OF ASPECT ANALYSIS: New Perceptions in Astrology by Bil Tierney $8.95, 288 pages. Ground-breaking work! The most in-depth treatment of aspects and aspect patterns available, including both major and minor configurations. Also includes retrogrades, unaspected planets & more!

A JOURNEY THROUGH THE BIRTH CHART: Using Astrology on Your Life Path by Joanne Wickenburg $7.95. Gives the reader the tools to put the pieces of the birth chart together for self-understanding and encourages creative interpretation by helping the reader to think through the endless combinations of astrological symbols.

THE JUPITER/SATURN CONFERENCE LECTURES: New Insights in Modern Astrology by Stephen Arroyo & Liz Greene $8.95. Talks included deal with myth, chart synthesis, relationships, & Jungian psychology related to astrology. A wealth of original & important ideas!

THE LITERARY ZODIAC by Paul Wright $12.95, 240 pages. A pioneering work, based on extensive research, exploring the connection between astrology and literary creativity.

NUMBERS AS SYMBOLS FOR SELF-DISCOVERY: Exploring Character & Destiny with Numerology by Richard Vaughan $8.95, 336 pages. A how-to book on personal analysis and forecasting your future through Numerology. Examples include the number patterns of a thousand famous personalities.

THE OUTER PLANETS & THEIR CYCLES: The Astrology of the Collective by Liz Greene $7.95. Deals with the individual's attunement to the outer planets as well as with significant historical and generational trends that correlate to these planetary cycles.

PLANETARY ASPECTS: FROM CONFLICT TO COOPERATION: How to Make Your Stressful Aspects Work for You by Tracy Marks $8.95, 225 pages. This revised edition of HOW TO HANDLE YOUR T-SQUARE focuses on the creative understanding of the stressful aspects and focuses on the T-Square configuration both in natal charts and as formed by transits & progressions. The most thorough treatment of these subjects in print!

THE PLANETS AND HUMAN BEHAVIOR by Jeff Mayo $7.95. A pioneering exploration of the symbolism of the planets, blending their modern psychological significance with their ancient mythological meanings. Includes many tips on interpretation.

PRACTICAL PALMISTRY: A Positive Approach from a Modern Perspective by David Brandon-Jones $8.95, 268 pages. This easy-to-use book describes and illustrates all the basics of traditional palmistry and then builds upon that with more recent discoveries based upon the author's extensive experience and case studies. A discriminating approach to an ancient science that includes many original ideas!

THE PRACTICE AND PROFESSION OF ASTROLOGY: Rebuilding Our Lost Connections with the Cosmos by Stephen Arroyo $7.95. A challenging, often controversial treatment of astrology's place in modern society and of astrological counseling as both a legitimate profession and a healing process.

REINCARNATION THROUGH THE ZODIAC by Joan Hodgson $6.50. A study of the signs of the zodiac from a spiritual perspective, based upon the development of different phases of conciousness through reincarnation.

RELATIONSHIPS & LIFE CYCLES: Modern Dimensions of Astrology by Stephen Arroyo $8.95. Thorough discussion of natal chart indicators of one's capacity and need for relationship; techniques of chart comparison; using transits practically; and the use of the houses in chart comparison.

SEX & THE ZODIAC: An Astrological Guide to Intimate Relationships by Helen Terrell $7.95, 256 pages. Goes into great detail in describing and analyzing the dominant traits of women and men as indicated by their Zodiacal signs.

THE SPIRAL OF LIFE: Unlocking Your Potential with Astrology by Joanne Wickenburg & Virginia Meyer $7.95. Covering all astrological factors, this book shows how understanding the birth pattern is an exciting path toward increased self-awareness.

A SPIRITUAL APPROACH TO ASTROLOGY: A Complete Textbook of Astrology by Myrna Lofthus $12.95, 444 pages. A complete astrology textbook from a karmic viewpoint, with an especially valuable 130-page section on karmic interpretation of all aspects, including the Ascendant & MC.

HEALTH BUILDING: The Conscious Art of Living Well by Dr. Randolph Stone $8.95. A complete health program for people of all ages, based on vital energy currents. Includes instructions on vegetarian & purifying diets and energizing exercises for vitality & beauty. The author is the originator of Polarity Therapy.

HELPING YOURSELF WITH NATURAL REMEDIES: An Encyclopedic Guide to Herbal & Nutritional Treatment by Terry Willard, Ph.D. $11.95. This easily accessible book blends 20th century scientific & clinical experience with traditional methods of health maintenance. Allows you to select natural remedies for over 100 specific problems, all arranged in alphabetical order & with a complete index.

POLARITY THERAPY:VOL.I & II The Complete Collected Works by Dr. Randolph Stone, D.O., D.C. $25.00 each. The original books on this revolutionary healing art, available for the first time in trade editions. Fully illustrated with charts & diagrams. Sewn binding.

For more complete information on our books, a complete booklist, or to order any of the above publications, WRITE TO:

CRCS Publications
Post Office Box 1460
Sebastopol, California 95473
U.S.A.